KU-142-156

VISUAL
RESEARCH
METHODS

Image, Society, and Representation

GREGORY C. STANCZAK

Editor

SAGE Publications

Los Angeles · London · New Delhi · Singapore

Copyright © 2007 by Sage Publications, Inc.

All rights reserved. No part of this book may be reproduced or utilized in any form or by any means, electronic or mechanical, including photocopying, recording, or by any information storage and retrieval system, without permission in writing from the publisher.

For information:

Sage Publications, Inc.
2455 Teller Road
Thousand Oaks, California 91320
E-mail: order@sagepub.com

Sage Publications India Pvt. Ltd.
B-42, Panchsheel Enclave
Post Box 4109
New Delhi 110 017 India

Sage Publications Ltd.
1 Oliver's Yard
55 City Road
London, EC1Y 1SP
United Kingdom

Sage Publications Asia-Pacific Pte Ltd
33 Pekin Street #02-01
Far East Square
Singapore 048763

Printed in the United States of America

Library of Congress Cataloging-in-Publication Data

Stanczak, Gregory C., 1967-
Visual research methods: Image, society, and representation/Gregory C. Stanczak.
    p. cm.
Includes bibliographical references and index.
ISBN: 1–4129–3954–2 (pbk.: alk. paper)
    1. Social sciences—Research. 2. Social sciences—Study and teaching. I. Title.
H62.S39 2007
300.72—dc22   2006031955

This book is printed on acid-free paper.

07   08   09   10   11   10   9   8   7   6   5   4   3   2   1

Acquiring Editor:	Lisa Cuevas Shaw
Editorial Assistant:	Karen Margrethe Greene
Production Editor:	Beth A. Bernstein
Copy Editor:	Jacqueline Tasch
Typesetter:	C&M Digitals (P) Ltd.
Indexer:	Rick Hurd
Graphic Designer:	Candice Harman

169473

VISUAL

RESEARCH

METHODS

Contents

Chapter	Title	Summary	Primary topics	Thematic topics	Methodology
1	Introduction	Overview of collection and chapter outline	Epistemology, methodology, and theoretical contributions	Historical sketch	Overview of approaches
2	Observing Culture and Social Life	Similarities and differences between the social sciences and documentary image makers	Observational research, data collection, commitments, and modes of inquiry	FSA, global culture, gender, adolescence, social change	Comparison and overview
3	All Photos Lie	The constructed nature of photographs	Technical aspects of photography and vision, assumptions about photographic reality	Scientific photography, Doisneau, photojournalism	Technical and subjective aspects of taking photographs
4	Capturing the Visual Traces of Historical Change	Rich potential of missionary photographic archives as social and historical data	Photographs as visual documentation of colonial interaction and social change	Religion, gender, cultural exchange, colonial politics	Historical/Comparative archival methods
5	The Failure of "The President's Choice"	Photography in social policy is affected by the under-analyzed experience of viewing	Contrasting positions about the role of photography, emotional experience of viewing	Political use of images, aesthetic assumptions	Historical archival methods

Chapter	Title	Summary	Primary topics	Thematic topics	Methodology
6	Using Photography in Studies of Immigrant Communities	Reflection upon years of various photographic research with immigrant communities	Visual orientation, rapport building, digital benefits, use in analysis	Community studies, labor, gender, ethnicity	Qualitative methods and rapport building techniques
7	Inner-City Children in Sharper Focus	Assessment of PEI in research on the everyday lives of immigrant children	How to conduct auto-driven PEI, potentials and pitfalls	Childhood, immigration, education, gender, inequality	Auto-driven photo elicitation
8	When Words Are Not Enough	Assessment of PEI in cross-cultural research on adolescent Sri Lankan monasticism	Strengths and weaknesses in auto-driven PEI for abstract concepts, breaking cross-cultural assumptions, shooting scripts	Religion, Buddhism, childhood/adolescence	Auto-driven photo elicitation
9	Signs of Resistance	Documenting visual forms of public discourse and political resistance	"Fixing" ephemeral visual discourse as data through photography, interdisciplinary contributions with visual research	Political discourse, deviance, global vs. local communication, social control, gentrification, post-colonial discourse	Images as documentation of discourse

of socioeconomic demographics, gender achievement in standardized testing, or the intersection of age, race, and religious participation in civic life. We have come to accept and even expect such visual representations as signifiers of complex calculations, backed by a methodological rigor that is offered (perhaps more often required) as a staple within most social scientific curricula. We are trained to decipher particular kinds of visual representations in order to be scholars in our respective fields.

On the other hand, until recently, what we most often think of as visual imagery—photographs and more recently video and virtual images—functioned as illustration. I use the past tense confidently, if not somewhat optimistically, given the changes in the status of the image in academic fields over the past decade. Admittedly, anthropology has carried the mantle of visual analysis throughout its disciplinary tenure; however, the chapters presented in this book indicate that visual or image-based research is reemerging with significant untapped potential and vigor across a broader scope of disciplines. It is in this spirit that the current collection was compiled. Each of the chapters incorporates the image in slightly different ways and across remarkably different issues. Yet, what remains consistent is that images are not merely appendages to the research but rather inseparable components to learning about our social worlds. The selected chapters in this book strike vivid and highly accessible connections between the everyday world that we take in through our eyes and the cognitive, analytic framework that we apply through our scholarship and pass along in our teaching.

In this opening chapter, I will lay out the guiding structure of this collection and offer some different ways to access the text. My hope is that readers will find one or more of these pieces resonating with their own projects in some way, either methodologically or substantively. More than that, I hope these chapters as a whole spark conversations concerning the "hows" and the "whys" of incorporating images into various research agendas and, in doing so, prompt us to rethink what images tell us about the image maker, the viewer, the way in which images are shared and talked about, and the entire academic process of generating credible social knowledge.

Guiding Themes

Although this is a book about methods and each chapter provides clear examples and concise explications of methodological approaches, this is not a conventional methodological handbook. There are few step-by-step guidelines. Methodologies are highly contingent on epistemological positions, populations, researcher interests, rapport, and confidentiality, among a host of other concerns. Each chapter discusses in detail its author's uniquely tailored methodology, but extending these methodologies to other projects requires each reader/researcher to hone his or her own craft accordingly. With this in mind, each author instead describes and reflects on the situated way he or she uses images for particular purposes and notes the potentials and pitfalls that images provide in building or extending research questions. Connecting these differences are three main themes or threads that run through each chapter: epistemological concerns, methodology, and theoretical or substantive contributions. Each of these three terms can seem overly abstract, and admittedly, they are often used in very circuitous ways. For this collection, I use these three themes as practical points to engage, question, and reflect on the visual research process within and across chapters.

Epistemology

Instead of a "how to" compilation of visual methods or an exploration of substantive findings alone, this text is an interactive epistemological odyssey engaging the authors, the readers, and various disciplines. Epistemology, for our purposes, asks several broad questions. How is it that we come to know what we know, and what are the underlying assumptions of this pursuit? In other words, what is our process of inquiry? What are our disciplinary, sub-disciplinary, and personal expectations about what information is valid for what purposes? Moving the image both figuratively and literally into social scientific research has epistemological implications that raise widely applicable questions of validity, subjectivity, and rapport. Questions such as these are not new; they have a long intellectual history of prodding researchers and image makers since the advent of photography. That history is examined more deeply elsewhere, but let me spend some time to trace a sketch that loosely contextualizes the contours of the subsequent chapters.

Perhaps not too surprisingly, the camera and positivism emerged together (Berger & Mohr, 1982). Both photographic technology and philosophical framework stem from the aligned notions that the truth can be discerned empirically from objective facts observed in the world and that systematic documentation of these facts can lead to the harnessing of certain social processes and outcomes. The camera held promise as a valued tool for the strict empirical construction of knowledge in Western science, a promise that was embraced for medical, philanthropic, and legal advances and claims (Tagg, 1993). For example, in the United States, the camera served quite well for those hoping to reveal emergent social patterns during the shifts toward urbanization and industrialization. Paging through Jacob Riis's (1890) *How the Other Half Lives* over a century after its publication confirms this early role of photography as an influential vehicle for social critique. Riis's images of orphans and of alcohol dens illustrate the advances and applications of new technology (including rudimentary flash photography) as well as the social conscience with which the camera could be used.

In a similar social vein, Lewis Hine was a pioneer of visual social science who earned a graduate degree in sociology from Columbia University while freelancing for the National Child Labor Committee. Hine focused his developing sociological lens on the social and economic disparities of the industrial city (as well as multiple other projects, such as child labor and immigration), using Pittsburgh, Pennsylvania, as one particular case study. Sociologically informed, Hine's aim was to promote a rational, public dialogue about these inequities that would encourage social change. However, even given Hine's integration of sociological perspectives, the empirical promise of photography was relatively short-lived for the social sciences. With the exception of visual anthropology, the epistemological direction of the social sciences by mid-century became unhooked from the use of visual tools as valid modes of analytic inquiry.

Within 20th-century social sciences, epistemological assumptions regarding what constitutes valid research agendas fell along two main divisions or avenues of inquiry: qualitative and quantitative. Although the two are by no means mutually exclusive, qualitative approaches were and are based on the assumption that close, often intimate connections to the lived experiences of a particular phenomenon—gender socialization in junior high school or the effects of global technology on national identity in rural India, for example—produce the clearest and most informed understanding of the topic, whereas quantitative approaches fundamentally assume that the most reliable indicator of a phenomenon is represented through systematic analysis of large representative samples of a population about whom one is curious. Visual data receded as quantitative methodologies refined surveys and questionnaires that tracked the demographic and social shifts of the 20th century and as Robert Park's qualitatively oriented Chicago School perfected a notably text-based or verbal approach to exploring lived experiences through sociology (Platt, 1996).

Broader changes in the social location of photography may have also contributed to this shift away from mainstream social science epistemologies. By mid-century, photographs increasingly were held under the auspices of the state and within the walls of the museum. The special photographic division of Roosevelt's Farm Security Administration (FSA), headed by Roy Stryker, became one of the most influential and enduring legacies of the New Deal. The images from this program exist in our collective memories as the face of the Dust Bowl and the Great Depression; they simultaneously conjure the desperation and resilience of the everyday American experience. We might forget, however, that from its inception, the photography of the FSA was critiqued as a politically motivated campaign to sustain support for New Deal policies by conjuring just such responses. This critique persisted—although motivated by different political agendas—when the division was transferred over to the Office of War Information in 1942, at which time it patriotically and unabashedly documented the country's mobilization for war.

Years later during the boom following World War II, the anthropological role of photographs merged with mainstream culture in the Museum of Modern Art's *The Family of Man* exhibit. Edward Steichen (1955), a champion of the aesthetic and artistic designation of photography, conceived of the exhibit as one that would present the "gamut of human relations," ultimately revealing our universal connections. It proved to be the most heavily attended exhibit of photography of its time, drawing capacity crowds throughout the United States before moving on to 69 venues in 37 other countries (Sandeen, 1995).

Since then, there has been a steady stream of social commentary within the walls of the museum. Suspicious of co-optation by governmental programs or the editorial constraints of photojournalism, the Riises and Hines of the second half of the 20th century voiced their critiques through stunning content and equally stunning aesthetics in galleries, coffee-table books, and now websites. Over the same period that documentary photographers were weaving compelling narratives laden with social institutional implications about the family, poverty, unemployment, urban problems, drug abuse, or religion, photographs in art galleries were losing much of their policy punch and nearly all of their utility within the social sciences (Becker, 1974). The ideological malleability of images by the state and the sentimentality of images such as in *The Family of Man*—not to mention ubiquitous family photo albums—were at odds with the modern march of social scientific rigor in the academy at mid-century, and an epistemological wariness still challenges the validity of images as data today.

Still later in the 20th century, critical documentary image-work in photography and increasingly video moved forward again as television and image-based technologies proliferated. Media studies reemerged from its Frankfurt School roots as the analytic arena for understanding the impact of images on society, producing a vibrant yet bounded discourse. This disciplinary shift toward media studies moved the focus onto institutional carriers and producers of images and audience responses. Findings were aimed as much at the industry as at the academy—a changed agenda from using images as data or as methodologies for exploring the social world. Yet, the critical connection between image and society enabled and continues to spark productive collaborations within certain pockets of the social sciences. By the late 20th century, photographic criticism, epistemological debate, and sociological implications (broadly used) emerged in the work of authors as varied as Susan Sontag, Roland Barthes, and Jean Baudrillard.

The social and academic position of photography sheds some light on the disciplinary shifts with regard to images. At the core of these relationships are epistemological assumptions about subjectivity versus objective empiricism. For both conventional and image-based projects, this continuum poses perennial challenges for the social sciences and requires us to stake out a position for or within qualitative, quantitative, or combined approaches to research. When considering images, the line between subjectivist and objectivist-realist assumptions—that images capture something "real" and that images are constructions—is continually moving. Indeed, images often ask us to hold both positions simultaneously to greater or lesser degrees. Roland Barthes (1981), for example, championed the deeply personal, emotional intimacies with which we relate to certain photographs while simultaneously asserting what he believed was the unquestionable realist basis of photography; photographs demand that we accept that "this has been." The connection between subjectivity and realism is instructive for social scientific analysis. Rather than demanding only an objective reading, images also elicit various subjectivities from our participants that—instead of being bracketed away—can be probed and analyzed.

Just as subjectivity and realism interact in the space between the image and the viewer, the same occurs between the producer of the image and the subject or content. We may select in time and space what we want to capture, but the mechanical operation of the camera will document all that is before it in that moment. In other words, the camera is susceptible to the selectivity of the operator, but it is not selective once the shutter is opened (Collier & Collier, 1986). 主观

As images reemerge as data within the social sciences, we must acknowledge the empirical components of the image while embracing the compelling challenges and opportunities of subjectivity and the potential emotional impact of making and reading images. Yes, cameras crop, adjust for lighting, and create moods in their captured environments; increasingly, they zoom and pan. And yes, questions regarding the selection of content within the frame, close-ups or wide angles, and a slew of technical considerations in general (digital versus analog, black and white versus color, SLR versus automatic) should be of significant interest as we address the epistemological concerns related to visual data. However, neither the camera's capacity to affect what is captured or the ways that images can be used by other social institutions such as museums or the state should rule out the camera as a research tool for other disciplines. Images need not—in fact, should not—be considered the province of one discipline or held to one set of readings. This is especially true in an era after the so-called cultural turn, when we no longer assume the pure objectivity of unbiased academic research and allow for or even expect transparent subjective reflexivity in many projects. In fact, the same questions of selection and technique that we pose about cameras have already been asked and answered regarding our epistemological assumptions about nonvisual approaches to research. We select which questionnaire items to contrast with others in our regression models. We select, for example, the interactions of gender with religious-based voluntarism rather than (or in combination with) socioeconomic status. We choose certain interview fragments over others to bring to life our ethnographies. We selectively reconstruct the setting of an inner-city elementary school by describing as much or as little from our fieldnotes as we believe is needed to evoke our situated observation or to lend support to our arguments. In narratives, we verbally zoom and pan, taking the reader down one path chosen from among many others. Visual approaches to understanding and inquiring about aspects of the social world need not fall outside the parameters set by the epistemological assumptions and rigors regarding how we collect valuable information. In fact, many times, they already fit snugly within them.

By saying this, I do not want to overemphasize a subjective defense. There are empirical benefits of the mechanical and digital workings of the camera that we may still accept epistemologically, even given this caveat. William Henry Fox Talbot (1844/1969), the founder of paper-process photography, was immediately attuned to this mechanical operation and wrote in *The Pencil of Nature,* "It frequently happens, moreover—and this is one of the charms of photography—that the operator himself [sic] discovers on examination, perhaps long afterwards, that he has depicted many things he had no notion of at the time" (notes to Plate XIII). Talbot's observation, indeed the very title of his book, suggests the empirical sense in which the camera was imagined at its origins. While the photographer carefully sets up the shot, the camera captures more than the photographer's eye can take in. Thinking about visual data through the surprise of discovery holds potential in a range of research agendas today. The empirical projects in this collection suggest that employing images in our methodologies often reveals surprising new knowledge that we as scholars, students, and researchers may not have recognized through conventional means.

Unexpected discovery might be interpreted through a strict empirical epistemology of what actually existed at that moment when the shutter was depressed—cars in a parking lot provide a quantifiable estimate of the socioeconomic standing of a local congregation but, when used later in a project on spatial demographics, might reveal the percentage of cars from each state in a tri-state region. Strict empiricism emphasizes "indexicality" or the one-to-one relationship between the image produced by the camera and the object in the social world. On the other hand, the grounded theory approach of qualitative empiricism is easily amenable to the potential of discovery when, as with fieldnotes, patterns emerge in our interpretation of details that we did not know existed (or did not think were meaningful) when we clicked the shutter—the seating arrangements and proximity of family members while at church over the course of a year might mark the internal relationship struggles that the husband and wife experienced but tried to keep private until their ultimate divorce. In this instance, the camera captures something that the photographer/researcher was unable to see without the interpretative collaboration of participants. In the realm of research, these surprises are as much an outcome of our methods as they are the outcome of discovery, as Talbot suggested so many years ago.

While I argue that images have great flexibility within our disciplines, the chapters that follow have a qualitative bent. Even so, the chapters are varied and do not suggest one global epistemology for images. In this spirit, these projects reflect many epistemologies already at play across and within disciplines. Incorporating images into these assumptions strengthens, amends, challenges, advances, and if nothing else, makes us think about our epistemological bases. In short, images help us to ask what we know about the social world and how we know it.

As is evident by now, discussions about epistemology and discussions about methodology continually collapse upon each other. These are two sides of the spinning coin of social inquiry. Epistemological assumptions affect the types of methods that we choose, just as the methods that we use—their strengths and their limitations—act on our ways of thinking about the way we generate valid social knowledge. Given this dialectic relationship between epistemology and methods, this collection is rooted in a practical or pragmatic epistemology. Howard Becker (1996) suggests something similar for qualitative approaches to social science in general. From a pragmatic epistemology, we allow each case or each topic to shape our epistemological assumptions. We even expect changes in those assumptions as a project moves forward. The same may be applied to visual research. Images will trigger different insights depending on the different questions that we ask of them (Becker, 1986; Suchar, 1989). Knowles and Sweetman (2004) suggest a pragmatic realism as a working stance that brackets definitive definitions of images and enables bounded research within various disciplines. The combination of these two stances works best for me. Pragmatic epistemology provides variation in assumptions but steers clear from holding the realism of the image as a unifying constant across projects. In other words, the epistemological assumptions in these chapters work well for the topics and questions at hand yet should not be read as fixed truths about the way to construct research agendas on these or other topics.

Methodology

Methodology, as I will use it here, is distinct from epistemology. Methodology considers the innovative ways in which researchers employ visual tools and techniques in the field to generate rapport and gather data. Although distinct, methods are always related to epistemological assumptions even if they do not always follow directly from a particular epistemological base. Jon Wagner suggests in Chapter 2 that at times methods and epistemology are tightly synchronized while at others they are loosely associated. The pragmatic epistemology that I suggest allows for a wide array and combination of epistemological assumptions and methodologies. Because of this, certain approaches in the chapters that follow will be immediately recognizable. Often, techniques are appropriated from established methodological traditions. At other times, newly emergent tactics are employed. Most often, these two paths intertwine in ways that draw on conventional means while pushing the boundaries to best use the image-based methodological tools. Across the types of approaches used, methodologies also vary from explicit empirical uses of documentation—a realist position—to storytelling approaches built on sequences of images—a narrative position—to integrative techniques that incorporate interviews or participants' own photographs and points of view—a reflexive position. These positions refer to commonly debated social scientific methodological assumptions rather than to the epistemological assumptions surrounding photography or images alone. Like methodological techniques, methodological positions often intertwine, although many researchers implicitly privilege one position over others.

Following the strict empirical assumptions of visual research, images are direct representations of the field once we have left. If we extend the example of church parking lots used earlier, care would be taken to frame the image so that a particular field was captured; if subsequent images were taken, the identical camera position would recapture the same field and allow for comparative analyses of correlating data. Collier and Collier (1986), in their classic *Visual Anthropology*, outline methods for recording the public landscape as well as creating a cultural inventory of private spaces. Drawing on the empirical/realist tradition of images for data collection, the Colliers remind us that the camera, as opposed to the researcher's eye, is relatively indefatigable and precise, and the image traces captured on film (or now digitally) are not susceptible to the fading memory to which even the most astute researcher is vulnerable. In other words, when we leave the field, we are no longer dependent on the few notes we could scribble while there or our recall, which is often filtered by our original research questions or the acknowledged and unacknowledged assumptions that we carry with us. We now have additional data—limited, of course, by the way we framed each shot, the focus and lighting, and the number of images we captured. Although these data are equally susceptible to filters and assumptions, the camera, as Talbot promises, will also capture data that we may not have been attuned to but can access later.

Taken at this stage alone, these explicitly empirical methodological suggestions for constructing typologies and creating indexical markers of public and private social landscapes are deeply linked to realist assumptions. Yet most often, visual research such as the richly detailed analyses that the Colliers craft is simultaneously tied to a narrative methodological position, in which images are more than the sum of their material traces. Rather, they gain meaning and depth from their use and placement in relation to each other. Images as data can be used to construct visual stories that become the building blocks of an argument. The narrative turn in the Colliers' methodology is based on systematic methods of review in which the researchers comb through images until patterns become evident. From these patterns, images are rearranged and a more narrow focus is applied that addresses and compares particular instances of this pattern. These patterns can turn into new methodologies or at least new directions for the guiding questions under consideration. Returning to the field, we may take more focused images that highlight these emerging patterns. Shooting scripts, like interview questions, are works in progress that may shift over the span of a project as new insights reveal themselves and as narratives congeal (Suchar, 1989). Within these designs, the images remain rooted in a realist methodological position, even as the methods attempt to convey visual narratives of the field. However, narrative methodological positions can be constructed using a reflexive base assumption as well.

Reflexive epistemologies of visual research hold that the meaning of the images resides most significantly in the ways that participants interpret those images, rather than as some inherent property of the images themselves. Doug Harper's (1987; see also, Harper, 2002) *Working Knowledge* illustrates this reflexive approach well by using photo elicitation. In photo elicitation methodology, images are used as part of the interview protocol (Collier & Collier, 1986). In conjunction with or as an alternative to conversational questions, participants are asked open-ended questions about a photograph. Prompting a participant with "tell me about this photograph," for example, shifts the locus of meaning away from empirically objective representations of objects or interactions. Instead, images gain significance through the way that participants engage and interpret them. Auto-driven photo elicitation takes this method one step further by removing the researcher from the image-making process altogether. Auto-driven photo elicitation can be relatively broad in focus, by asking participants to photograph or video anything they want about their life, or quite narrow, by giving them a set of specific questions to answer with their images.

The reflexive methodological position allows for the greatest malleability of conventional approaches. In fact, some suggest that unique configurations of each individual project require correspondingly new or tailor-made methods. Sarah Pink (2001), in her careful explanation of visual ethnography, argues that images cannot, or more particularly should not, fit into the already existing methodologies of the social sciences. Rather, we must develop new methodologies for this new analytic tool and data source, which will fit new ways to think in and about various social worlds. Pink's perspective is seductive for ethnographic research, and I agree that visual research requires closer methodological and theoretical attention to developing the unique grammar of images, both as data and more broadly as guiding points in everyday life. This book is one step in sparking such a discussion, but it does not attempt to accomplish that feat alone. Yet, this collection does not advocate for one methodology or propose another but rather suggests that visual methods work well in combination with others. Images and videos add an additional layer of data from which a critical reader may triangulate between statistical data, theoretical or conceptual argumentation, and the subjectively interpreted lived experience of the participants. Doing so challenges our methodologies and invigorates our inquiries.

Substantive/Theoretical Contributions

Finally, this book articulates the unique substantive findings that visual methods produce. In addition to epistemological concerns and innovative methodologies, the case studies below highlight new knowledge that might have gone unnoticed had these methods not been employed. This collection highlights new ways of thinking about a topic and new ways of understanding how our participants think about the world. By theoretical contributions, I do not mean the relatively narrow metatheoretical discourse regarding the construction of photographic or video meanings—although this may be part of the contribution—but rather the potential to think differently about the topic that we set out to investigate. Visual research reveals new insights that our conventional methodologies can miss. Such insights occur frequently in reflexive approaches when images open up internal worlds and interpretations of our participants regarding issues that we might not otherwise think to probe. More generally, the methodological contributions of deepening rapport can unlock what otherwise might be closed off. Steven J. Gold makes particular note of this in Chapter 6. Of course, we have to acknowledge that these benefits come with consequences. Whereas certain doors may be open, others may be closed. Whereas some issues may be tapped by images, other issues may go unnoticed. The camera may invoke rapport in one situation and shut it down in another. In addition to generating substantive findings, communicating these contributions of visual research, as Stephen Papson, Robert Goldman, and Noah Kersey do in Chapter 12, requires nimble translation and a challenging search for a suitable—and acceptable—home.

Outline of Chapters

The collection is loosely clustered around four sections. Chapters 2 and 3 deal with conceptual aspects of photography. Chapters 4 and 5 look at archival research. The middle of the collection—Chapters 6 through 9—consists of four various approaches to using still cameras directly in empirical research. Finally, the book concludes with three chapters that offer new directions beyond the still image.

Jon Wagner takes on the supposed divide between image makers in the social sciences and image makers as documentarians in Chapter 2. Wagner neatly encapsulates this perceived tension by suggesting that academics view documentarians as overly concerned with aesthetics while documentarians view academics as too reliant on theory-driven protocols. In unraveling this presumed tangle of disciplinary claims, Wagner asks, what makes an image credible or empirical and with whom do these decisions reside. Wagner answers these questions through historical grounding and detailed case studies that reveal epistemological similarities between these approaches and the analytical and theoretical benefits of critically reading across them.

In the third chapter, Barry M. Goldstein, a practicing photographer with a background in the medical sciences, explores through personal reflection and epistemological argument the extensive subjectivities that are bound up socially, culturally, politically, and technologically in photographs. Goldstein's title is a conscious barb intended to cut through much of the ambivalence of photographic discourse. Rather than starting from the premise that all photographs contain elements of truth, Goldstein argues that acknowledging the opposite makes us better readers and creators of images. This chapter combines methodological concerns such as social context and rapport with the often unacknowledged biases of framing, lighting, shutter speed, and even the quasi-sacred photographic dictum of the "decisive moment." Much more "decided" than decisive, all images must be understood not only by the image maker's decision process but also by the interface with the viewer.

Missionary societies of the 19th and early 20th century were meticulous record keepers of European and American colonial expansion. Photography provided a novel and efficient technology for documenting the work of mission societies, the powerful political and economic actors with whom they came in contact, and the daily and ceremonial life at the junctures of cultures. Today, digital scans of these extensive archives are increasingly available through collaborations between mission societies, scholars, and research institutions, reinvigorating a new analysis of these visual artifacts and the intricate power dynamics bound up within them. In Chapter 4, Jon Miller explores comparative/historical methodology and vividly represents the academic potential for reconsidering this data. Miller invites us—visually and conceptually—to consider potential interpretations of these archival images and to actively create our own questions about the images located in the Internet Mission Photography Archive.

In 1964, President Lyndon Johnson declared a "war on poverty," sparking policy shifts and legislation, many of which remain in certain form today. Perhaps not as well remembered was the cultural shift that Johnson also hoped to produce, in part by recruiting advisers to select photographs representing the human face of government. Erina Duganne excavates the Johnson archive in Chapter 5, tracing this short-lived project and assessing the change that was hoped for and the complications that ultimately undermined its potential. Duganne illustrates that the images and text found in the archive reveal only partial answers to her questions. Instead, Duganne suggests that we must critically consider the conflicting, underlying, and often unexamined aesthetic idiosyncrasies that influenced the multiple ways that photography was evaluated and used. By doing so, Duganne raises interesting concerns regarding the historical role and the continued assumptions of photography.

The next four chapters explicitly represent the methodological benefits and constraints of using photography as part of a broader research agenda and the new insights that can be gained from visual empirical work. Departing from the early anthropological use of cameras to illustrate a concept or a set of relationships that the researcher had already identified as relevant (Ball & Smith, 1992), these chapters reference John Collier's metaphorically rich call to employ photography as a "can opener" for deeper reflection and discussion within the interview process (Collier & Collier, 1986, p. 25). Eliciting responses through images brings the "subject" into the research process as an interpreter or even an active collaborator, rather than as a passive object of study. Steven J. Gold begins this discussion in Chapter 6 by reflecting on his years of experience researching immigrant communities in the United States. Throughout this career, photography has influenced his work in different ways and at different times. The breadth of Gold's work provides a long view of this type of qualitative approach, noting the strengths and weaknesses of the camera in the field. What is interesting about Gold's chapter is the way he reveals the manifest and latent effects of the camera in uncovering patterns of ethnic labor or gender relations within his communities of study. At times, as a result of the visual needs of the camera, Gold goes behind the scenes to document labor practices *in situ* rather than simply interviewing significant contacts in isolated office spaces. Similarly, the way that individuals respond to the camera unintentionally indicates gender patterns (both public and private) that pervade these communities. What's more, images at times contradict narrative interviews and thus provide an additional research node from which to interpret or triangulate findings.

In Chapter 7, Marisol Clark-Ibáñez thoroughly details photo elicitation as a methodological technique that circumvents elements of the researcher/subject divide. Her work among school-age children in south Los Angeles is richly substantiated and sympathetically illustrated. Clark-Ibáñez lays out the steps by which to conduct auto-driven photo elicitation research, a process in which the participants in the study capture images that are subjectively salient to their own lived experiences. One of the benefits of such an approach is the "a-ha" moment that can arise as the participants reveal segments of their lives unknown to the researcher. Clark-Ibáñez highlights the difference between her outsider eye and the children's insider view with refreshing honesty and insight. Balancing theory and on-the-ground experience, Clark-Ibáñez suggests that bringing the subject into the research as an active participant reduces the voyeurism of older models of visual research that allowed "us" to view "them" (Banks & Morphy, 1997; Lutz & Collins, 1993).

Jeffrey Samuels's Chapter 8 offers an insightful counterpoint to Clark-Ibáñez's portrait of inner-city youth. Samuels conducted extensive fieldwork within a Sri Lankan community of monks, asking questions about the aesthetic attractions leading to ordination and the ways these are transformed or reinforced as the young teen novitiates age. In his more recent trips to Sri Lanka, Samuels put cameras in the hands of the monks and asked them to take photographs of often-abstract spiritual precepts or to simply take photographs of something that "attracted their heart." The results are compelling. Samuels neatly articulates the arc in his own thinking about his research as he reviews the photographs taken by these young monks. The revelations continue as he elicits detailed and sometimes unanticipated responses during photo-driven interviews. But in addition, Samuels meticulously extracts the marked differences between the trip in which he provided a shooting script and the trip in which he allowed greater range in the choice of subject matter. His reflections raise fascinating and sensitive questions that are situated at the core of visual work.

In Chapter 9, Emmanuel David brings to life the residual evidence of political protest, social control, and local resistance through the visually evocative remnants of public art and ad hoc symbolic communication. Focusing on political posters, graffiti, and the ongoing attempts by police and others to remove these, David notes the visual aspect of public discourse and the symbolic struggles being waged over defining public space. In doing so, David's insights illustrate the everyday potential of local visual methodologies to generate theoretically compelling stories and critical assessments of the often taken-for-granted world around us.

The final three chapters in this volume push the boundaries of visual research. Although their authors have very different research agendas, these chapters suggest that our knowledge about the social world is in part constrained by the ways in which we are able to present, discuss, critique, and improve on that knowledge. New forms of visual technology and visual documentation require new forms of presentation and dissemination. As with other forms of data, visual data are influenced by the methodological approaches, ideological assumptions, and technological apparatuses used to capture them. Put succinctly, the imprint of the approach affects the outcome of the image.

Ruth Holliday addresses precisely this concern in Chapter 10, arguing that newer forms of video research, in the form of auto-driven video diaries or "confessionals," allow for greater flexibility and control among subjects in tailoring their reflexive presentation. Holliday's queer video methodology encourages the gray areas in which identities, selves, and sexualities are played with and performed. Holliday couches the empirical outcomes of this methodology in an extensive theoretical framework. Beyond the benefits for research designs, Holliday raises the prescient point that text-based disciplines are not able to adequately engage this video format without condensing it into a conventional text-based narrative. And yet it is precisely the presentation of the moving image that Holliday suggests will provide informed critiques and an open scholarly dialogue in the future.

In Chapter 11, Yolanda Hernandez-Albujar, constrained by the dynamics of her field of research, pushes against the conventional parameters of visual methods. Hernandez-Albujar explores the emotional complexities of migrant mothers working as domestic servants in the heart of Rome. Some mothers have their children with them whereas others make agonizing decisions to leave their children behind. Hernandez-Albujar argues that as a ubiquitous form of contemporary life, video has the potential to unlock reflexive and emotional responses from viewers in a way that text-based analysis cannot. However, Hernandez-Albujar's participants, many of whom were undocumented workers, were unwilling to be videotaped. Rather than forgoing the contributions that she believed video can evoke, Hernandez-Albujar's experiments with mixing the symbolic and metaphoric images of filmmaking with analytic inquiries of the social sciences. Her approach prods debates at the core of visual methodologies regarding constructed images, epistemological assumptions, and theoretical claims on social knowledge.

Stephen Papson, Robert Goldman, and Noah Kersey conclude this collection by posing a similar future-looking challenge—in their case, the epistemology of hypermedia. This team has compiled an extensive website of commercial advertising images of global capital. Publishing findings on the Web allows for vivid representations of advertising, including streaming videos, and has imaginative pedagogical applications. At the same time, virtual analyses present a variety of perplexing new questions that the conventional author need not consider. For example, Chapter 12 makes us consider the role of aesthetics for the virtual reader. How can the author attempt to direct or control the nonlinear navigation of the user/reader's surfing style? What happens to television commercials when they are remediated on the Web? And who peer-reviews a website in ways that are recognizable and valued within the academy? Such questions may be ahead of most of our curves at this point, but they clearly represent one imminent direction for our disciplines. After years of hypertext writing and website design, Papson, Goldman, and Kersey ambivalently pull back from a Web-only approach and suggest that mixed formats will serve well as a bridge to the pending but not yet secured digital future.

Reading Across Chapters

Although this book can be read in ways that attempt to amalgamate perspectives and methodological approaches into a grand toolkit, a stronger tack is to read these perspectives against each other and against the grain of their own internal positions. Contributors were selected with the hope of sparking internal conversations across the chapters. For example, Wagner's discussion (in Chapter 2) of the credibility of images among social scientists and documentary photographers is neatly balanced with a reflective piece by Goldstein (in Chapter 3), a professional photographer who operates outside the traditional bounds of academic social inquiry. Miller's historical-comparative methodology of missionary organizations (in Chapter 4) details an overarching argument for the utility of archival research, while Duganne (in Chapter 5) presents the findings of just such an archival project.

Beyond the chapters contained within these pages, comparisons should be extended to ongoing and future projects. How are the epistemological assumptions about creating social knowledge in one project applicable to your own? How might these be appropriated or nuanced for the types of questions you want to ask or for the populations you want to consider?

Let me start with the epistemological and methodological considerations first. Earlier, I suggested that reading these chapters should be an interactive epistemological odyssey engaging the authors, the readers, and various disciplinary positions. How might the assumptions embedded within one approach be lifted up and placed down within another context? How would the approach change? What might it reveal? For example, how might Miller's rereading (in Chapter 4) of archival missionary photographs depicting cultural encounters resonate in similar and different ways from Samuels's use of the camera among Sri Lankan monks (in Chapter 8)? What driving assumptions about the role of power or the translation of visuals across cultures can be assessed in each project? Do we assume different or similar meanings when we view images of different eras and from different hands? How do we clarify these distinctions in the questions we ask or the interpretations we make of these texts? What supporting or corroborating data might we seek out as we assess these distinctions? In general, each of these chapters can be juxtaposed to others in asking how we know what we know about the social world.

The overall structure of the book reinforces the clusters of methodological, theoretical/conceptual, and epistemological themes. Grounded in historical arcs, the first four chapters raise explicit theoretical, epistemological, and methodological issues with an eye toward the past as well as the present. On the other end, the final three chapters, while also empirically based, suggest interesting new questions, future directions, and the current limitations of the text-based social scientific research and reporting. These discussions book-end the four contemporary field studies nicely. As such, they raise interesting questions: How are aesthetic assumptions or truths bound up in the process of image making, selecting, and reading? How does Wagner's argument (in Chapter 2) about the construction of credible images, for example, play out in the documentation of South Central Los Angeles neighborhoods or the political graffiti in New Orleans? How do publishing constraints affect the circulation and readability of image-based projects such as visualizing immigration? What are the benefits and potential limitations of rapidly developing technology, as Gold points out in Chapter 6, for rapport and relationship building? Reading in this direction—from epistemology to empirical research—is productive, but reading in the opposite direction also offers potential insights. How might the fieldwork sharpen or be incorporated into the conceptual arguments? How might photo elicitation with archival images inform photographic use, interpretations, and memory? How will auto-driven projects document the way that certain populations experience hypermedia or advertising?

In addition to the epistemological and methodological considerations of this collection, the book may be read with an eye toward substantive interests or similarities within populations. Gender, for example, is a central concern within the social sciences. Reading across these chapters with that focus uncovers fascinating textures in the ways in which gender is displayed, performed, elicited, and resisted. Wagner, Miller, Hernandez-Albujar, Gold, and Holliday (Chapters 2, 4, 11, 6, and 10, respectively) engage this issue directly, alternating between structures and agency as genders are reproduced across starkly different times, places, and spaces. Through comparisons, we may ask how different methodologies set different parameters regarding what we can know about gender at any given time or in any given place. How might various approaches work similarly or differently if applied in different contexts or within different populations?

Children are another common concern within these projects. Clark-Ibáñez (Chapter 7) and Samuels (Chapter 8) place children at the core of their research, and Wagner (Chapter 2), Holliday (Chapter 10), and even Miller and Duganne (Chapters 4 and 5) at times add to the internal conversation about representations of and by children and teens. What works best for which set of children? How do certain approaches fit with certain populations but not others? How do representations of children function given their setting or when compared to images of adults? What might be alternative approaches to employing visual methods or visual data with children and teens?

Most social scientists who are engaged in fieldwork are concerned about cross-cultural interactions, which must be thoughtfully considered when using visual methods. Miller (Chapter 4) reminds us that the complicated and bumpy terrain of colonial encounters cannot be understood from one point of view alone; rather, cultural contact—often illustrated through photographs—involved circuitous and contradictory patterns of exchange. Samuels renegotiates this carefully in Chapter 8 while Wagner (Chapter 2) and Papson, Goldman, and Kersey (Chapter 12) unpack the process by which global cultures are documented and circulated.

Other issues crisscross through these chapters including stratification, immigration, and politics. Reading substantively scrapes along the tip of the iceberg for visually thinking through various methodological approaches to the recurring core issues within the social sciences. Rather than providing fixed answers alone, perhaps these examples will generate additional forays into visually exploring gender or childhood development or immigration, forays that will enrich those conversations.

In conclusion, visual research is not objectively better than other methodological approaches. Yet, as our world is increasingly inundated with visual representations that contribute to the meanings that our participants carry around in their heads—through advertisements, television, film, home videos, the Internet, and camera phones—image-based research holds great potential for supplementing other forms of social knowledge that will strengthen, challenge, and contradict the way we understand the social world of ourselves and others. I hope the conversations within this collection work toward that end and that these conversations extend in other projects long after this book is closed.

Note

1. Because I did not consider these as visual data at the time I took the photographs, I did not seek signed consent from the boy's guardians and therefore am unable to reproduce the images here.

References

Ball, M. S., & Smith, G. W. H. (1992). *Analyzing visual data*. Newbury Park, CA: Sage.

Banks, M., & Morphy, H. (Eds.). (1997). *Rethinking visual anthropology*. New Haven, CT: Yale University Press.

Barthes, R. (1981). *Camera lucida: Reflections on photography*. New York: Hill & Wang.

Becker, H. (1974). Photography and sociology. *Studies in the Anthropology of Visual Communication, 1*, 3–26.

Becker, H. (1986). *Doing things together*. Evanston, IL: Northwestern University Press.

Becker, H. (1996). The epistemology of qualitative research. In R. Jessor, A. Colby, & R. Shweder (Eds.), *Ethnography and human development: Context and Meaning in Social Inquiry*. Chicago: University of Chicago Press.

Berger, J., & Mohr, J. (1982). *Another way of telling*. New York: Pantheon.

Collier, J., Jr., & Collier, M. (1986). *Visual anthropology: Photography as a research method*. Albuquerque: University of New Mexico Press.

Harper, D. (1987). *Working knowledge: Skill and community in a small shop*. Chicago: University of Chicago Press.

Harper, D. (2002). Talking about pictures. *Visual Studies, 17*(1), 13–26.

Knowles, C., & Sweetman, P. (Eds). (2004). *Picturing the social landscape: Visual methods and the sociological imagination*. New York: Routledge.

Lutz, C., & Collins, J. (1993). *Reading* National Geographic. Chicago: University of Chicago Press.

Pink, S. (2001). *Doing visual ethnography: Images, media, and representation in research*. Thousand Oaks, CA: Sage.

Platt, J. (1996). *A history of sociological research methods in America*. Cambridge, UK: Cambridge University Press.

Riis, J. (1890). *How the other half lives*. New York: Charles Scribner's Sons.

Sandeen, R. J. (1995). *Picturing an exhibition:* The Family of Man *and 1950s America*. Albuquerque: University of New Mexico Press.

Steichen, E. (1955). *The family of man*. New York: Museum of Modern Art.

Suchar, C. (1989). The sociological imagination and documentary still photography. *Visual Sociology, 4*(2), 51–62.

Tagg, J. (1993). *The burden of representation*. Minneapolis: University of Minnesota Press.

Talbot, W. H. F. (1969). *The pencil of nature*. Cambridge, MA: Da Capo Press. (Original work published 1844–1846)

2

Observing Culture and Social Life

Documentary Photography, Fieldwork, and Social Research

Jon Wagner

Issues of methodology and epistemology are lodged at the heart of many forms of inquiry, but they are rarely examined as such outside philosophy or the natural and social sciences. This is both understandable and somewhat unfortunate. It's understandable because the language of science and philosophy of science is the language in which these and other *ology* words semantically reside. But anyone trying to support a claim about the world will inevitably take an epistemological position, if only by championing one kind of evidence over another—stories, for example, or spreadsheets; government or news media reports; surveys or personal experience; photographs or hearsay. In much the same way, selecting one strategy over another for collecting, organizing, or analyzing these different kinds of evidence is a methodological choice, even when made by people who never use that term.

Social scientists preoccupied by their own epistemology and methodology may not think to examine these terms as they apply to other forms of inquiry. There are lessons to be learned when they do, however, not only for people who conduct other forms of inquiry but also for social scientists themselves. As I hope to illustrate in the following pages, this is very much the case for the kind of inquiry involved with social documentary photography. From one side of the equation, this examination can reveal some of the implicit epistemological and methodological choices that shape the work of photographers interested in documenting culture and social life. From the other side, it raises questions about related choices that social researchers make, only some of which are routinely acknowledged.

My interest in social research and documentary photography was catalyzed by reading what Howard Becker and John Collier Jr. wrote about the subject several decades ago. Collier's 1967 book, *Visual Anthropology: Photography as a Research Method,* provided a thoughtful and encouraging account of how photographs could be used to make durable visual records of culture and social life and to interview research subjects through a process of photo elicitation. Although he had worked previously as a documentary photographer in the federal Farm Security Administration, Collier's 1967 monograph argued that the kind of image making most appropriate to the social sciences was systematic, deliberate, and well articulated with conventional research designs. Becker's 1974 essay on "Photography and Sociology" (published as a chapter in Becker, 1986) set aside the kind of systematic recording Collier recommended to make the somewhat different claim that, on its own terms, social documentary photography shared important elements of inquiry and representation with sociological work.

Both Becker and Collier commented on photographic practices that implicate the relationship between epistemology and methodology. One way of thinking about this relationship in general is that each research method is linked through the logic of inquiry to a distinctive set of epistemological principles. Within this perspective, methodological strategies, such as Likert scales, double-blind experimental designs, openness with field informants, confidence-building sample sizes, randomized or thematic photographic inventories; see, for example, Mead & Bateson, 1976), have a one-to-one relationship with epistemological principles.

A second way of thinking about this relationship is that it's arbitrary. Instead of a one-to-one relationship, epistemological principles and particular methodologies are aligned as one-to-many. Countless and varied approaches are equally viable, and conventions of research practice are just that, conventions, owing more to social circumstance than to epistemological rigor (Feyerabend, 1975).

Yet a third way of conceptualizing this relationship is that epistemology and methodology are "loosely coupled" (a phrase used by Weick, 1976, to describe links between levels of school hierarchies). Epistemology sets

Photo 2.1   A photograph made by John Collier, Jr., when he worked for the Farm Security Administration. The original caption reads, "Red Cross distributing knitting material. San Francisco, California, 1941."

SOURCE: Photo by John Collier Jr., courtesy of the Library of Congress.

parameters within which various (but not all) methodological approaches can be useful and methods of inquiry can support varied (but not all) logics of inquiry. Within this perspective, the conventional practices of different research communities rest on both social and epistemological foundations. Some departures from convention might be epistemologically indefensible whereas others are not only defensible but more appropriate and productive than conventional practice and, as a result, equally or more consistent with scientific inquiry.

Drawing on this notion of a loose coupling between methodology and epistemology, I will argue that social documentary photography and social science fieldwork are distinguished less by different epistemologies than by contrasting social practices. As a companion argument, I will propose that documentary photography and social science fieldwork—as complementary modes of observation-based inquiry—may have more in common with each other epistemologically than fieldwork has in common with other forms of social research.

In presenting these arguments, I'll first describe what I mean by empirical social inquiry and where that fits within documentary studies and social scientific practice. I'll then examine how ideals of empirical inquiry were articulated within three thoughtful documentary projects. Taken together as a point of both correspondence and contrast, these projects reveal three taken-for-granted practices of social researchers that warrant further consideration. These include preparing research designs that exclude personal accounts of observation and data collection, relying on academic communities to define new knowledge, and attending to explicit rather than implicit statements of social theory.

Treating these practices as social conventions of professional social researchers, rather than as derivatives of an empirical epistemology per se, could bring increased attention to their alternatives, including the practice of social documentary photography. That attention could stimulate new forms of observational study and enrich visual inquiries within the social sciences themselves. To take full advantage of these opportunities, however, will require dispositions and skills that are rarely taught in graduate research methods courses and that few social researchers have acquired on their own.

Field Methods, Documentary Studies, and Empirical Inquiry

For purposes of this chapter, I'll define *empirical social inquiry* as an effort to generate new knowledge of culture and social life through the systematic collection and analysis of sensory evidence and other forms of real-world data. This definition falls across and somewhat outside the conventions of both academic social science and professional documentary photography. It contrasts, for example, with the narrow view held by some social researchers: that empirical studies are necessarily quantitative. It also contrasts with the convictions of some image makers: that personal vision and field photography skills are all that's required to document culture and social life—a kind of "photographic faux-realism" that is more likely to undermine than affirm empirically sound inquiry.

The idea of tying inquiry to sensory evidence and other real-world data is at first blush a relatively simple matter, but it bears only an indirect relationship to how researchers tend to think about empirical social research for several reasons. First, sense data may be "real," but they can also reflect distortions of perception and memory. Eyewitness accounts and photo or video recordings may provide evidence not available in any other form, but they can also introduce judgments that depart from the facts of a matter. Material artifacts are similarly useful and problematic, not because artifacts make judgments but because the variations, arrangements, and modifications that make artifacts meaningful to researchers can reflect both naive and manipulative human agency.

The vagaries of sense perceptions and material artifacts in natural settings have led more than a few social researchers to search for more reliable indicators of culture and social life. Among the most prominent candidates are texts and numbers generated by institutions or by researchers themselves. Census data, survey responses, financial accounts, tabulations of experimental trials, health records, employment policies, achievement test scores, and so on have special attractions in this regard. Although these data rest on varied forms of self-reporting, conversation, and note taking, the uncertainties of their origins are routinely excised through standardized reporting formats. Large data sets that reflect this kind of redaction, aggregation, and reduction are an essential feature of the "hard data" romance—that is, the notion that, removed far enough from the social circumstances in which they were created, numbers and words are unambiguously objective. For many researchers, the "reliability" of these data appears as a firmer foundation for conducting empirical social inquiry than artifacts and behavior observed in natural settings.

Taken together, these considerations reflect an abiding irony of social scientific work: Investigations based on data that have been pared away from their real-world origins are regarded by many researchers as more empirically sound than investigations (including the work of documentary photographers) based on direct observations in natural settings. This inversion rests on confounding empirical value with how easily different kinds of data can be analyzed systematically. As a related instance of reliability trumping validity, direct observations of natural settings are valued less than the kinds of text and numbers that are relatively easy to reduce, aggregate, compare, and manage.

A second irony emerges, however, when we resist this kind of reification so forcefully as to reject data management of any sort. Both social researchers and documentary photographers are understandably suspicious, for example, of photographs that reflect contrived poses or processing distortions or that come with captions that misrepresent an image's origins or typicality. Posed photographs, however, provide valuable evidence of how people want to be seen by others (Pinney, 1997; Ruby, 1995), and photographed re-enactments can generate credible visual records not otherwise available (Kroeber, 2002; Rieger, 2003). Similarly, although page layouts featuring severely cropped and juxtaposed images can create false impressions, they can also highlight theoretically significant details and comparisons. The irony is that keeping data as "raw" as possible can also reduce their usefulness in answering empirical questions we care about.

Photo 2.2   Using a "peeling spud" made from an old car spring, semi-retired logger Ernie Toivonen demonstrates in 1990 the handcraft of debarking a tree in Ontonagon County, Michigan. In the course of an interview with the sociologist Jon Rieger, Toivonen offered to "show him how it was done" prior to mechanization of the pulp wood industry in the 1970s and 1980s. Following up on Toivonen's invitation to re-enact this technique, Rieger photographed aspects of a logger's craft that were no longer practiced and for which no historical images were to be found.

SOURCE: © Jon Rieger; used with permission.

These ambiguities complicate the challenge of determining whether projects of social scientific and documentary work are empirically sound. However, they also suggest how social science fieldwork and documentary photography are joined at the epistemological hip in ways that also distinguish them from nonobservational forms of social research. Documentary photographers and social science fieldworkers—ethnographers and participant observers, in particular—both regard direct observation as an essential step toward understanding culture and social life. This is not to say that nothing valuable can be learned through other methods of inquiry—surveys or laboratory experiments, for example, or the analysis of institutional data. However, as Tope, Chamberlain, Crowley, and Hodson (2005) concluded from their extensive review of the research literature about work, some things learned through direct observation in natural settings are difficult or impossible to learn in any other way.

As a correlative to this shared epistemological principle, most field researchers and documentary photographers are willing to regard photographs as durable and useful records of what was visible in a cultural or social setting at a particular time and from a particular point of view. They recognize that it's not always easy to make those records in the way we will later find most useful, nor is it a simple matter to understand what's depicted fairly in images made by others. But these uncertainties fall inside, not outside, the scope of their epistemology and point to questions that field researchers and documentary photographers are comfortable working with and around. That's not necessarily the case for social researchers who work at greater remove and who consider photographs to be more credible if they are "untouched by human hands" or dismiss the evidentiary value of images for which that's clearly not the case.

Social documentary photographers, and many social science field researchers, will argue that the idea that photographs and other machine-recorded data can be generated without human agency is both naive and misguided. They regard in similar terms the idea that a photographer's selectivity in one dimension makes an image wholly suspect in all others (Schwartz, 1999). In contrast to more extremist views, field researchers and thoughtful documentary photographers are less interested in the absolute truth of an individual image than in the partial and multiple truths of image collections related to a particular project or study. As a counterpoint to this common epistemological ground, however, the practices by which they describe and contextualize field inquiries are not at all the same.

Research Designs and Personal Accounts

One tool for helping researchers and others determine what a set of photographs might contribute to a project of empirical inquiry is a written proposal or research design, an explicit description of how a study is organized and how the right kind of evidence can be brought to bear in answering predetermined questions. By and large, that's where social scientists place their own trust and hope. Regardless of the kinds of data they choose to examine, a good research design advances the claim that the researcher has conducted (or is about to conduct) an empirically sound investigation, a study for which methods and epistemology are in harmony.

Relying on research designs to advance these claims suggests that the main threats to empirical inquiry are those that a research design can guard against. For example, statements by social scientists frequently do a good job of accounting for sample size, site selection, the wording of survey or interview questions, or the preparation of appropriate observation schedules and coding strategies. But social science research designs are typically silent about other potential pitfalls. They rarely note the full range of an investigator's interest in a topic or a study site, preview indeterminate features of the research process, or describe the researcher's honesty, interpersonal skills, or ability to elicit cooperation and useful information from research subjects. Leaving these potentially problematic elements out of a research design affirms an epistemology in which the researcher's role dominates the researcher, in which an investigator's formal plan transcends the crafts of observation and inquiry.

Personal accounts are another tool for establishing the credibility of empirical social inquiry. They're used rarely by professional social researchers (although efforts to clarify a researcher's "positionality" are of a kindred sort) but frequently by documentary image makers. Some such accounts are infused within the body of a documentary project itself, the way James Agee spoke for himself and Walker Evans in *Let Us Now Praise Famous Men* (1939/1960). In other instances, they appear as forewords, afterwords, and interviews that documentary image makers give about their work (Light, 2000; Loengard, 1998; Lyons, 1966; Morris, 1999). In the aggregate, these narrative accounts by documentary image makers affirm an epistemology in which people shape inquiry and in which the crafts of observation and inquiry transcend research designs.

In making connections between methodology and epistemology, research designs and personal accounts refer to complementary dimensions of empirical quality. Taken together, these dimensions circumscribe familiar issues of data collection and analysis. However, they also point to myriad other choices that investigators make as they go about their work—deciding when data are complete enough to warrant analysis, for example, or selecting details to report as illustrations and examples, choosing a starting point for introducing or framing a study, pitching descriptions to a particular level of abstraction or generality, identifying or cultivating audiences for which a study might be of interest, and so on.

By paying attention to how these choices affect the truthfulness of their work, social researchers and documentary image makers stand on the same side of the empirical divide. This distinguishes their work from other ways of approaching the world—divine revelation, for example, or fantasy making, psychological projection, speculation, or demagoguery. Alternatives to empirical inquiry also include forms of photographic work in which documentary appearances are pursued with great skill and thoughtfulness. Photographic faux-realism of this sort, for example, appears routinely in advertising and political campaigns (Bumiller, 2003; Heffernan, 2003) and in training manuals (for an exceptional example, see Pepin, 1976). A similar emphasis on projective imagery characterizes many (but by no means all) forms of journalism (Hagaman, 1993, 1996) and family photography (Chalfen, 1987, 1991). Scholars have examined the assumptions, fabrications, and projections that shape such imagery as intriguing evidence about culture and social life (Lesy, 1973, 1976, 1980; Ruby, 1995), but the most telling images for studies of this sort are made for completely different purposes.

Against the backdrop of these alternative perspectives, social researchers rest their case for the soundness of empirical inquiry on research designs, relative to which personal accounts play a minor role. The emphasis among documentary photographers is just the opposite. A related contrast appears in how inventions of the investigator are regarded within these two different forms of inquiry.

Inventions and Reflections

In explicating their method and epistemology, social researchers, photographers, and artists can be more or less self-conscious about what their accounts and reports add to what they've seen. Walker Evans, for example, referred to his work not as documentary photography but as "art done in a documentary style" (Hambourg, Rosenheim, Eklund, & Fineman, 2000). Other documentary image makers have been less careful or held contrary beliefs. In his prejudicial framing, selection, and printing of supposedly realistic images, W. Eugene Smith may be more the rule than the exception among well-known documentary photographers (de Miguel, 2002). Even realist landscape photographers such as Ansel Adams (who railed against the subjectivities of "pictorialism") have adjusted the tone, contrast, and framing of their photographs to better express their own strongly held ideas about how the places they photographed "should look" (Brower, 1998). Other documentary photographers have done much the same in depicting culture and social life.

Photo 2.3   The original caption reads, "Movie theatre on Saint Charles Street. Liberty Theater, New Orleans, Louisiana. 1935–36." Walker Evans described his work not as documentary photography but as "art done in a documentary style."

SOURCE: Photo by Walker Evans, courtesy of the Library of Congress.

In thinking through where the inventions of documentary image makers fit along what I've called the empirical divide, there's much to learn from the work of social researchers themselves. Stimulated in part by Becker (1986) and Collier (1967), scholarly writing in this area has increased substantially in recent years through monographs (Banks, 2001; Emmison & Smith, 2000; Harper, 1982, 1987, 2001; Pink, 2001; Ruby, 2000), edited collections (Prosser, 1998), and an expanded array of journals (*Visual Studies, The Journal of Visual Studies, The Journal of Visual Culture, Visual Anthropology, Visual Anthropology Review*, etc.). However, methodological treatments of image work within the social science literature are dominated by issues of research design to the neglect of personal vision and craft. This can push the latter outside the epistemological purview of social inquiry, but there's much to gain from keeping them in.

Personal accounts by documentary photographers can alert us to somewhat different ways of thinking about empirical visual inquiry. Dorothea

Lange, for example, displayed prominently over her desk the following quotation from Sir Francis Bacon, an early proponent of empirical inquiry: "The contemplation of things as they are, without substitution or imposture, without error or confusion, is in itself a nobler thing than a whole harvest of invention" (in Lyons, 1966, p. 67). Lange arranged, cropped, sequenced, and edited her photographs to make documents that went beyond—in meaning and social impact—her camera's capacity to record the visible details she aimed it at (Coles, 1997). However, she also appears to have taken Bacon's statement seriously, at the very least as an alternative to the commercial photographic work she produced prior to her better known and explicitly documentary projects.

Photo 2.4   These two images were both made from the same Dorothea Lange photograph. Lange printed the image on the left "full frame" but cropped it to create the image on the right and focus on the man and his expression of despair.

SOURCE: Both photographs by Dorothea Lange, courtesy of the Library of Congress.

An empirical ideal for photographic work has also been championed by Wright Morris, a documentary photographer, fiction writer, and essayist. Morris (1999) argued that, "We should make the distinction, while it is still clear, between photographs that mirror the subject, and images that reveal the photographer. One is intrinsically photographic, the other is not" (p. 8). However, in what looks at first like a contradiction to the mirror ideal, Morris also noted that "only fiction will accommodate the facts of life," adding that "our choice, in so far as we have one, is not between fact and fiction, but between good and bad fiction" (p. 103).

Considered in light of his other writing, Morris's statement reveals what I've come to regard as a radical or root appreciation of empirical inquiry that is hard to find within the social science literature per se. At the heart of this epistemology are two key ideas that Morris developed more fully in both his photography and writing: First, that every account of "the facts of life" will reflect some form of inventiveness by investigators and reporters, not just in making photographs or putting words on a page or quantifying variables, but in linking observations of any sort to concepts, theories, or narratives— what Charles Ragin (1992) refers to as *casing*. Second, depending on the intention, skill, and integrity of the investigator, these inventions can move an account closer to or farther away from "things as they are."

Morris did not examine this provocative link between empirical inquiry and fiction in social scientific terms, but James Clifford (1986) did just that a few decades later, in characterizing "ethnography as fiction" (p. 6), but a kind of fiction that's not necessarily false or untrue. In Clifford's perspective, rhetorical inventions fall within both the fieldworker's tool kit and the epistemology of science, not as a substitute for detailed observation and systematic analysis but as their handmaiden. As Sarah Pink (2001), Doug Harper (1998), and others have noted, this argument applies as well to the rhetoric of photographic reports, within which the personal vision of social researchers—as an instrument of investigation—can contribute substantively to empirically sound accounts. Within this orientation, issues of representation are integral to the process of social inquiry, not just a dimension of inquiry products (e.g., articles, books, photographs, films).

Within the notion of loosely coupled epistemology and methods, incorporating invention as a necessary element of empirical inquiry does not mean "anything goes." However, to get comparable, empirically sound information, experienced field researchers recognize that they may need to alter a line of questioning from one informant to another. Along the same lines, it might be necessary to use different lenses, vantage points, or image-making strategies in one setting than in another. In some cases, a researcher might have to move objects around so that they can be better seen and recorded. It also might be necessary to use artificial lighting to make a photograph that looks like what we can see in the field under "natural light" or to resequence raw film footage so that events and settings are more comprehensible and clear. There's also much to be learned about culture and social life from how participants respond to outsiders, including outsiders who come with cameras, videotape recorders, and questions that might otherwise never be asked (Biella, 1988).

As Morris intimated, the choice is not between truth and invention but between inventions that lead toward truths and those that lead away from them. This ties the soundness of empirical inquiry not only to techniques and methods but to the ethics and integrity of the investigator. Although reflection and invention are not quite the same as objectivity and subjectivity, Robert Coles (1997) speaks to the epistemological dimensions of each in noting

> To take stock of others is to call upon oneself—as a journalist, a writer, a photographer, or a doctor or a teacher. This mix of the objective and the subjective is a constant presence and, for many of us, a constant challenge—what blend of the two is proper, and at what point shall we begin to cry "foul"? (p. 8)

Three Exemplary Projects

An epistemology that includes both reflection and invention as essential elements of empirical inquiry is hard to define beyond statements of principle such as those provided by Morris or Bacon, or critiques of scientism such as those offered by Marcus, Pink, and others, or a call to honesty and thoughtfulness such as that provided by Coles. It certainly doesn't turn neatly into a checklist of methodological do's and don'ts. And it falls far short of (or extends beyond, depending on your point of view) explicit guidelines for collecting or analyzing specific kinds of data—photographs or videotapes, interview transcripts, survey responses, or census tract figures. In the simplest terms, it calls for nothing more and nothing less than trying to ground ideas about the world as much as possible in observations of the world, to notice what's visible and account for it in ways that "get it right."

Many social scientists spend their working lives trying to come as close as they can to this ideal. As illustrated by the three projects described below, so too do some documentary photographers. Although none of these projects has been embraced as bona fide social research by professional sociologists or anthropologists, each reflects a systematic approach to empirical inquiry, the intent to create new knowledge, and an effort to extend and refine social theory. In these respects, the epistemology behind these projects overlaps considerably with the perspective of social research, and with fieldwork in particular. After briefly describing each project, I'll turn to two related questions: First, how do the practices that generated these three projects of empirical inquiry differ from what we've come to expect from social scientists? Second, what implications do these differences have for how social researchers are prepared to study culture and social life?

Material World

Few documents provide a more provocative depiction of social and economic inequality than the book, *Material World: A Global Family Portrait* (Menzel, 1994), a survey in photographs, text, and statistics of the household possessions and routines of a single family from each of 30 countries. In the six to eight pages allotted to each of these families, the authors present a wide range of data: a demographic profile and a paragraph or two about each country; an array of captioned photographs showing the "daily life" of family members; a summary of each family's possessions and living space, including the "most valued possession" identified by different family members; and a brief account by the photographer. For each family, we also are provided with what Menzel calls the "Big Picture," a single large photograph of family members standing or seated among all their possessions, outside their home. These provocative images are interesting in their own right. They are rendered more informative by a legend that identifies objects and people and a list in the Appendix (p. 253) of additional objects not included in the photo.

Both photographs and text of *Material World* are clearly designed for impact, but pains were taken to make the impact empirically credible. The book provides a list of references and data sources and a table comparing all 30 countries on 22 different demographic variables. The selection of families is also described in enough detail, individually and in the aggregate, to alert readers to important qualifications and sampling questions and to provide some sense of the immediate circumstances in which photographers worked.

Photo 2.5   The Namgay family, Shinka, Bhutan, 1993.

SOURCE: © 2006 Peter Menzel/menzelphoto.com.

In his own account of photographing the family portrayed in Photo 2.5, for example, Menzel (1994) writes,

> For six days I lived with the Namgay family in a twelve-house village an hour's walk from a 7-mile dirt road off a small paved road four hours from Thumphy, the capital. The Namgays had never seen a TV, an airplane, or for that matter a live American before and were as curious about me as I was about them. I had dinner with a different family every night, the same basic good food that I ate gladly with one hand as my legs ached from sitting cross-legged on the floor (My other hand fanned the flies from my food) . . . Wild marijuana grows everywhere, but villagers feed it to their pigs after boiling it. The sounds were incredible: women singing in the fields as they harvested wheat, the murmur of monks chanting, the squeal of children playing, all without the haze of electronic noise I have unfortunately come to take for granted. On the other hand, all was not paradisiacal. Animals and people excreted just outside the house and the family cooked inside on an open fire. (p. 78)

We don't know from this comment alone exactly how Menzel decided what to photograph, but we do get some insight into the cultural contrasts and personal dispositions that shaped his image making in the field.

A sympathetic reading of *Material World* requires that we ignore, at least for the moment, the cultural and economic diversity within each country.

Photo 2.6   An English lesson in the school attended by 12-year-old Bangum Namgay, an hour's trek from her home in Shinka, Bhutan, 1993.

SOURCE: © 2006 Peter Menzel/menzelphoto.com.

However, Menzel presents the book not to challenge or discourage that kind of complexity but to resist another kind of simplification. As he notes: "Newspaper, magazine and television stories almost always deal with the extremes: famine, flood, mass killing, and, of course, the life-styles of the rich and famous . . . I wanted to give some insight into the rest of the world" (p. 255).

The empirical value of *Material World* rests in part on the study design, in part on an ability to elicit cooperation from the families themselves. This cooperation was inextricably tied to both data collection and reporting. Indeed, the power of the *Material World* accounts, family by family and country by country, hangs on making the visual comparisons and contrasts somewhat systematic. This applies with special force to the "Big Picture." Inventories of household possessions have been described by anthropologists such as Collier (1967), Oscar Lewis (1965), and Janet Hoskins (1998). They are given added punch, however, by the technical virtuosity and documentary skill of the *Material World* photographers. As anyone who has tried it can attest, it is no small matter to arrange diverse materials so that they are all visible at the same time, let alone to light and focus the array in ways that will produce a well-exposed and legible image.

Photo 2.7   The Skeen Family, Pearland, Texas, 1993.

SOURCE: © 2006 Peter Menzel/menzelphoto.com.

The same technical and representational skills that *Material World* photographers used to create empirically sound images could also be used to misrepresent culture and social life. We don't know for a fact that they weren't used in just that way, although we have many indications that this was not the photographers' intent. It's also clear that families willing to sit for such extended and intrusive portraits might differ somewhat from those who were not so inclined. And the idea of finding one family from each country flies in the face of more comprehensive and differentiated surveys. Although the imperfections of this research design are acknowledged rather than concealed, some readers might take them seriously enough to wholly dismiss what *Material World* has to offer. However, a more appropriate test of empirical merit is framed by the following two questions: Do we know more about social and economic inequality between different countries as a result of this book, or less? And is what we know well grounded enough in empirical evidence to challenge speculation and ignorance? For some kinds of speculation and ignorance, I certainly think it is.

Photo 2.8   The Qampie Family, Soweto, South Africa.

SOURCE: © 2006 Peter Menzel/menzelphoto.com.

Girl Culture

The questions noted above are also worth considering in connection with Lauren Greenfield's documentary study, *Girl Culture* (2002). Like the creators of *Material World*, Greenfield seems intent on "getting it right" empirically—recording what she sees and what her subjects have to say in

Photo 2.9   Two 15-year-old girls try on clothes in a dressing room, San Jose, California.

SOURCE: Photo © Lauren Greenfield/VII.

ways that both document and raise questions about culture and social life. Indeed, the artful juxtaposition of comments and images from different but related scenes is, in her hands, a tool of both personal and collective inquiry. In one cluster of photographs, for example, she records a range of women and girls working on their appearance in mirrors. Through another set of photographs, she shows a diverse array of girls and women in different forms of "dressing up" (Photos 2.10, 2.11, and 2.12).

In putting together images of this sort, Greenfield suggests the fundamentally exhibitionist dimension of feminine identity, a theme that plays back and forth between mass-market icons and personal appearance. As Greenfield (2002) puts it,

> The body has become the primary canvas on which girls express their identities, insecurities, ambitions and struggles. I have documented this phenomenon and at the same time explore how this canvas is marked by the values and semiotics of the surrounding culture. (p. 150)

As an important variation on this theme, she also reminds us that the exhibitionist equation works well only for a few women whose physiognomy matches well-advertised icons, and not even that well for those. This encourages, as Greenfield sees it, the constant scrutiny and disaffection that women express toward their own bodies and heightens the temptations of plastic surgery or physical self-abuse.

Photo 2.10   Augusta, 22, the newly crowned Queen of the Cotton Ball, Chattanooga, Tennessee.

SOURCE: Photo © Lauren Greenfield/VII.

In much the same way that Erving Goffman (1963) called attention to the "total institution" as an ideal type that could characterize quite diverse organizations (prisons, monasteries, mental hospitals, boarding schools,

Photo 2.11   Exotic dancer Tammy Boom backstage at Little Darlings, Las Vegas, Nevada.

SOURCE: Photo © Lauren Greenfield/VII.

Photo 2.12   Elita, 6, at a birthday party where girls have their hair and makeup done, play dress-up, model in a fashion show, and have a tea party, Hollywood, California.

SOURCE: Photo © Lauren Greenfield/VII.

and so on), Greenfield's work calls attention to "girl culture" as an ideal typical configuration of values, practices, and ideas through which women define and display their sexual identity. As she puts it (Greenfield, 2002), "Understanding the dialectic between the extreme and the mainstream—the anorectic and the dieter, the stripper and the teenager who bares her midriff or wears a thong—is essential to understanding contemporary feminine identity" (p. 150).

Like the authors of *Material World*, Greenfield combines powerful photographs with other data, including extended interview comments by the subjects of her study. In keeping with her intentions, these commentaries give her treatment of "girl culture" empirical depth and complexity. "As the photographs are my voice," she notes, "the interviews give voice to the girls." The credibility of Greenfield's work is also enhanced by the candor and caution she expresses in describing her own "inventiveness" and vision. She acknowledges that while the photographs "are about the girls I photographed . . . They're also about me." At another point, she reminds

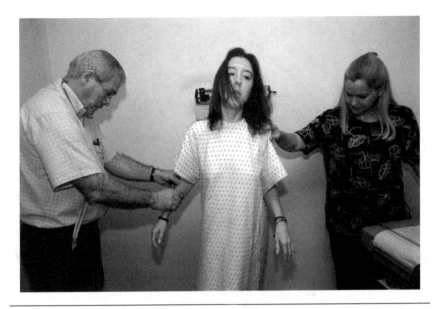

Photo 2.13   Erin, 24, is blind-weighed at an eating-disorder clinic, Coconut Creek, Florida. She has asked to mount the scale backward so as not to see her weight gain.

SOURCE: Photo © Lauren Greenfield/VII.

us that, "Infinite choices were made in the subject matter, the point of view, in the moment I depressed the shutter, in the editing. Ultimately, *Girl Culture* looks at a wide spectrum of girls through a very narrow prism" (all quotes on page 152).

In another parallel to *Material Culture*, it's not just the photographs and interviews that create the "new knowledge" of *Girl Culture*, but the comparative framework within which Greenfield has placed them—in this case, comparing women across age groups and social status instead of countries. Thoughtfully framed and sequenced, her photographs create a credible multidimensional account, a kind of meta-image that both references and questions other images of women with which we are already familiar.

The Great Central Valley

The *Great Central Valley: California's Heartland* is a collaborative social history prepared by photographers Stephen Johnson and Robert Dawson

Photo 2.14   Wind gap pumping station, California Aqueduct, Kern County, 1985.

SOURCE: Photo by Stephen Johnson.

and the essayist and novelist Gerald Haslam (Johnson, Dawson, & Haslam, 1993). The book combines an extraordinary array of visual materials and a lengthy text that includes personal accounts, observations and reviews of scholarship from a wide range of disciplines—economics, agronomy, anthropology, and so on. These varied materials are organized as convincing empirical evidence of the changing life and culture of the Central Valley of California. In the same chapter, we can find FSA photographs from the 1930s, contemporary black and white photos made in the same geographical area (that look as if they could have been taken by FSA photographers), contemporary color photographs of both old and new icons, other old photographs (some of which have been rephotographed), satellite photographs, maps, and the reproduction of a landscape painting.

Like the creators of *Material World* and *Girl Culture,* the authors of *California Heartland* describe the process of their own creation, in this case through another book by Johnson called *Making a Digital Book* (1993). This companion volume provides additional details about how *California Heartland* was designed and put together, both technically and conceptually. We learn that a prerelease version of Adobe Photoshop allowed Johnson to improve the clarity of old photographs by removing "cracks, serious scratches,

Photo 2.15   Johnnie, Merced, California, 1975.

SOURCE: Photo by Stephen Johnson.

and other artifacts of age" and that he also altered "contrast and brightness" to make some images more legible, but that the digital photo editing only went so far: "I was careful to respect the integrity of the original, however, and did not remove or add any real objects" (p. 9). Johnson's account of how ideas within the book came forth is equally explicit.

> Once I had settled on a basic grid (for the design), my primary task was to find a relationship between the text and photographs that was integrated, but not directly illustrative. That really was the largest single design challenge, and the most time consuming. I had to know the photographs, read every word of the text, and imagine relationships. (p. 15)

We might like to know more about the process by which Johnson "imagined" relationships between words and images in preparing *California Heartland,* but the detail he has provided—including how he chose to present this study to others—goes well beyond what we'd expect from a social science research design.

Photo 2.16   Used cans, crop-dusting airstrip, Newman, California, 1984.

SOURCE: Photo by Stephen Johnson.

Photo 2.17   Discovery Bay, San Joaquin Delta, California, 1985.

SOURCE: Photo by Stephen Johnson.

Documentary and Social Scientific Practices

How did the photographers and writers who created these three projects approach the ideal of sound empirical inquiry? And where do the documentary practices they relied on depart from the conventions of social research?

In trying to answer these two questions, let me begin by noting that all three documentary studies make extensive use of recorded images to represent how culture and social life looks in particular times and places and that the images themselves provide a kind of information that's difficult to represent in text alone. This is true not only for the sheer wealth of visual detail but for the precise imaging of physical and social environments from particular viewpoints, the juxtaposition of contrasting images, and the sequences and formats in which we encounter images as readers. Indeed, the photographs in these three studies go well beyond the common social science trope of "illustrating" ideas that are otherwise well accounted for in text. They provide instead a form of content that is analytically interesting in its own right.

In arguing for the empirical credibility of this content, these documentary image makers give more attention to challenges of recording good evidence than do most social researchers. In *Material World*, for example, we find not only a description of how the photographs were made in general, but individual accounts from photographers about each family photographed. The two photographers working on *California's Heartland* offer individual accounts of what they were doing photographically in studying the Great Central Valley, as does Greenfield for her work with *Girl Culture*.

The origins of these documentary studies are also described in terms that are more personal and situational than is typical for social science study designs. Greenfield notes that she was "enmeshed in girl culture before I was a photographer, and I was photographing girl culture before I realized I was working on *Girl Culture*." Johnson reports (1993) that he "embarked on the Central Valley project to better understand the place that made me a landscape photographer" (p. 43). Menzel's (1994) account of what led him to the kind of data reported in *Material World* refers not only to the United Nation's International Year of the Family (1994) and his previous work as a photojournalist, but also to a program he heard on the radio about marketing a sex-fantasy book by the pop star Madonna: "The book and the singer seemed to hold more interest for people than the pressing issues of our day. I thought the world needed a reality check" (p. 255).

Evidence about how individual images were made and about the personal interests of investigators does not necessarily make studies more empirically sound—see Biella (1988) and Ruby (1976) for contrasting views on this. However, it can help us determine how close a study comes to hitting its empirical marks. In mainstream social science reporting, an explicit research design is called on to help make that determination. The documentary studies reviewed here don't provide that, but they do offer some sense of where the data come from and where the authors think the findings of their studies might or might not apply. For example, Greenfield (2002) contends that "*Girl Culture* is my photographic examination of an aspect of our culture that leaves few women untouched." However, she also cautions that the book "does not attempt to represent the experience of all girls in American, or even the full and rich experience of any girl I photographed" (both quotes from p. 150). Similar efforts to focus and delimit empirical significance appear within the other two studies.

Many realistic-looking photo studies have been created by reducing a large collection of photographs to a carefully edited display of just a few. In contrast to less thoughtful efforts, however, the imagery of the three studies reviewed here seems well selected, sequenced, and spaced to represent analytical themes. Individual images and image sets provide the core content of each study. However, they also are articulated with data from other sources—including interviews, direct field observation, historical records, and demographic statistics. The authors and photographers of these studies also have taken some pains to describe their work processes and to characterize the empirical warrant of their work.

Although they depart from conventional social science reporting practices, these features help create a kind of harmony between data, methodology, and epistemology that we have come to associate with sound empirical work. Somewhat similar patterns appear in how these studies address two other challenges I noted earlier: framing empirical observations to highlight new knowledge and challenging existing social theory.

Highlighting New Knowledge

Social researchers define and present new knowledge by publishing articles and books for specialized academic communities and markets. For them to regard knowledge as "new," it has to be new for colleagues already hard at work studying related questions and phenomena. Documentary image makers approach this challenge somewhat differently. They're not particularly interested in creating knowledge that appears to be "new" only to small groups of social scientists. Like social researchers, they want their work to be recognized and well regarded by professional peers. However, documentary image makers also pitch their inquiries to other audiences, including the subjects of their study and members of the public who may already harbor ideas about the visual evidence the image makers have put together.

As one step toward reaching this broader audience, some documentarians (including those I've described here) frame their work as the result of a personal journey that led to new insights and understanding. Johnson (1993) notes that while making photographs for *California Heartland* began in territory familiar to him, it "grew into the discovery of a place I didn't know very well. It became an exploration of land use, water use, agricultural practices, racism and poverty" (p. 43). In establishing points of personal connection with both professional and public audiences, Greenfield (2002) reports that "*Girl Culture* has been my journey as a photographer, as an observer of culture, as part of the media, as a media critic, as a woman, as a girl" (p. 149). This personal and public rhetoric contrasts with how social researchers index their own reports to specific research publications and communities (Richardson, 1991).

The documentary image makers reviewed here also give much more attention than social researchers usually do to issues of editing, layout, and visual representation. Not only do they make explicit the aesthetic dimensions of this work, they link design issues directly to both analysis and audience. I've already noted Johnson's extended account of what it took to prepare *California Heartland* in book form; Menzel and Greenfield also offer explicit commentary about designing their books. As another illustration of this emphasis, Greenfield (2002) distinguishes her contributions to *Girl Culture* from other instances in which the same photographs appeared for other purposes: "While I often can't control the picture editing, writing and design in my work for magazines, the selection and presentation of photographs in this book are my own" (p. 152).

For all three documentary image makers and authors, the boundary between research subjects and public communities is also blurred, all the more so because each has encouraged distribution of this work in other forms. *California Heartland* was at first a documentary project, then an exhibit in the Central Valley itself and a symposium, then a book, and later a book about the book. *Girl Culture* also began as a documentary project, elements of which appeared in mass market publications, and the book is now complemented by a traveling photo exhibit and a website that includes an online photo gallery, transcripts of all 20 interviews reported on in the book, a teaching guide, links to organizations working on related issues, video interviews with Greenfield, and an opportunity to participate in related online forums. The work brought together in *Material Culture* has also appeared in other publications, and a CD–ROM is now available that both replicates and extends the content of the book. Taken together, these activities and media provide a larger and more variegated public presence than we would expect from a publication alone, let alone a publication addressed primarily to social scientists.

The "new knowledge" available to research subjects and the public through these documentary materials is available to sociologists and anthropologists as well, but it's not inscribed in mainstream social science journals. Indeed, the rhetorical conventions of that literature—the emphasis on words and numbers, accompanied at times by figures and charts, organized around arguments and summarized "findings"—are problematic for documentary image makers.

These problems become apparent when we try to imagine converting any of these three studies into standard social science reports. An abstract or synopsis of each might be noteworthy, but it would also fall far short of the new knowledge we're likely to acquire from reading each work as a whole. Some of this new knowledge is acquired in a process of elicited meaning and inquiry. As Paul Kennedy notes in his introduction to *Material World* (Menzel, 1994), "The real benefit to learning that the reader can extract from this project depends on going into the details, especially on a comparative basis. New kinds of valuable inquiry can be generated by such detailed observation" (p. 7; i.e., "observing" the book itself).

As a related point of contrast, the balance between evidence and interpretation in the documentary projects reviewed here is weighted more toward evidence than is customary for social science research reports. In all three cases, materials are presented, for example, without being fully interpreted or analyzed, with the expectation that some dimensions of analysis are appropriately left to the reader or viewer. That may make documentary studies somewhat more ambiguous than social scientific reports, but it does not make them any less empirical.

Challenging Social Theory

Girl Culture includes an introduction by Joan Jacobs Brumberg, a professor of human development and women's studies at Cornell University, and in her own commentary, Greenfield refers to a few scholarly studies that helped shape her thoughts. *California Heartland* is heavily referenced to the work of historians, geographers, and policy analysts. And *Material World* lists numerous sources that someone could consult to learn more about the countries and issues it examines. However, just as none of these projects take social researchers per se as their primary audience, neither do they frame insights to readers as a contribution to academic scholarship. Johnson (1993) is quite explicit about his interest in avoiding both romantic and academic genres: "None of us wanted this project to become another photography book idealizing a landscape," he notes, "Nor did we want the book to become an historical dissertation" (p. 15).

This apparent neglect of disciplinary scholars goes hand in hand with the interest of documentary image makers in attracting other audiences. However, it also reflects alternative ideas about where social theories are most likely to be found, acquired, and contested. Social scientists pay the most attention to theories inscribed explicitly in published social science texts. Documentarians might acknowledge this kind of theory as well, but they also attend to a wide range of cultural materials in which social theories are more embedded than explicated—texts, of course, but also news accounts, folklore, and mass media imagery. Instead of contesting theories and hypotheses, the documentary projects I've described here are designed to challenge ideas and imagery.

These image-based challenges to social theory can mirror exchanges among academics about different theoretical perspectives, interpretations, and data sets, but they can take other forms as well. For example, Johnson and his associates reproduce in *California Heartland* some policy documents and photographs that they then call into question through juxtapositions with other documents, their own photographs, or the testimony of local participants. Greenfield both photographs and critiques some of the images that the people she studied respond to in constructing their identities. With admirable candor, she notes that as a journalist, she even helped make some of the images that fall within her critiques. Menzel (1994) saw *Material World* as a way not only to illustrate "the great differences in material goods and circumstances that make rich and poor societies" (p. 7) but also to challenge less credible ideas, some of them supported by images he had helped create through previous photographic assignments. In each case, the documentary photographs presented by these authors are framed to challenge other images that reflect existing, largely implicit, and widely held ideas about culture and social life—elements of social theory, by any other name.

Observational Methods, Evidence, and Meaning

In terms of empirical social inquiry, the three documentary studies I've described are exemplary. Other studies might be called *documentary* because they include realistic photographs of people and places. In looking to documentary image making for empirically sound accounts of culture and social life, however, I suggest we seek out works similar to those I've reviewed here, studies that not only offer interesting imagery but also reflect a concerted effort, in Morris's (1999) words, to "mirror the subject" that they purport to depict.

Having said that, if we think of *Girl Culture, California Heartland,* and *Material World* as merely documentary work, we isolate what we can learn about empirical inquiry through projects of this sort from how we think about social research. A more productive strategy is to consider each project as an instance of empirical social inquiry, analytically defined. Instead of asking, "What's the difference between documentary photography, narrative accounts, and sociology or anthropology?" we might ask, "How does empirical social inquiry look when practiced by skilled sociologists or anthropologists, and how does it look when practiced by skilled documentary photographers, journalists, and essayists? Given an epistemology of empirical social inquiry, where can we go and what can we see through these varied forms of practice?"

As a partial answer to these questions, I've summarized in Table 2.1 some of the contrasts noted above between social science and documentary studies. These contrasts suggest that, in some circumstances, one approach to empirical social inquiry might work better than the other. For example, if we want to build a written literature around a distinctive set of concepts and questions—a disciplinary tradition, so to speak—the conventions of social science have the most to offer. Why? Because they require that new work be tightly indexed to the work of other scholars who have wrestled in writing with similar questions and concepts. This kind of intertextuality both reflects and stimulates the evolution of a literate community. But if we care less about literature building in academia than community building in the field, documentary work with images has real advantages of its own.

These advantages certainly apply to the challenge of informing public discourse, but they also have special relevance for human service professionals. In studying local clients and communities, for example, teachers, social workers, community organizers, and health care professionals may find documentary conventions more agreeable and productive than social scientific approaches. They don't need to know if new ground is being broken for the disciplines of psychology, sociology, or anthropology to learn something of value and relevant to their work. Without referring to the literature of social research per se, "new" knowledge and insights can come their way by looking at videotapes of student small-group discussions, by making and examining photographs of institutional events and routines, or by working with young and old community members to document neighborhood and family traditions.

The contrasting merits of documentary study and social research as resources for field-based professionals extend as well to undergraduate curricula and students. Social scientific knowledge is essential to an informed citizenry, but so too are documentary studies and the ability to think clearly

Table 2.1 Two Modes of Empirical Social Inquiry

	Social Science	Documentary Study
Purpose	Develops new knowledge and understanding of culture and social life through empirical investigation and scholarly works	Develops new knowledge and understanding of culture and social life through empirical investigation and public works
Research design	Dedication to explicit research design, including a priori rationale for linking questions with appropriate data sources, scope of data desired, identification of analysis strategies, and so on; emphasizes testing ideas through narrowly bounded inquiry; separation of personal interest from logic of inquiry	Casual attention to research design; implicit and diffuse statement of research questions, data sources, and so on; emergent rather than a priori focus and questions; emphasizes exploring, investigating, and examining phenomena, places, people, or ideas through broadly bounded inquiry; integration of personal interest and logic of inquiry
Data collection	Emphasis on getting enough data points to meet requirements spelled out in research design; larger sample size frequently preferred to more detailed observation of particulars	Explicit attention to recording challenges and media; interest in presentation of quality documents and data sources; more detailed observations preferred to larger sample size
Data analysis	Precursor to reporting and representation; systematic use of discrete analysis strategies; analysis restricted to bounded data sets	Closely integrated with issue of representation; push toward coherence and clarity through multiple analysis strategies; unrestricted data sources
Reports and representations	Representation as afterthought to data analysis; focus on matching reports to publication options; primacy of summary, report, and argument	Great attention to issues of representation, aesthetic ideals/principles; reports designed for power and effect; primacy of narrative, example, and collage
Audiences	Specialized research community as primary audience, but passing interest in public and popular constituencies, including policymakers	Public and popular constituencies as primary audience, but passing interest in specialized communities (policymakers, researchers, research subjects, etc.)
Framing new knowledge	New knowledge as extension, complement, or alternative to existing and explicit social theory	New knowledge as images, concepts, and perspectives that are new to the public or to targeted communities
Theory building	Emphasis on propositions inscribed in the social science research literature; "competing propositions" as primary content drama	Emphasis on ideas and principles embedded in public media and discourse; "contrasting images" as primary content drama

about credible images of culture and social life. Engaging students in producing and questioning the kinds of documentary studies I've examined here—and struggling with related questions about evidence, representation, audience, imagery, and ethics—represents a good investment in young people and civic culture, a better investment, perhaps, than the kind of disciplinary specialization that is currently typical for a liberal arts education.

These implications follow closely from the contrasting dimensions of practice displayed in Table 2.1, but a somewhat different picture emerges from several epistemological principles to which these practices are loosely coupled. Table 2.2 provides a complementary comparison of social research that does not involve fieldwork, observation-based fieldwork, or documentary studies and a fourth perspective that I referred to earlier as photographic faux-realism—an approach to making photographs that presents images of the world as if they are realist accounts but does so without worrying much about "getting it right." This comparison makes visible some parallels between documentary photography and social science fieldwork that Table 2.1 conceals. It might also help distinguish documentary photography that is empirically sound from photographic studies in which empiricism is more trope than substance.

The parallels between observational field studies and documentary photography displayed in Table 2.2 could be explored further in thinking about how social researchers are trained and how they report their work. This exploration might begin by explicating key features of observation-based fieldwork, on the one hand, and other forms of social research on the other. These features transect the familiar split between quantitative/qualitative and empirical/interpretive and point to alternative configurations of methods and epistemology.

What might it look like, for example, if social researchers were to spend as much time working on observational skills, methods, and theorizing as they do on nonobservational data (quantities in particular, but also some forms of text)? What kinds of guided opportunities could help students to learn about field-recording technologies, the relative merits of open and code-based observation strategies, the design of photographic inventories and surveys, photo elicitation interviews, and other forms of observational data collection? What kinds of training might follow these to address issues of data analysis and reporting? Does it indeed make sense to provide students with advanced coursework about transcribing, coding, and aggregating visual records; or articulating images and text; or using multimedia software to generate and test hypotheses? Stated far too baldly to sway departmental curriculum committees, does training graduate students to observe culture and social life require that they spend lots of time and attention looking at it? Does it require concerted, incremental, and

Table 2.2 Epistemological Correspondence Among Four Kinds of Inquiry

		<< *Observational Studies* >>		
	Nonobservational social research	Observation-based social research	Documentary photography	Photographic faux-realism
Direct observation	No	Yes	Yes	Yes
Participant role in field setting	None	Participant or nonparticipant observer	Participant or nonparticipant observer	Participant or nonparticipant observer
Data collection role	Data collector and manager	Investigator as instrument of observation, data collector, data manager, and analyst	Investigator as instrument of observation, data collector, data manager, analyst, and editor	Photographer as instrument of observation and editor
Commitment to "getting it right"	Strong	Strong	Strong	Weak
Multiple data sources	Yes	Yes	Yes	No
Study explication	Research design	Research design	Personal account	Personal account or no account at all
Inquiry purposes	Scientific inquiry and representation	Scientific inquiry and representation	Documentary inquiry and representation	Photo illustration
<< *Analytical Studies* >>				

long-term attention to recording what they can observe and examining what that portends for the next time they look—as well as for refining knowledge in their chosen field?

Acknowledging a core distinction between observational and nonobservational studies also has implications for research reporting. There's little in existing curricula to prepare students for making reports of any kind: few courses on writing, fewer still on designing tables and charts, and even fewer on articulating text and images or multimedia editing. As writing is, in its rhetorical aspects, the medium of analysis, helping students develop their writing skills makes sense for both observational and nonobservational studies. That said, even accomplished report writers can find a lot to learn when they try to give a good account of observational detail, either in writing alone or through a combination of text and still images.

Of particular interest in this regard are opportunities for research reporting that extend beyond the printed page. It's difficult to convey fully the richness of many observational studies within the limitations of traditional print media. For social researchers who have the interest, alternatives can be found in a wide range of formats, from illustrated talks at conferences or class sessions to stand-alone DVDs, different forms of Internet hosting, webcasts, and public performances.

One format for reporting observational field studies that seems particularly appropriate is that of a multimedia archive or database (Pink, 2001). Both the *Girl Culture* and *Material World* projects have associated online archives of this sort, as do many other projects of social documentary photography (David Bacon's website provides one of many notable examples: http://dbacon.igc .org/). Social researchers receive little or no training and support for developing complex, multimedia reports of this sort. Most scholars probably see that only as a matter of limited time and attention. However, it might also represent an instance where conventions of social science reporting hold at bay alternative ways of representing knowledge that are epistemologically more sound.

Some sociologists and anthropologists have found ways of putting photographs and videotape recordings to extremely good use within their own research and teaching. However, their accomplishments reflect little institutional support and great individual initiative. Few if any social science programs take a deliberate approach to observational studies and the attendant challenges of educating students about what it takes to "see" culture and social life. Their graduates are left to discover on their own the complexities of visual representation and the promise of visual studies or to become acquainted with what it takes for photographs, films, and videotapes to provide empirically sound accounts of culture and social life.

The lack of formal social science training in observational studies is not a fatal flaw, and other skills are well worth acquiring in graduate school. However, continuing neglect of observational methods and epistemology within the social sciences makes it all the more important that social researchers learn what they can from documentary photographers and filmmakers, at least some of whom celebrate both art and empiricism and who aim for both telling images and telling truths.

References

Agee, J., & Evans, W. (1960). *Let us now praise famous men.* Boston: Houghton Mifflin. (Original work published 1939)

Banks, M. (2001). *Visual methods in social research.* Thousand Oaks, CA: Sage.

Becker, H. (1986). Photography and sociology. In *Doing things together: Selected papers* (pp. 221–272). Evanston, IL: Northwestern University Press.

Biella, P. (1988). Against reductionism and idealist self-reflexivity: The Ilparakuyo Maasai film project. In J. R. Rollwagen (Ed.), *Anthropological filmmaking* (pp. 47–72). New York: Harwood.

Brower, K. (1998, May). Photography in the age of falsification. *Atlantic Monthly, 281*(5), 92–111.

Bumiller, E. (2003, May 16). Keepers of Bush image lift stagecraft to new heights. *The New York Times,* p. 1.

Chalfen, R. (1987). *Snapshot versions of life.* Bowling Green, OH: Bowling Green University Popular Press.

Chalfen, R. (1991). *Turning leaves: The photograph collections of two Japanese American families.* Albuquerque: University of New Mexico Press.

Clifford, J. (1986). Introduction: Partial truths. In J. Clifford & G. E. Marcus (Eds.), *Writing culture: The poetics and politics of ethnography.* Berkeley: University of California.

Coles, R. (1997). *Doing documentary work.* New York: Oxford University.

Collier, J., Jr. (1967). *Visual anthropology: Photography as a research method.* New York: Holt, Rinehart, & Winston.

de Miguel, J. (2002, July). *Reconstructing social reality: Community, power, and social control in the Spanish Village photographic project by W. Eugene Smith.* Paper presented at the International Visual Sociology Association, Annual Meetings, Santorini, Greece.

Emmison, M., & Smith, P. (2000). *Researching the visual: Images, objects, contexts, and interactions in social and cultural inquiry.* Thousand Oaks, CA: Sage.

Feyerabend, P. (1975). *Against method.* London: New Left Books.

Goffman, E. (1963). *Asylums: Chapters on the social situation of mental patients and other inmates.* Garden City, NJ: Anchor.

Greenfield, L. (2002). *Girl culture.* San Francisco: Chronicle Books.

Hagaman, D. (1993). The joy of victory, the agony of defeat: Stereotypes in newspaper sports feature photographs. *Visual Sociology, 6*(2), 48–66.

Hagaman, D. (1996). *How I learned not to be a photojournalist.* Louisville: University Press of Kentucky.

Hambourg, M. M., Rosenheim, J. L., Eklund, D., & Fineman, M. (2000). *Walker Evans.* New York: Metropolitan Museum of Art / Princeton University Press.

Harper, D. (1982). *Good company.* Chicago: University of Chicago.

Harper, D. (1987). *Working knowledge: Skill and community in a small shop.* Chicago: University of Chicago Press.

Harper, D. (1998). An argument for visual sociology. In J. Prosser (Ed.), *Image-based research* (pp. 24–41). London: Taylor & Francis.

Harper, D. (2001). *Changing works: Visions of a lost agriculture.* Chicago: University of Chicago.

Heffernan, V. (2003, December 16). Camera down the hole, and the world follows it. *The New York Times,* p. 1.

Hoskins, J. (1998). *Biographical objects.* New York: Routledge.

Johnson, S. (1993). *Making a digital book: Art, computers, design, and the production of the great Central Valley: California's heartland.* Pacifica, CA: Stephen Johnson Photography.

Johnson, S., Dawson, R., & Haslam, G. (1993). *The great Central Valley: California's heartland.* Berkeley: University of California Press.

Kroeber, T. (2002). *Ishi in two worlds: A biography of the last wild Indian in North America.* Berkeley: University of California Press.

Lesy, M. (1973). *Wisconsin death trip.* New York: Pantheon Books.

Lesy, M. (1976). *Real life: Louisville in the twenties.* New York: Pantheon Books.

Lesy, M. (1980). *Time frames: The meaning of family pictures.* New York: Pantheon Books.

Lewis, O. (1965). *Five families: Mexican case studies in the culture of poverty.* New York: New American Library.

Light, K. (2000). *Witness in our time: Working lives of documentary photographers.* Washington, DC: Smithsonian.

Loengard, J. (1998). *Life photographers: What they saw.* Boston: Little, Brown/Bullfinch Press.

Lyons, N. (Ed.). (1966). *Photographers on photography.* Englewood Cliffs, NJ: Prentice Hall.

Mead, M., & Bateson, G. (1976). "For God's sake, Margaret." *Co-Evolution Quarterly, 10,* 32–44.

Menzel, P. (1994). *Material world: A global family portrait.* San Francisco: Sierra Club.

Morris, W. (1999). *Time pieces: Photographs, writing, and memory.* New York: Aperture.

Pepin, J. (1976). *La technique: The fundamental techniques of cooking: An illustrated guide.* New York: New York Times Books.

Pink, S. (2001). *Doing visual ethnography.* London: Sage.

Pinney, C. (1997). *Camera indica: The social life of Indian photographs*. Chicago: University of Chicago Press.

Prosser, J. (Ed.). (1998). *Image-based research: A sourcebook for qualitative researchers*. Bristol, PA: Falmer Press.

Ragin, C. C. (1992). "Casing" and the process of social inquiry. In C. C. Ragin & H. S. Becker (Eds.), *What is a case? Exploring the foundations of social inquiry* (pp. 217–226). New York: Cambridge University Press.

Richardson, L. (1991). *Writing for diverse audiences*. Newbury Park, CA: Sage.

Rieger, J. (2003). A retrospective study of social change: The pulp-logging industry in an upper peninsula Michigan county. *Visual Studies, 18*(1), 156–177.

Ruby, J. (1976, March). In a pic's eye: Interpretive strategies for deriving significance and meaning from photographs. *Afterimage, 3*(9), 5–7.

Ruby, J. (1995). *Secure the shadow: Death and photography in America*. Cambridge, MA: MIT.

Ruby, J. (2000). *Picturing culture: Explorations of film and anthropology*. Chicago: University of Chicago.

Schwartz, D. (1999). Pictorial journalism: Photographs as facts. In B. Brennen & H. Hardt (Eds.), *Pictures in the public sphere: Studies in photography, history, and the press*. Champaign: University of Illinois Press.

Tope, D., Chamberlain, L. J., Crowley, M., & Hodson, R. (2005). The benefits of being there: Evidence from the literature on work. *Journal of Contemporary Ethnography, 34*(4), 1–24.

Weick, K. E. (1976). Educational organizations as loosely coupled systems. *Administrative Science Quarterly, 21*, 1–19.

3

All Photos Lie

Images as Data

Barry M. Goldstein

The Historical Debate

For more than 150 years, photographers have argued over the degree to which they should manipulate their subject, their viewer, and themselves and whether such manipulation is good or bad. The most obvious examples occur frequently in these days of digital photography, where the content of an image can be altered in any way imaginable. But the debate also encompasses more subtle issues about the honesty or integrity of images. When this property is thought to be lacking, the implication is that the photographer has somehow manipulated his or her subject in a way that deceives or misleads the viewer, either intentionally or unintentionally. The premise in these discussions (which can take up a remarkable amount of text for a visual medium) is that there exists some benchmark of physical or social reality that is more closely approached by one camp or another. Here's a random sampling of some of the better known quotes from the literature:

> The photograph has an added realism of its own; it has an inherent attraction
> not found in other forms of illustration. For this reason the average person

believes implicitly that the photograph cannot falsify. Of course, you and I know that this unbounded faith in the integrity of the photograph is often rudely shaken, for, while photographs may not lie, liars may photograph. (Lewis Hine, 1909, early 20th-century social documentary photographer)

Honesty no less than intensity of vision is the prerequisite of a living expression . . . The fullest realization of this is accomplished without tricks of process or manipulation through the use of straight photographic methods. (Paul Strand, 1917, early 20th-century modernist photographer)

Of course, the camera is a far more objective and trustworthy witness than a human being. We know that a Brueghel or Goya or James Ensor can have visions or hallucinations, but it is generally admitted that a camera can photograph only what is actually there, standing in the real world before its lens. (Hannah Höch, painter and photomontagist, quoted in Roditi, 1959)

By the precision of their instrument, by the very mechanical limitations of shutter, lens, and film, they are invested with credibility; simple honesty will render to their pictures the dignity of fact; feeling and insight will give their fraction of a second's exposure the integrity of truth. And truth, universal and applicable as a measuring stick to life, is the objective of the documentary attitude . . . Of course, the line between an "honest" and a dull photograph may be as thin as a knife's edge. There are times when you simply have to pose your model. The difference is in the *kind* of posing. It can be honest and dishonest, interesting and as wooden as a cigar store Indian. (Roy E. Stryker, 1943, head of the Depression-era Farm Security Administration documentary photography project)

"I don't care what you do with that negative, you can retouch it, you can spit on it, you can grind it underfoot. The only thing that matters is if it is honest. If [the picture] is honest, you and everybody can tell. If it is dishonest, you and everybody can tell" . . . that explains what good photography and any good art is all about. (Portrait photographer Arnold Newman, 2003, paraphrasing a conversation with American photo icon Alfred Stieglitz)

Our task is to perceive reality, almost simultaneously recording it in the sketchbook which is our camera. We must neither try to manipulate reality while we are shooting, nor must we manipulate the results in the darkroom. These tricks are patently discernable to those who have eyes to see. (Henri Cartier-Bresson, 1952, master photojournalist and founder of Magnum photo agency)

For me the true business of photography is to capture a bit of reality (whatever that is) on film . . . if, later the reality means something to someone else, so much the better. (Gary Winogrand, quoted in Lyons, 1966, quintessential American street photographer)

Although there is nothing unprejudiced about any representation, in the modern era, attempts at a necessarily false objectivity in relation to meaning have periodically been made . . . Photography, dressed as science, has eased the path of this feigned innocence, for only photography might be taken as directly impressed by, literally formed by, its source. (Martha Rosler, 1981, contemporary artist and critic)

Of course, the counterargument has been made as well:

I believe that this whole question of some photography being "true" and some "untrue" is a non-question. Photography is not objective; it never was objective. It has never told the truth any more than any other form of artistic communication can . . . Some people accept this but still argue that the photograph remains in some way uniquely honest . . . They cling to the idea that the photograph is an inherently "real" or honest image and as such is always on a different plane from an obviously subjective form of visual communication such as painting. (Tibor Kalman, 1994, designer and editor of Benetton-sponsored magazine, *Colors*)

Nothing is more misleading than the old adage that "the camera does not lie" . . . And when it is further shown that the ability of the camera to "lie" can be controlled and used in a creative sense, one must admit that photography does provide possibilities for doing artistic work. For the word *lie* used in connection with a photograph merely means "deviation from literal reproduction" . . . That one of the greatest misconceptions about photography is expressed in the saying that "the camera does not lie," anyone who has ever been disappointed in a photograph should gladly agree. (Andreas Feininger, 1953, author of the classic textbook, *Feininger on Photography*)

We know that sensory phenomena are transcribed, in the photographic emulsion, in such a way that even if there is a causal link with the real phenomena, the graphic images can be considered as wholly arbitrary with respect to these phenomena. (Umberto Eco, 1982, novelist and philosopher)

Photographers know perfectly well that the pictures represent a small and highly selected sample of the real world about which they are supposed to be conveying some truth. They know that their selection of times, places, and people, of distance and angle, of framing and tonality, have all combined to produce an effect quite different from the one a different selection from the same reality would produce. (Howard S. Becker, 1986, sociologist)

Images as Data

Why then revisit this less-than-fertile ground? Readers might expect that I, as both a scientist and photographer, would be particularly invested in this debate, because both disciplines are clearly concerned with representations of reality. As a practitioner of the photographic craft, I fall solidly in the skeptic's camp. However, my working perspective is short and to the point: All photos lie.

It's fashionable these days to bring scientific references into the humanities, so let me begin with an admittedly unusual point of departure for an essay on photography: the laws of thermodynamics. These are sometimes paraphrased as "you can't win, you can only break even," and this can only happen at a single unobtainable state: absolute zero. If by "winning" in the photographic sense, we mean presenting some state of absolute truth, then this pessimistic view of the universe is also a fair summary of the inevitable result of these arguments. A photograph, under the most technically ideal, well-intentioned circumstances, can never represent reality. I repeat: Every photograph lies. This is for some trivial and some not-so-trivial reasons, both technical and cultural. Some time and ink may be saved by reviewing, for nonphotographers, some of the obvious and not-so-obvious reasons why this is unavoidable.

However, acceptance of the fact that "all photos lie" is neither as nihilistic nor as useless as readers may suppose, for the next question becomes "how do they lie" followed by "is this important to me, the viewer?" If we are looking at an image of soldiers at war, our tolerance for manipulation is likely to vary depending on whether we want to know what type of equipment they carry versus what happened during the conflict or how individuals respond to the stresses of combat. What we require from the image will determine how much deviation from the "truth" we're prepared to accept.

Put in slightly more academic terms, I propose that we treat photographic images in the same way a scientist treats data. No experimentalist assumes that data are perfect. Indeed, all data are assumed to have a variety of types of error (i.e., deviation from "truth"). The question then becomes not "do these data represent reality," but rather "are the deviations from reality I know to be present relevant to the question I'm asking?" In attempting to obtain an answer, scientists use their familiarity with the methodology to estimate error. They can then determine whether or not the data are adequate for their purposes or need to be reacquired using some more accurate technique. Thus, a measurement of 20 pounds with an error of ±1 pound may be sufficient to determine that your cat is overweight but is unlikely to suffice for calibrating a satellite's payload.

Quantification of error in an image is, of course, less straightforward, but the viewer's methodology can, in principle, be the same as that of the scientist. Viewers should not approach an image with the assumption that it represents reality. They should assume it does not. As has been noted, every image is the result of a large number of technical and aesthetic choices made by the photographer. Each choice introduces subjective elements into the content. Even in a completely automated image acquisition system, software and hardware choices ensure that the mapping of the world onto a two-dimensional image will create distortions relative to how our senses perceive reality. An understanding of the technical and subjective choices inherent in creating an image permits the viewer to identify these sources of error and then make the decision as to whether or not such factors are important.

Unfortunately, the process is complicated by the same effects experienced by Heisenberg's experimentalist, who influences the system he measures. This applies not only to the photographer's influence on the subject but also to the viewer's own assumptions and cultural biases. Nevertheless, the process of viewing must start with at least a minimal awareness of the technical aspects of image acquisition, processing, and presentation, followed by an understanding of the cultural context. Because the technical reasons are easy to describe and conceptually simple, I will discuss these first. The cultural context (meaning anything not easily quantified) is the topic of numerous texts, articles, and lectures. I'll touch on these but leave the brunt of these arguments to others.

Cameras Cannot Replicate Human Vision

The most trivial reason that a photograph can never represent reality is that it's a two-dimensional representation of a three-dimensional world. Even if we were to define *real* as "what our eye sees," we know that two eyes view a scene from slightly different angles. The brain interprets this information as a third dimension, or depth. This stereo effect can be very nicely simulated in either a dual stereo image (19th-century technology) or a two-dimensional screen using special glasses (20th-century technology), and no doubt this limitation will be overcome by the use of holography and virtual imagery at some point in the not too distant future. However, at the moment, photographs remain pretty much two-dimensional representations.

It is also curious that early proponents of "straight" or "honest" photography rarely mention that most of us perceive the world in color. Indeed, color perception, like depth perception, is an important evolutionary trait, allowing the identification of food sources and the tracking of objects. Again, it is pointing out the obvious to note that, for much of the history of the medium, photographic images were rendered in monochrome.

A more subtle reason that a photograph cannot portray what the eyes see is that film and imaging chips do not "see" light the way the human eye does. Under a fixed set of conditions, the human eye and brain can discern detail over an approximately 10,000-fold range in light intensity. This is called the dynamic range. Photographers measure the amount of light in f-stops, each stop representing a twofold increase or decrease in light intensity. Thus, the eye has a dynamic range of 13 to 14 stops ($2^{13} \approx 8,000$). This can be increased even further by changes in pupil diameter to more than 20 stops. In comparison, with some care, reversal film can record detail over an effective range of approximately 100-fold (seven stops, or $2^7 = 128$). Slide film has an even narrower "dynamic range" (about five stops). Digital imaging chips have a dynamic range comparable to that of film. Photographers have been aware of this limitation for some time and have developed strategies to deal with it.

In digital photography, it is now common practice, particularly among landscape photographers, to acquire multiple images of the same scene. These are combined to produce an image with the appearance of an expanded dynamic range. For example, an image is recorded in which the sky is correctly exposed (Figure 3.1, left). The limited range of tonalities that can be captured by the recording medium then renders the foreground a dark, underexposed area lacking detail. A second image is then acquired with the foreground correctly exposed (Figure 3.1, right). This demands that the sky appear overexposed and featureless. The final composite image consists of the correctly exposed areas of the two component images (Figure 3.1, bottom). It is argued that such HDR (high dynamic range) composites more closely approximate what we see because they compress the range of tonalities visible to the human eye into an image capable of being rendered on some display medium—a monitor or paper, for example.

Before this technique is condemned as proof of the shameless manipulation common in the digital world, it should be noted that it has been used, in one form or another, for well over a century. As the English critic, Lady Elizabeth Eastlake, noted 150 years ago, "If the sky be given, therefore, the landscape remains black and underdone; if the landscape be rendered, the impatient action of light has burned out all cloud form in one blaze of light" (Rosenblum, 1997, p. 105).

Early photographers had even less dynamic range to play with and so employed the method of composite printing. Thus, a landscape might be printed from one plate exposed correctly for the foreground and a second plate (often from a collection) exposed correctly for the sky. Later,

Figure 3.1   Merging of two digital images to increase dynamic range.

SOURCE: © 2006 Barry Goldstein.

photographers and cinematographers employed split, neutral-density filters to compress the tonal range of images so that more detail could be recorded on film. Regardless of the method employed, photographers have been routinely manipulating images to compensate for the significantly reduced dynamic range of film relative to human vision since the inception of the medium.

Intensity is only one of light's properties. Light is usually described in photographic terms as having three additional attributes: color, direction, and quality (the latter being what we might generally refer to as contrast: the abruptness of the transition between a dark and light area). Of course, photography means "writing with light," so it should come as no surprise that the intensity, color, direction of application, and quality of the ink will, by definition, have a profound effect on the appearance of an object. This is self-evident to readers who have enjoyed the yellow tones of a late afternoon "golden hour," cringed at the appearance of their face under a bare bulb, or attended a feature film.

We have already discussed how the eye can accommodate a much greater range of intensities than our recording media. There are also very significant differences in how the brain and eye, compared to film or digital sensor, handle color. Consider the sickly greenish cast of a photograph taken under fluorescent light. Film photographers routinely use filters and gels to adjust the color of light (technically described by *color temperature*) reaching the recording medium. The brain, which has an automatic white balance filter, renders the scene as more neutral. Modern digital cameras either automatically adjust color temperature or allow the user to do so with varying degrees of sophistication.

Similarly, photographers commonly manipulate the other attributes of light, and cinematographers are masters at this. The location of the light source relative to the subject and camera, and the subsequent location of shadows, will determine how the subject is perceived by the viewer. The use of Rembrandt-style lighting in portraiture speaks to the many hundreds of years that painters have understood this. The famous 1963 Arnold Newman photograph of the arms merchant, Alfred Krupp, in which the low angle of the light source gives the subject a ghoulish appearance, offers one of innumerable examples of the editorial uses of lighting. Softboxes, umbrellas, and scrims are but a few of the many light modifiers pressed into service to control how hard or soft a shadow will appear in an image. However, even decisions about whether to photograph a subject in direct sun or in shade, whether to use a polarizer filter to reduce reflections or a red filter to make clouds appear more dramatic in black and white images (a favorite of some photojournalists), represent quite conscious decisions about how to convey the photographer's own brand of reality.

The choices made in the simple operation of the camera itself offer several examples of the differences between what the camera records and what the eye sees (or, more accurately, how the brain interprets what the eye sees). The first of these concerns depth of field. This is the width of a slab of space perpendicular to the direction of gaze within which objects appear sharp. All else being equal, this width, or depth, is fixed in a photograph by the diameter of the aperture, or iris, in front of the lens. The photographer (or the software in an automated camera) must make a deliberate decision about how much depth of field to incorporate in an image. Ansel Adams and others in the f/64 school of landscape photography employed small apertures for maximum depth of field, rendering both the boulder in the foreground and the mountain in the distance sharp. However, the use of wide apertures to produce a shallow, or selective depth of field is also a common technique. The viewer's attention is focused on a particular part of the image by blurring the contents of the frame in front of and behind the point of interest.

In human vision, depth of field is constantly changing. Selective depth of field can be achieved by fixing one's gaze on a single point (for example, your thumb placed a foot in front of your nose." However, under normal circumstances, perceived depth of field is much greater. This results from frequent changes in the direction of our gaze, accompanied by rapid changes in the aperture of our iris and other factors. Thus, the photographer's selection of a correct aperture to most closely approximate reality will immediately fix the depth of field to a limited subset of what our eye perceives.

Another basic difference between what the camera and what the eye sees is in the field of view. Without moving your head, you will be aware of objects within an approximately 180-degree arc centered on your nose. However, only a subset of this—about 50 degrees—is perceived as sharp. In normal vision, we overcome this restriction by movements of our head and gaze, accompanied by rapid refocusing. As with depth of field, this creates the perception of a wider angle of view.

The field of view seen by a camera is determined by the focal length of the lens. Lenses with short focal lengths are called wide angle lenses because they provide a large field of view. Conversely, lenses with long focal lengths (telephoto lenses) have narrow fields of view. Most people are familiar with changing the focal length via operation of a zoom lens, usually to adjust framing. What is less widely understood is the fact that, as the focal length of the lens changes, so does the relative size of near and distant objects. This is called perspective.

In vision, perspective changes by adjusting relative distances. The closer we are to an object, the larger it appears relative to its background. We cannot make large changes in the focal length of our eyes. However, the experienced photographer makes a conscious choice of focal length, not just to adjust the angle of view but also to produce the desired perspective.

A camera with a lens having a 50 mm focal length yields about the same perspective as human vision, and for this reason, it is called a normal lens. Telephoto lenses with long focal lengths diminish the effect of perspective, making near and far objects appear of similar size. This produces the familiar photographic effect of stacking, where, for example, people on a crowded street are made to appear to be walking on top of one another. More subtly, such lenses are commonly used in portraiture because the results are considered flattering. Conversely, wide angle lenses with short focal lengths exaggerate perspective, making near objects appear larger than normal and distant objects smaller. Adherents of a particular school of contemporary German photography make portraits with a wide angle lens held close to the subject. This exaggerates the features (particularly the nose) and is considered droll.

The wide angle look is also very popular today in photojournalism, not only because it crams more information into the frame, but also because of the dramatic effects it can achieve by exaggerating perspective. Think of the trope, seen commonly in newspapers, of a cropped face looming in the foreground (a soldier?), the main action occurring in the midground (a burning vehicle?), and some content offering ironic comment on the whole affair in the distant background (perhaps a child with a toy?).

Falling back on our language of images as data, we might expect the viewer to have little tolerance for error in the products of photojournalism. However, little criticism is heard of manipulation of the truth by using wide angle lenses. This may simply be due to the fact that most viewers are unaware of the photographer's ability to manipulate perspective.

There is one last difference between what we see and what the camera records. It may seem obvious, but it probably has the most profound effect on the medium of photography; indeed, this difference defines the medium. Thus, I'll set this property off by itself:

A photograph records a brief moment in time.

This may seem self-evident but bears some thinking about. Consider an artist working in a two-dimensional medium who wishes to convey impressions about something. For simplicity, let's pick an obviously time-dependent event—say, a boxing match. Painters might go to a number of matches over the course of days, weeks, or years and later produce a work that integrates their impressions over time; a summation of experiences over a potentially lengthy period with the intent to capture some property that is important to the artist.

Photographers may do the same thing but are limited to capturing a two-dimensional image over a period somewhere in the range of 1/1000 of a second to 1 second. Of course, photographers can capture as many of these images as they want, but the practicalities of presenting the work would limit their ultimate choices to a few tens of images, at most. In the middle of the spectrum, videographers might capture segments that are many minutes or hours long (although the segments may be chosen over any period). Even in the case of so-called static subjects, changes in the environment (such as the direction, intensity, and color of light) will not be captured by the still photographer.

Not only is this static view of the world vastly different from what our visual system processes under normal circumstances, it can be argued that this is wholly alien to how our brains evolved to perceive the world. For example, we are much more sensitive to, and stimulated by, movement in our field of view. Yet, it is widely argued that the temporal limitation of a photograph is one reason that such images are so compelling. Whereas our immediate perceptions consist of three-dimensional, ever-changing views, photographs are seen as metaphors for our long-term visual memories. Thus, a static image has the power to evoke very strong emotional responses. The relationship between photographs and visual image processing and storage is the subject of a large literature. For now, however, we'll just consider an important corollary of this time-freezing property of photography.

The "Decisive Moment" Is Really the "Decided Moment"

The photographer Henri Cartier-Bresson (who died recently at the age of 95) is widely known. Associated with his name is the concept of the "decisive moment," that is, that single point in time that captures some truth/essence/jene sais quoi about the subject. The photograph that is often used to illustrate this idea (*Place de l'Europe, Paris, 1932*) shows a man jumping over a puddle, caught by the shutter in midair (Figure 3.2, center).

Figure 3.2   The "decided moment," before and after (with apologies to Cartier-Bresson). Center Image: Henri Cartier-Bresson *Place de l'Europe, Paris, 1932*. © Henri Cartier-Bresson/Magnum. Left and right images © Barry Goldstein.

This is a compelling image, for many reasons, and has been extensively analyzed. However, consider the moments before and after the image was taken (Figure 3.2, left and right). Did the man stand at the edge of the dry ground and ponder thoughtfully his next move, or did he take a running leap with abandon? Did he land gracefully or slip comically? Neither of these moments was of interest to Cartier-Bresson. His *intent* (more on this term later) was to capture the particular moment between these events, in which the subject is figuratively (and literally) suspended in time. This moment was not so much decis*ive* as deci*ded*. Any photograph represents a choice by the photographer to depict one among an infinite number of moments. This choice may be made during the moment of capture (consider even this language) or during editing. It may be conscious or unconscious, but a choice it is.

Temporal and Spatial Editing

The choice of the decided moment might itself be considered a subset of the process of editing—in this case, the choice of one moment over another—that we might refer to as *temporal editing*. A more familiar form of temporal editing is the process of selecting one image over another—each, of course, representing a different moment in time. We might contrast this with *spatial editing,* the selection of one portion of an image over another. Photographers call this cropping, and those concerned with truth fight wars over the subject.

Why this occurs is a puzzle. The act of making an image is itself one of cropping or selecting a subset of the field of view to record. Thus, cropping begins with the choice of where to point the camera. However, the term usually refers to the postacquisition act of removing a portion of the frame that has already been recorded. This is often discouraged, and in more extreme cases, it is considered cheating. This is the reason some images are shown with the film border preserved in the print, a form of saying, "I did this without cropping." The vilification of cropping goes well beyond the sensible encouragement of beginning photographers to carefully consider all elements within the viewfinder before acquisition. It is as if the 35 mm film frame had somehow become a sort of standard for photographic reality, which, once all acquisition choices have been made, is never to be altered. The paradox created by this mode of thinking is illustrated by the following *gedanken* experiment.

Suppose a photographer (in this case, W. Eugene Smith, in his famous 1948 *Life* magazine photo essay, "Country Doctor") set up several stationary cameras of varying common formats, all having a lens of the same focal length and linked to the same shutter control. At the same "decided moment," he records a scene (Figure 3.3). If, after examining all images, he selects one over the other, is this cropping? Does the act of recording all the images simultaneously require that all be displayed? It is interesting to me that those who do all of their cropping "in camera" rarely feel compelled to

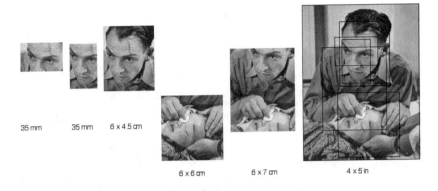

Figure 3.3 A gedanken experiment: spatial editing using different film formats. Original image: H. Eugene Smith. Untitled (Dr. Ceriani with injured child) 1948, From "Country Doctor," *Life* Magazine, September 1948 © The Heirs of W. Eugene Smith.

mention that the image displayed is one of many from a contact sheet or memory card. Temporal editing is generally more permissible than spatial editing.

However, if a photographer is fortunate or unfortunate enough to have produced an iconic image, all editing becomes fair game. Thus, much is made of the fact that Diane Arbus's dour boy with his toy grenade is seen in other images on the contact sheet to be behaving like, well, like a boy. It is as if the recording and display of the more famous frame required that the 10-year-old subject spend his entire life posing as a sociopath.

There is no question that postacquisition editing, whether subtle or massive, will influence our perception of the particular reality that was recorded. To offer another famous example, consider Nick Ut's 1972 Pulitzer Prize-winning Vietnam War photograph of Phan Thi Kim Phuk, the "napalm girl." The version that is most often published and displayed is shown at left in Figure 3.4. The full frame is shown at right in Figure 3.4, revealing another photographer on the right-hand edge of the frame who, according to a gallery talk by Ut in January 2001 at the George Eastman House, was reloading his camera.

Both images are horrific, although perhaps for different reasons. However, is one more real or more honest than the other? Those who argue that the full frame should be displayed might also argue that a larger format should have been used, so that even more of the subject's context could be recorded. Why not argue that only motion picture film should have been used so that

Figure 3.4   Spatial editing via cropping.

SOURCE: Photograph: Trang Bang 8.6.72: Vietnam Napalm, © 1972 Nick Ut/AP.

we could see a larger subset of the infinity of decided moments? But would a motion picture without sound be doctrinally permissible in this case? Any witness to such events will also tell you that smell is a significant component of the horror—a sense whose recording is mercifully beyond current technology. The *reductio ad absurdum* of these arguments quickly becomes apparent.

Every Photograph Results From a Series of Choices

We have considered perhaps the most important choice a photographer can make: when to trip the shutter. We have also considered the choice of aperture and focal length, as well as postacquisition editing. However, any number of other choices are also made.

I've not addressed any of the other postacquisition manipulations that are common in both traditional and digital photography: toning, contrast adjustment, dodging, burning, sharpening, color balance, and a host of other possible modifications. One example may suffice; the now notorious case of the June 27, 1994, *Time* and *Newsweek* magazine covers showing O. J. Simpson's mug shot at the time of his arrest for killing his wife and her companion. The *Time* image was vignetted and adjusted to a darker tone and different hue relative to that used on the cover of *Newsweek*. A great deal of discussion addressed the manipulations used in *Time*'s version, as well as the fact that this made the subject appear more threatening. Of perhaps equal interest was the tacit assumption that the *Newsweek* cover was a better reference to the "truth."

We have also not discussed the medium and method the photographer chooses to display the image: electronic or print, framed on a wall or flat on the page, as a single image or part of a series. But even if we consider only the purely technical decisions, we've seen that they are numerous. Thus, we come to a great truth about photography:

Every photograph is manipulated.

Try as I might, I can conceive of no photograph that is not manipulated in some way, simply by dint of the many choices that are made between image capture and presentation. Every photograph represents the photographer's choices, hence his interpretation of reality. Even if the photographer wants to capture some absolute reality (which, of course, many do not), we've seen that, for purely technical reasons, this is unobtainable with current technology. However, when critics or theorists talk about the honesty or integrity of work, they are rarely referring to the purely technical aspects of the process. In fact, many ignore the process altogether, a stunning omission given the fact that these technical choices can represent a large component of the artistic interpretation. However, it is certainly true that technical choices are not the only factor that will determine the viewer's response to the image. The photographer's choices will determine content. The viewer's response will depend not only on content, but on context and assumptions about intent.

Content, Intent, and Context. Oh My!

When looking at a photograph, it is useful to first consider all of the technical choices made by the photographer. All of these result in the content of the image: what's in the frame (or, more accurately, what's before us, since the frame itself may be an important part of the image). However, the more interesting question is often why the photographer made these choices. Were they conscious or unconscious? What did he or she intend that we notice, and why? Do we see something that was perhaps unintended? If we decide that a certain intent is present, does it work effectively, or could other choices have been more effective? What makes these questions interesting is that they often have more than one answer, or no answer at all. Nevertheless, volumes are written about this because the relationship between content and intent is at the heart of this question of honesty.

We've seen that every image results from manipulations (i.e., choices) on the part of the photographer. These produce some response from the viewer. The question then is, did the photographer intend the viewer to be aware of these manipulations when responding to the image? We tend to feel pretty clever when we respond to something, and, after some thought and analysis, can say why. This may be a gratifying experience. We can also enjoy responding to something without having a clue as to why. However, viewers tend not to react kindly when they're fooled. If we respond in one way (say, compassion for war refugees) and then find that the image was staged (the war refugees are out-of-work actors, requiring a wholly different form of compassion), we tend to be pissed off. Here the photographer intended that we remain unaware of his or her choices, and we may interpret this as deception. Of course, being fooled can itself be a positive experience, as long as we're in on the joke.

The issue of deception in photography is, of course, most often raised in news and documentary work. To what extent did Mathew Brady rearrange corpses in his Civil War photography? Was Joe Rosenthal's image of the raising of the American flag over Mount Suribachi on Iwo Jima staged? Does it matter? Again, the question can be reframed in terms of the photographer's intent, the viewer's interpretation of that intent, and the viewer's reaction to any discrepancies between the two. Theorists talk about our expectation of *indexicality* in a photograph: that the subjects were, at some point, as they appear in the image. Nor does this question apply only to obvious manipulations of the image or subject. Can a photographer from Background A (pick one: privileged, urban, male . . .) adequately/effectively/honestly represent subjects from Background B (poor, rural, female . . .) is a question that generates a great deal of critical ink. Again, the question reduces to that of the degree of mismatch between photographic intent and viewer interpretation.

Last, we shouldn't forget that the lens has two sides. We've discussed how the photographer's intent may lead to manipulation of the subject, either via technical choices, literal staging, or more subtle influences. However, the subject will have an intent of his or her own, and depending on the power relationship that exists, the subject's intent may easily lead to manipulation of the photographer. Anyone who has photographed the rich and famous understands how the photographer may end up subservient to the demands of the subject.

Is it possible to find any image in which the intent is straightforward, the level of manipulation well defined, and the viewer's interpretation entirely consistent with the photographer's goals? Consider Figure 3.5. As you may recognize, this is a mammogram, a technical image obtained using a

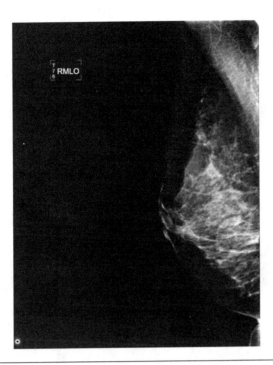

Figure 3.5   An objective image?

SOURCE: © 2001 Trustees of Dartmouth College.

controlled set of highly standardized choices (subject position, light [x-ray] and camera properties, recording medium, post-processing, etc.). The first viewer is generally the photographer, that is, the radiologist, whose intent also seems well defined: obtain diagnostic information about the presence or absence of a tumor. The fact that the patient, another highly interested viewer, has subjected herself to this procedure also suggests that she understands the photographer's intent.

Have we finally found, in technical imagery, the closest we're likely to come to the absolute zero of truth? As Malcolm Gladwell (2004) points out, despite ever improving technical accuracy, a content-intent mismatch still exists. It turns out, not surprisingly, that different viewers (radiologists) see different things, and even when they do agree on what they see, they will often differ about its significance. As Gladwell notes,

> Would taking a better picture solve the problem? Not really, because the problem is that you don't know for sure what you're seeing, and as pictures have

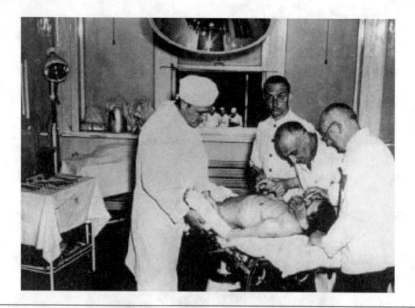

Figure 3.6   Viewer response depends in part on context.

SOURCE: Reprinted with permission of United States Holocaust Memorial Museum.

become better, we have put ourselves in the position where we see more and more things that we don't know how to interpret. When it comes to [breast cancer], the mammogram delivers information without true understanding. (p. 80)

In fact, one can take the argument further and note that, even if one removes the camera entirely from the equation, two individuals observing the same reality may disagree. One need only consult the literature on the unreliability of eyewitness testimony.

Of course, some would argue that it is meaningless to even consider the relationship between the photographer's intent and the viewer's interpretation because the latter will change according to the viewer's time and culture: that is, context. Everyone these days is acutely aware that the interpretation of content depends on context. Consider an image of men dressed in doctor's gowns working over a supine body on a hospital gurney (Figure 3.6). Our response to what appears to be a rather uninspired example of medical documentary photography changes dramatically when we learn that the picture was taken in Buchenwald. The fact that the intent of the photographer was merely to document a scene, while not irrelevant to our response, is probably not central to it.

Despite the fact that our interpretation of content will always rest on the shifting sands of context, I would argue that it is always a useful exercise to question the intent of the photographer in creating content. At a minimum, it makes us question our own background and biases and thus broadens our point of view. Furthermore, it may help add some precision to terms such as honesty, integrity, and deception. Most important, it makes us think about what we're looking at, and this is the greatest compliment we can pay any work.

Looking at Images as Data—and Not

To summarize my arguments:

1. Every image is manipulated, thus no image represents reality.

2. Content depends on a large number of technical and aesthetic choices made by the photographer, based on his or her intent.

3. The response of the viewer to the image will be based on
   - Content
   - Perception of intent
   - Context

How to make use of this photographic worldview? When looking at an image, first and foremost, I note my emotional response: disgust, envy, heat, sensuality—my first eye–brain impressions. I then catalog as best I can the choices made by the photographer, technical and aesthetic, before, during, and after image acquisition, and I ask myself how these contribute to my response. From a professional point of view, I may note some of the techniques employed, with an eye toward copying them myself. Based on these and any other available information (text, context), I question the photographer's intent. Is my response consistent with the perceived intent, counter to it, or a combination of the two? In other words, how am I being manipulated? Again, I assume that the data (i.e., the image) have some limits of error (i.e., deviates from reality as I might have perceived it) for all the reasons discussed above. My only concern is how I feel about this. In more analytical terms, is the degree of error acceptable based on what I require from the image? The answer will differ depending on whether the photograph hangs on a gallery wall, appears in a newspaper, illustrates a scientific journal article, or is presented in any of the innumerable other ways in which images confront us in life. What I will never do is ask, is this photo real? I know it is not.

Awareness of these factors does not disappear when my role changes from viewer to photographer. Indeed, intent and the craft to execute it are recruited to convey, not reality, but some consciously transformed version of it that I want the viewer to experience.

Having offered this rather dispassionate prescription for looking at images, I will make a confession. Despite my potential knowledge of all of the methodology employed, the intent of the photographer, and the context in which the image was made and despite my assumption that photographic truth, like absolute zero, can be approached, but never attained, I now admit that some images strike me as far more honest than others. How can this response coexist with my arguments that photographs can never represent reality? The cynic will argue that what I am responding to is the appearance of honesty—a combination of masterful technique and advantageous context that simultaneously draws attention away from technical artifice while encouraging a perceived intent on the part of the photographer to remain invisible. On the other hand, this begs the question as to whether honesty has anything to do with reality.

Having occasionally made light of others' attempts to address these questions, I now admit to offering little in the way of an alternative. In the end, I am convinced that theorizing about photography is similar to theorizing about sex—one can indeed come up with some creative and useful insights, but a bit of practice will tell you much of what you need to know. I therefore encourage all who engage in the debate to occasionally pick up a camera and make your own truth. The exercise may provide some fresh insight into a medium that, at least for me, still retains a few mysteries.

References

Becker, H. S. (1986). Do photographs tell the truth? In *Doing things together: Selected papers* (pp. 273–292). Evanston, IL: Northwestern University Press.

Cartier-Bresson, H. (1966). Introduction to the decisive moment. In N. Lyons (Ed.), *Photographers on photography: A critical anthology* (pp. 41–51). Englewood Cliffs, NJ: Prentice Hall. (Reprinted from *The decisive moment,* by H. Cartier-Bresson, 1952, New York: Simon & Schuster)

Eco, U. (1982). Critique of the image. In V. Burgin (Ed.), *Thinking photography* (pp. 32–38). London: MacMillan.

Feininger A. (1953). Feininger *on photography.* New York: Crown.

Gladwell M. (2004, December 13). The picture problem. *The New Yorker,* pp. 74–81.

Hine, L. (1980). Social photography: How the camera may help in the social uplift. In A. Trachentenberg (Ed.), *Classic essays on photography* (pp. 110–113). New Haven, CT: Leete's Island Books. (Reprinted from *Proceedings, National Conference of Charities and Corrections,* 1909)

Kalman, T. (1994). Photography, morality, and Benetton. In J. Myerson (Ed.), *Design renaissance* (pp. 41–43). West Sussex, UK: Open Eye.

Lyons, N. (1966). *Toward a social landscape*. Rochester, NY: Horizon Press and The George Eastman House.

Newman, A. (2003). Interview. *The Digital Journalist*. Retrieved September 20, 2006, from http://www.digitaljournalist.org/issue0312/an_intro.html

Roditi, E. (1959). Interview with Hannah Höch. *Arts, 34*(3), 24–29.

Rosenblum, N. (1997). *A world history of photography* (3rd ed.). New York, London, Paris: Abbeville Press.

Rosler, M. (1981). In, around, and afterthoughts (on documentary photography). Halifax, Canada: In 3 Works (pp. 59–87) Press of the Nova Scotia College of Art and Design.

Smith, W. E. (1948, September). Country doctor. *Life* Magazine. Retrieved September 20, 2006, from http://www.life.com/Life/essay/country_ doctor/sec2/page4.html

Strand, P. (1917, August). Photography. *Seven Arts Chronicle, 2,* 524–526.

Stryker, R. E. (1943). Documentary photography. In W. D. Morgan (Ed.), *The complete photographer* (Vol. 4, pp. 1364–1374). New York: National Educational Alliance.

4

Capturing the Visual Traces of Historical Change

The Internet Mission Photography Archive

Jon Miller

Scholars from many disciplines in the humanities and social sciences are paying attention to the visual record that marks the expansion of Western influence around the world in the 19th and 20th centuries. Material artifacts, technology, art, and photographs add a distinct category of information to what can be learned from the more familiar text-based archives that have long been the primary sources for studying the period. When it comes to historical photographs in particular, the archives of Christian overseas missionary societies are especially important.

However the impact of these religious organizations is estimated, the fact is that for well over a century, they represented the international face of one of the largest and most ambitious social movements in Europe and North America. Mission representatives went abroad in large numbers and were energetically active from the very beginning of the period of colonial and imperial expansion. The New Testament language that provided their motivation, known as the Great Commission, is unequivocal: "He said to them,

Go into all the world and preach the gospel to every creature" (Mark 16:15). To say that missionaries took that religious imperative seriously is to underestimate their sense of purpose. By the time of the First World War, male and female mission agents had succeeded in establishing outposts wherever the influence of the West had penetrated. Sometimes they were willing participants in the "Western project," and sometimes they were not, but whether in the mode of support or the mode of criticism or somewhere between the two, they were alert observers of the global political and economic transformations of the period. Indeed, propelled and fortified as they were by their intense religious energy, they were able to reach into remote regions where other Western interests sometimes declined to go. For this reason, they were often the primary Western witnesses to events in those places.

For reasons that were both religious and mundane, Western missionaries were consummate record keepers, and with the advent of photography, they began to use captured photos to compile a visual record of their activities. In the 1850s, some missionaries were already creating daguerreotypes and calotypes in the regions where they worked, although few of these fragile photos have survived in their original form. As lighter, more robust, and more portable cameras were developed, as factory-made negatives became available, and particularly as missionary societies became more sophisticated about the educational and fund-raising potential of photography, repositories of pictures began to grow, expanding exponentially from the 1880s onward. As a consequence, most missionary societies or the libraries that hold their archives have accumulations of historical pictures taken for a variety of purposes and in various styles and levels of technical skill, from amateur snapshots to the very best in photojournalism. They range from a few musty, uncataloged boxes or albums at one end of the scale to carefully preserved, well-organized, and professionally documented collections numbering in the hundreds of thousands of photos at the other. Families also hold significant collections that have not yet found their way into organized repositories.

Of course, the missionaries who took these pictures had an agenda, and the collections that survive document their religious endeavors, reflect their experiences, and record their views of communities and environments abroad. Thus, as expected, many examples of the physical influence of the mission presence can be found in the archives, in particular, churches and school buildings, mission compounds, workshops, and construction projects. There are also abundant examples of the intended and unintended cultural impact of mission teaching and Western influence, from the early development of missionary-founded congregations that, by now thoroughly indigenous, are often a major force in contemporary society, to school activities and training programs, to Western technology and fashions.

Scholars who are themselves identified with the evangelical cause, as well as more secular scholars of religion, are naturally drawn to the documentary record displayed in these diverse photos. But the scholarly significance of the collections is much broader. Although the acknowledged motive of the missionaries may have been to record their own evangelizing activities in order to educate and impress their superiors and supporting publics at home, their lenses inevitably captured a great deal more than what was explicitly and deliberately religious in nature. From the variety of images they captured, those holding the cameras seem to have been curious about everything that appeared and happened around them, whether or not those objects and events were specifically religious. Moreover, they could not always control what was transpiring before their lenses, nor is it likely that they always noticed what was taking place around the edges, as it were, of their primary subjects. The result is that the themes illuminated by the pictures in these collections are not limited to the mission-built Christian religious environment or to photos that display or validate the missionary agenda. These images can be quite powerful in capturing much broader currents of cultural diffusion and the economic, political, and technological transformation of traditional societies. For this reason, their appeal across a wide array of scholarly disciplines should be apparent.

Internet Mission Photography Archive

Despite their scholarly potential, the usefulness of these historical photographs has been limited by their fragility and by their unorganized state and inaccessibility, distributed as they are across many widely separated mission repositories. Researchers who have sought to tap into this resource have typically had to travel to the places where the photographs are held and then thumb through the collections in the hope of finding just the right photos that will illustrate a text, illuminate some scholarly theme, or provide visual confirmation or disconfirmation for an argument or empirical claim. Some collections have been scanned and cataloged for use onsite in the archives, thus achieving the goal of protecting the originals from handling and making the photographs easier to work with. More often, however, the success of a search through the paper files has been a function of the sheer persistence and good luck of the investigator.

The situation began to change a decade ago, when Paul Jenkins and Barbara Frey-Näf, working in the archive of the Basel Mission in Switzerland, began the laborious process of digitizing and cataloging some 29,000 photographs accumulated by that organization over the past century and a half. The result is BMPIX, the first significant searchable repository of mission photography available to anyone with access to the Internet. Inspired by this Basel example, the Internet Mission Photography Archive (IMPA), a project jointly undertaken by the Center for Religion and Civic Culture and the Digital Archive at the University of Southern California, has addressed the next challenge, namely, the need to consolidate searches across several physically and administratively separate collections. With such a confederation of archival source materials, it is possible to collate what is learned in one mission collection with what can be found in another. With an initial grant from the Getty Grants Program, IMPA has to date created a digital database that contains about 15,000 photographs. This project, which is still under way, uses a common Dublin Core metadata template to assure that information about the content and circumstances under which a photo was captured—photographer, time and place, persons and events depicted—were entered in the same format for the photographs taken from the various participating collections. As a result, a researcher can search quickly through thousands of photos from several separate archives, refining the search by time, place, and conceptual theme and sorting the results according to the categories, descriptors, and keywords used to catalog the photos as they were scanned and added to the record.

In IMPA's first stage, pictures from eight collections held in six separate repositories based in the United States, Britain, and continental Europe were included. Because this was a pilot project, IMPA focused its limited resources on the best organized collections in each of these places. The Moravian Church (Die Herrnhuter Brüdergemeine), established in 1722, was the first Protestant missionary society to send its agents to West and South Africa. Because of its location in what was formerly East Germany, the historically important collection in the Unitätsarchiv in Herrnhut has hitherto received little attention from those interested in Africa. IMPA's selection of Herrnhut photographs focuses on two missionary fields in Africa: "Nyasa" in what is now southern Tanzania and "South Africa West," the area just outside Cape Town. In both cases, the photographs in IMPA date almost entirely from the period 1890 through 1940, with the peak numbers from the late 1920s and early 1930s.

The Leipzig Mission (Evangelisch-Lutherisches Missionswerk Leipzig), founded in 1836, was and is active principally in East Africa, India, and Papua–New Guinea. The archive in Leipzig possesses some 20,000 photos, including about 3,500 from northeast Tanzania, notably Kilimanjaro, Arusha, and Pare. IMPA concentrated on the photographs from those regions that were supplied by the missionaries Wilhelm Guth (who worked mainly in

Pare, 1913–1917 and 1927–1938) and Leonhard Blumer (active mainly in Arusha, 1912–1913 and 1924–1926). Also included are colored postcards published by the mission, principally before World War I.

The Catholic Foreign Mission Society of America, Inc. (Maryknoll Fathers and Brothers) was established in 1911 at Maryknoll, New York, and sent its first missionaries to China in 1918. The photographic archive, established to support *The Field Afar* and *Maryknoll* magazines, contains between 1 million and 1.5 million prints, lantern slides, glass negatives, and film slides that capture mission activities in 38 different countries. The Maryknoll Mission Archives were established as a collaborative venture in 1990 to care for the records and photos of the Maryknoll fathers and brothers, Maryknoll sisters, and the Maryknoll lay missioners. IMPA has confined its selection to the China series of photos dated 1912 through 1945.

The photograph collection of the Norwegian Missionary Society in Stavanger is extensive, well preserved, and among the best organized and best cataloged collections. Overall, it comprises about 100,000 items, including photograph albums, glass plate negatives, and lantern slides, representing regions as diverse as South Africa (Natal and Zululand), Madagascar, China (Hunan, Hong Kong), Cameroon (Adamawa), Japan, Taiwan, and Ethiopia. IMPA has assembled pictures from just three regions: Madagascar (from the period 1890 to 1920), South Africa (taken between 1866 and 1940), and Cameroon (taken between 1925 and 1950).

The selection from the nearly 30,000 prints and 470 lantern slides held in the missionary society collections at the School of Oriental and African Studies (SOAS) is a sampling of photos from Africa, Burma, China, the Caribbean, Madagascar, South India, Sri Lanka, and Papua–New Guinea. The photographs come from the collections of four missionary societies: the Council for World Mission (formerly the London Missionary Society), the [Weslyan] Methodist Missionary Society, the English Presbyterian Mission, and the China Inland Mission (now called the Overseas Missionary Fellowship). Some of the photographs were taken by missionary workers in the field, such as the lay mission worker John Parrett (1841–1918), who served as a printer for the London Missionary Society in Madagascar from 1862 to 1885, and the Reverend Harry Moore Dauncey (1863–1932), who served with the same society in Papua–New Guinea, mainly in the Delena district, for 40 years from 1888 to 1928. There are also collections that overseas missionaries acquired from non-mission sources, for example, a fine collection of albumen prints of China in the early 1860s taken by an unknown Russian photographer.

Finally, the archival and manuscript collections of the Yale University Divinity School's Day Missions Library include, among other things, several thousand photographs documenting missionary and educational work in China from the late 19th century to 1950. Photographs in the archives of the United Board for Christian Higher Education in Asia focus on the work of the 13 colleges and universities founded by Protestant mission agencies in China. Photographs in the personal papers of missionaries, who served under a variety of agencies in numerous provinces, provide a broad-based view of the spectrum of Protestant mission work in China. Medical, educational, and evangelistic endeavors are documented, as well as famine relief, rural reconstruction, athletics, and other aspects of the lives and work of American and British missionaries and their Chinese students and colleagues.

The contributing archives retain ownership of the original photographs and determine the circumstances under which they can be reproduced in publications. Each archive's staff scanned and cataloged the pictures and posted them to the central IMPA database in the Digital Archive of the University of Southern California Library. The pictures appear on the user's screen as thumbnails, previews, or full-screen photos. The latter are medium-resolution jpegs; they can be downloaded (right-clicked), and they are quite adequate as reference copies. These downloads are not, however, of publication quality. For publication purposes, users can follow a link to the contributing archive's policies regarding conditions of use, permissions to reproduce, and charges for high-resolution copies.

The individual items in these collections vary widely in the richness of their metadata. IMPA's coding template assured that essentially the same categories of data could be entered in the same format for each photograph, but in some cases, pictures were included for which the available documentation was less than ideal. Scholars often bring their own special knowledge to the assessment of a photograph, and it is better for an interesting picture to be available for scrutiny, even if it is less than optimally documented. There is always the possibility that knowledgeable viewers who are familiar with the time, place, and people involved might be able to contribute information that IMPA can consider for incorporation into the electronic record. The online database, thus, inevitably contains some photos with only the minimally acceptable cataloging information, alongside photographs for which a great deal of associated information is available. In the final form of the IMPA website, each photo will contain a link to a page where viewer comments can be entered. These comments will reside alongside the official record so that users can examine them, but they will not be incorporated into the metadata unless and until they are verified for accuracy by the curator of the collection that contributed the photograph. It is also important to note that the archives participating in IMPA also possess a great many text-based historical records, open for scholarly use, which contain information that can often be linked to the individuals, events, and subjects depicted in the missionary photographs. Work with the IMPA photographs is, therefore, not narrowly confined to the information contained in the online photo and its accompanying metadata.

Using the Collections

Two versions of the same African family portrait are juxtaposed in Figure 4.1 to illustrate some of our technical judgments in preparing this chapter. The user who visits the IMPA Internet repository will note immediately that, like the example on the left, the online pictures are not edited, corrected, altered, or in any other way "prettied up" for presentation. IMPA's mandate in scanning the photographs was to capture as much of the visual information in the existing photos as possible, given current technology. That included imperfections, damage, captions, and in some cases handwritten notes on the surfaces of the prints—editorial comments, for example, or simply informal notes jotted down by previous owners or viewers. Many pictures are glued into albums, and these were scanned in those mountings rather than risking damage by removing them for scanning. If there were duplicate photos, both were scanned in most cases. Although most of the photographs are in black and white, that term actually covers a range of tones and shades. For this reason, most of IMPA's scanning was done in color, and the calibrating color "targets" that can be seen on many of the pictures (see the one on the left in Figure 4.1) are not on the originals. Those bars were placed alongside the pictures during the scanning process so that professionals who use the online collections can judge the color fidelity of the scans. The remaining photographs in this chapter, like the one on the right in Figure 4.1, are not presented in color, and the originals were altered in small ways to be consistent and to enhance the visual presentation. Specifically, they have been cropped to the edges of the original compositions and then straightened, and light and contrast have been adjusted to bring out more detail. In every case, the unaltered version of the picture can be seen in the online IMPA archive.

Figure 4.1   Group portrait of Christian family, Sierra Leone, May 1906.

SOURCE: © Trustees for Methodist Church Purposes, used by permission of Methodist Publishing House.

These visual collections can be used in ways that are limited only by the curiosity of the researchers who visit the website. In the pages that follow, I have selected photographs linked to four distinct topics to provide a feeling for the richness of the materials: the built environment, women in missions, cultural encounter, and political change. I chose the topics because they mirror my own interests and because they serve as a good introduction to the potential of the IMPA project. The pictures that I "cherry-picked" for display here are necessarily only a small fraction of those that I could have shown. They are likely to raise as many questions as they answer and for this reason should be taken as they are intended, that is, as tantalizing illustrations but not the product of any serious or conclusive analysis. By showing them here, I hope to stimulate other investigators to examine them and many others in the IMPA repository so that they can conduct their own investigations into what the images do or do not portray.

The Physical Stamp of the Missionary Presence

Conducting a search for *churches* in the IMPA database provides an easy first point of entry into these archival materials. Whatever else they tried to do, missions were church-planting enterprises, and the physical structures they created are often the most arresting marker of their presence in a place. Not surprisingly, among the 15,000 pictures in the database, there are some 1,300 that show churches. Several hundred more depict the more inclusive category of *mission stations* or *settlements,* which typically include a church and the institutional structures grouped around it, such as schools, farms, houses, workshops, and the like. Documenting the missionary footprint shown by these structures could be relevant for a variety of different research questions.

There is no room here to explore any of these questions in depth, but just to suggest some examples, a sizable subset of the 1,300-plus church pictures show buildings in various stages of construction in different locales, giving insight into questions of architecture, construction techniques, available local resources, and often the division of tasks between Europeans and indigenous people providing the labor in emerging Christian communities. Alternatively, viewers could be alert to evidence of the ecclesiastical relationships among European missionaries and indigenous church members. What do the pictures reveal about norms of precedence and church hierarchies, for example? How often do they depict native versus European pastors, and does this change over time? What about the presence or absence of key religious markers and symbols? Attention could be aimed at important differences from one sending society to another in the approach to church building (Catholics versus Protestants, for example), or the focus could be on variations in building types from one geographic region to another (African churches versus Chinese ones, for example, or urban churches designed for large memberships versus small village chapels). For some purposes, the importance of the pictures might lie simply in the evidence they provide of the increasing size and progressive elaboration of religious buildings over time—the expanding Christian footprint, as it were. But they can also suggest intriguing questions about the relations of missions with local populations, including the local traditional authorities that had to allow those building projects to proceed. The small selection of photos shown here illustrates several but not all of those themes.

The simple Nigerian Methodist church in Photo 4.1, for example, falls clearly in the "modest beginnings" category, and I selected it to define one end of a continuum of church presence. The building's purpose and its familiar peaked roof and rectangular shape are European, but the scale and materials are distinctly local.

In comparison to this simple building, the next two pictures show more elaborate and ambitious installations, often indicative of a firmer grounding in the locale. Like Photo 4.1, Photo 4.2 also depicts a village chapel that employs materials and construction reflecting the place, in this case India, but the structure is considerably larger and more elaborate than the one in Nigeria.

Photo 4.1   Village church, Nigeria, 1915.

SOURCE: © Trustees for Methodist Church Purposes, used by permission of Methodist Publishing House.

Photo 4.2   Missionary outside village chapel, Nagercoil, Tamil Nadu, India, ca. 1890.

SOURCE: © Reproduced from London Missionary Society/Council for World Mission Archives.

Even more imposing is the European-style anchor church for a Moravian settlement in Tanzania shown in Photo 4.3. In the early years, large structures like this one were most often built without the more highly evolved and labor-saving building techniques and machinery that were available in Europe and North America at the time. Making beams (Photo 4.4) and hoisting roof timbers aloft (Photo 4.5) are far more daunting (and muscular) tasks where sawmills and construction cranes are not part of the local technical infrastructure.

Looking at the larger surrounding context for buildings such as these, Photos 4.6 and 4.7 show the remote mission settlement of Utengule in Tanzania, which surrounds the church shown in Photo 4.3. The pictures were taken at some distance so that the details appear small, but they nevertheless suffice to show how church building most often went hand in hand with community building. Missionaries quickly learned that when Christian converts left their native religion, they were often excluded from traditional ways of living in the local culture. Many evangelical organizations learned from experience that effective and lasting conversion relied on a supporting institutional structure of houses, schools, clinics, farms, and production shops that could sustain a stable way of living. In the absence of these resources, the attraction to Christianity was likely to be ephemeral.

Photo 4.3   Missionaries Kootz and Kruppa in front of the church, Utengule, Tanzania, ca. 1898–1918.

SOURCE: © Reproduced by permission of the Moravian Archives, Herrnhut. LBS 01320, ca. 1903.

Photo 4.4   Sawing beams at the joiner's workshop, Mbozi, Tanzania, ca. 1906–1929.

SOURCE: © Reproduced by permission of the Moravian Archives, Herrnhut. LBS 04699, ca. 1927/28.

Photo 4.5   Pulling parts of a roof onto the church building, Mbozi, Tanzania, [s.d.] (undated).

SOURCE: © Reproduced by permission of the Moravian Archives, Herrnhut. LBS 04691, ca. 1927/28.

Photo 4.6   Mission houses and church, Utengule, Tanzania.

SOURCE: © Reproduced by permission of the Moravian Archives, Herrnhut. LBS 01318, ca. 1903.

Photo 4.7   Christian settlement, Utengule, Tanzania, 1912.

SOURCE: © Reproduced by permission of the Moravian Archives, Herrnhut. LBS 01317, ca. 1903.

Photos 4.8 and 4.9 redirect viewers' attention from the architectural meaning of *church* (a building dedicated to worship) to the human meaning of that word (a body of believers). These pictures, chosen from hundreds of similar ones, animate the concepts of *community* and *institution* by showing the large Christian congregations that filled and enlivened the religious structures that appear behind them. These congregational portraits also serve to illustrate why church buildings and mission stations were often the largest structures in the areas they were built to serve. When dramatic growth in the converted mission population occurred, it was soon echoed in equally dramatic growth in the physical structures of Christianity. Religions commonly announce their claim to legitimacy and permanency by putting down a visible stamp, erecting imposing structures that cannot be ignored, and the Christian communities founded by missionaries in far-flung parts of the world clearly reflect that impulse.

Finally in this brief sequence about churches, the Catholic cathedral in China shown in Photo 4.10 (the picture is from the Maryknoll collection, but the church was probably built by a French Catholic mission) stands in quite dramatic contrast to the small Methodist church shown in Photo 4.1. If that small, simple structure defined the *modest* pole on a scale of architectural

Photo 4.8   Large group portrait of church congregation, Axim, Ghana, 1914.

SOURCE: © Copyright © Trustees for Methodist Church Purposes, used by permission of Methodist Publishing House.

Photo 4.9   Congregation gathered outside the church, Ivary, Ambato, Madagascar, 1906.

SOURCE: © Reproduced by permission of the Norwegian Missionary Society Archive.

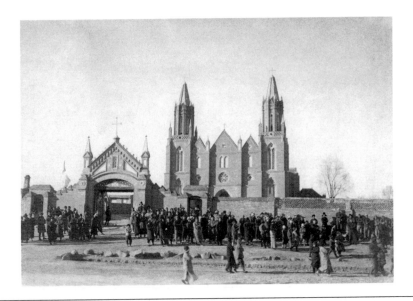

Photo 4.10   The cathedral at Manzhoukuo, China, 1934.

SOURCE: © Reproduced by permission of Maryknoll Mission Archives.

elaboration, this last one surely stakes out the opposite end of the continuum. Although this is not the place to address them, the differences between these two structures make it almost impossible to resist questions about how building styles may signal differences in religious approaches to local culture.

Women in Mission

Participation by women in the Western missionary movement of the 19th and early 20th centuries has been the subject of strong opinions and sharp disagreements in the scholarly literature. The available collections of photographs alone cannot resolve these arguments, simply because we are unable to assume that they capture a random sampling of all the ways—active or passive, conservative or forward looking—in which women took part in mission work. Neither is the small sample of pictures presented here a fair representation of the vastly larger number included in IMPA. But even this small selection displays a sufficient variety of women's occupations to make it difficult to cling to easy oversimplifications.[2]

The first of these pictures, Photo 4.11, is unsettling, but it provides a good point of reference for discussion. If we start with the assumption that

Photo 4.11   Aagot Kjeldseth rides a filanjana (palanquin) on her way to church, Antananarivo, Madagascar, ca.1896.

SOURCE: © Reproduced by permission of the Norwegian Missionary Society Archive.

Western women joined the missionary movement as lesser participants and that they modeled an essentially conservative view of appropriate gender and race relations, this contrived studio confection might be taken as strong visual confirmation. When Aagot Kjeldseth of the Norwegian Society went to church, four men and two female attendants were apparently necessary to take her there.[3]

Other pictures that convey such hierarchy and cosseted privilege can be found in the IMPA database, but any systematic search would reveal a far more diverse engagement of women in the mission field. Photos 4.12 and 4.13, for example, were taken around the same time as Photo 4.11 and in the same mission field, Madagascar. Although they are also professionally composed and executed, these exquisite portraits of two friends in the London Missionary Society, who like Aagot Kjeldseth are clearly privileged materially, nevertheless give a radically different impression from the scene with the sedan chair in the garden. The intimacy of these compositions suggests anything but cultural distance between the two women, but is it significant that Elsie Sibree, the European, is named and her "friend" is not?

Does the reversing of the higher/lower seating arrangement between the two pictures hint that the question of precedence was explicitly addressed by

Photo 4.12   Portrait of Elsie Sibree and friend, Madagascar, 1903.

SOURCE: © Reproduced from London Missionary Society/Council for World Mission Archives.

Photo 4.13   Portrait of Elsie Sibree and friend, Madagascar, 1903.

SOURCE: © Reproduced from London Missionary Society/Council for World Mission Archives.

the photographer or by the person who commissioned the portraits? Is there any significance in the change of clothing between the two sittings? Is one picture a correction of the other ("No, it is really this way . . ."), or is one a completion of the other ("Both views are necessary to capture this relationship . . .")? Does the fact that both versions were printed and preserved suggest that in someone's editorial judgment the two are equal in importance or aesthetic worth? Studied closely, these pictures raise more questions than they answer, but neither of them reproduces the aura of domination and separation that suffuses Photo 4.11.

An abundance of other pictures in the database display mission women involved fully in mundane but vital tasks, and, in a different way from the portraits of the two friends, these also are difficult to reconcile with Aagot Kjeldseth floating to church in her elite conveyance. Photos 4.14 through 4.17 are quite diverse, but all of them show women laboring in clearly professional teaching and medical capacities in circumstances that show no hint of sheltering or separation: a nurse examining a slide under a microscope; a teacher surrounded by her pupils, the wife of a missionary vaccinating children, and a missionary doctor paying very close attention to something a small child is telling her.

Photo 4.14   Sister Frieda Wetzel working with a microscope, Tanzania, ca. 1927–1938.

SOURCE: © Reproduced by permission of the Evangelical-Lutheran Mission of Leipzig.

Photo 4.15   Agnes Simmons with children, Jammalamadugu, Andhra Pradesh, India, ca. 1908–1912.

SOURCE: © Reproduced from London Missionary Society/Council for World Mission Archives.

Photo 4.16   Missionary's wife vaccinating child, Yunnan, China, ca. 1942.

SOURCE: © Trustees for Methodist Church Purposes, used by permission of Methodist Publishing House.

Photo 4.17   Missionary doctor and child, Karimnagar, Andhra Pradesh, India, ca. 1915.

SOURCE: © Trustees for Methodist Church Purposes, used by permission of Methodist Publishing House.

Shifting the focus away from European and American women, Photos 4.18 and 4.19, both taken in Madagascar, are single frames from the record of native women at work in traditional occupations, in the first case fishing, in the second, craft weaving. The six succeeding photos (Photos 4.20 through 4.25) show native women at school and at work in mission and medical settings in Africa, Madagascar, India, Myanmar (Burma), and China in the first half of the 20th century. They are quite effective in pointing to the Western technical and professional training that was sometimes opened up to these women by their inclusion in the mission community.

The description following the title of Photo 4.23 (undated but likely taken before 1930) reads, "'A leader in Women's Work.' A former pupil of Mandalay's Girl High School and a leader in the Burmese Women's Missionary Society." Note that Photo 4.24 bears a striking resemblance to Photo 4.14, although it was taken a continent away, in a different mission, and by a different photographer. In addition to the subject matter of the two pictures—women involved in the application of science in a mission context—the skill of the photographer and the obvious attention to aesthetic quality joins the two pictures in a single genre.

Photo 4.18   Women fishing in the Anosy Lake, Mahamasina, Antananarivo.

SOURCE: © Reproduced by permission of the Norwegian Missionary Society Archive.

Photo 4.19   Malagasy woman plaiting a hat using rush, Madagascar, 1900.

SOURCE: © Reproduced by permission of the Norwegian Missionary Society Archive.

Photo 4.20   Large group portrait of female students, Ghana, ca. 1910.

SOURCE: © Trustees for Methodist Church Purposes, used by permission of Methodist Publishing House.

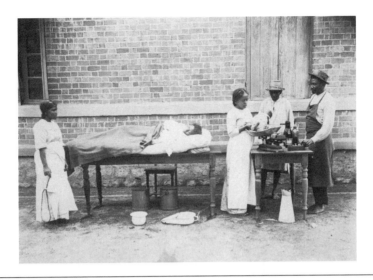

Photo 4.21   Midwife weighing newborn child, Madagascar, ca. 1910.

SOURCE: © Reproduced from London Missionary Society/Council for World Mission Archives.

Photo 4.22   Nurses' home, Ramayampet, Andhra Pradesh, India.

SOURCE: © Trustees for Methodist Church Purposes, used by permission of Methodist Publishing House.

Photo 4.23　Female Christian leader, Myanmar.

SOURCE: © Trustees for Methodist Church Purposes, used by permission of Methodist Publishing House.

Photo 4.24　A Chinese Sister practicing medicine at Jiangmen, China, 1949.

SOURCE: © Reproduced by permission of Maryknoll Mission Archives.

Photo 4.25   Smallpox vaccinations, Chengdu, Sichuan, China, ca. 1942.

SOURCE: © Reproduced by permission of Special Collections, Yale Divinity School Library.

Cultural Encounter/Colonial Intrusion

The intended and unintended effects that missions had on both the preservation and the alteration of indigenous cultural traits is the subject of ongoing debates. The photographs that missionaries produced can aid us in the way we think about these processes of continuity and change, but by themselves, they are not conclusive; indeed, sometimes they are full of paradox and surprise.

At the simplest level of assessment, the collections assembled over the course of a century capture cultural shifts as they were occurring. It is apparent, in fact, that straightforward documentation was often the photographer's goal, and putting aside disputes about how the photographs should be interpreted, the spread of Western influence is certainly on display in these pictures. That theme is bound to emerge as a dominant one for anyone who spends time studying the photographs. But the pictures can also be provocative when they capture profoundly ambiguous or counterintuitive events or when they present scenes that pull against common stereotypes. In such cases, they challenge taken-for-granted presuppositions and stimulate new ways of looking at social change. The sequence of six pictures below (Photos 4.26 through 4.31) serves as fairly uncomplicated examples of continuity and change in cultural traits. They require little comment. Photos 4.32 through 4.36, by contrast, offer a far greater challenge for interpretation.

Photo 4.26   Valiha musician and his wife, Sakalava, Midongy, Madagascar, 1901.

SOURCE: © Reproduced by permission of the Norwegian Missionary Society Archive.

Photo 4.27   "Lioma" music band, Midongy, Madagascar, 1900.

SOURCE: © Reproduced by permission of the Norwegian Missionary Society Archive.

Photo 4.28   Usambara brass band, Arusha, Tanzania, 1923.

SOURCE: © Reproduced by permission of the Evangelical-Lutheran Mission of Leipzig.

Photo 4.29   Students blowing their horns, Rungwe, Tanzania, ca. 1898–1914.

SOURCE: © Reproduced by permission of the Moravian Archives, Herrnhut. LBS 03238, ca. 1912/14.

Photo 4.30   Group of mothers and babies, Mailu, Papua–New Guinea, ca. 1905.

SOURCE: © Reproduced from London Missionary Society/Council for World Mission Archives.

Photo 4.31   Group portrait of South Sea and Papuan teachers and families, Kalaigolo, Papua–New Guinea, ca. 1908–1910.

SOURCE: © Reproduced from London Missionary Society/Council for World Mission Archives.

Photo 4.26 is one of several photographs that capture indigenous musical forms, in this case an instrument called a *valiha*, in Madagascar in 1901. Another picture taken at about the same time in the same region, Photo 4.27, shows the entry of a brazen and brassy competing musical idiom. Indeed, brass bands like the one in Photo 4.27 pop up with surprising frequency in the IMPA collections from different missions and from countries across Africa. Photos 4.28 and 4.29 are from Tanzania. The cross on the flag in Photo 4.28 is a reminder that these bands were typically of mission origin.

As is suggested by Photos 4.30 and 4.31, both taken in Papua–New Guinea before World War I, changes in the prevalent forms of dress and personal adornment, like changes in popular musical forms, can also be a dramatic indicator of the spread of Western conventions. Indeed, judging by the recurrence of the dress theme across the various archives, it seems clear that the adoption of Western standards of dress was considered one important metric, or prerequisite, for the progress of Christianity.

Shifting to a different zone of cultural expression, the next four photos also capture social change in a visually dramatic way, but it is a much greater challenge to read their significance. Photo 4.32 was taken in a Methodist boys' school in Ghana in 1926, and Photo 4.33, also from the Methodist archives,

Photo 4.32   School boys in formation outdoors, Ghana, 1926.

SOURCE: © Trustees for Methodist Church Purposes, used by permission of Methodist Publishing House.

Photo 4.33   Group portrait of missionary with scouts, Nigeria, 1929.

SOURCE: © Trustees for Methodist Church Purposes, used by permission of Methodist Publishing House.

is from Nigeria in 1929. In both of these scenes, religion, education, and organizational discipline are fused in a way that produces a strong sense of regimentation and cultural imprinting. This is one of those places where it would be important to explore the associated text-based archives from the period to see how the missions articulated the need for these organizational forms and how they described the anticipated benefits. Scholars of colonialism might well point to these pictures when they write about *the colonization of consciousness,* which is usually a pejorative term referring to attempts by Europeans to radically reshape the cultural premises and daily habits that defined indigenous cultures. Indeed, taking these photographs by themselves without exploring their context in more detail, it may be difficult to resist that interpretation.

But, while capturing or creating a certain kind of conforming consciousness may describe what is happening in these two African pictures, contrast the authoritarian aura that they give off with the apparent message of Photos 4.34, 4.35, and 4.36, which show a protest parade in Canton (Guangzhou), China, in 1925. Once again, we see young people in uniform, in this case students marching in precise order down an urban avenue, but in reading the titles and accompanying metadata for these pictures, there are several surprises. One is that the white-clad marchers in the center of the first two photographs are female university students (both pictures are dim but Photo 4.35 is slightly better in showing this); another is that all of those shown are marching in support of a national protest over the killing of 13 labor demonstrators by British police in Shanghai. The final surprise is that the demonstrators are from Canton Christian College. In other words, it would be quite plausible, indeed perhaps inescapable, to characterize this segment of the march as an anti-colonial protest by Christian university women. Which one of the three surprises about this public demonstration is the most startling (the demonstrators are women; they are protesting collectively and publicly; they are Christian) could reveal a lot about the presuppositions of the viewer, but putting that aside, there are simply too many counterintuitive elements in these photographs to allow any facile interpretation of how religion, Western influence, and social change are woven together.

Reflecting back on the two African scenes in Photos 4.32 and 4.33, Photo 4.36 adds yet another dimension of surprise by showing that Boy Scouts were also caught up in the demonstration. If there is a "common consciousness," putatively Western, at work in this mass political demonstration, it would appear to be *both* Christian *and* anti-colonial. The methodological point here is clear: The value of photographs such as these will lie not just in

Photo 4.34   Female university students in protest parade, Guangzhou, Guangdong, China, 1925.

SOURCE: © Reproduced by permission of Special Collections, Yale Divinity School Library.

Photo 4.35   Protest parade through city, Guangzhou, Guangdong, China, 1925.

SOURCE: © Reproduced by permission of Special Collections, Yale Divinity School Library.

Photo 4.36   Students and Boy Scouts at protest parade, Guangzhou, Guangdong, China, 1925.

SOURCE: © Reproduced by permission of Special Collections Yale Divinity School Library.

their ability to clarify events but also in their ability to call attention to nuances that otherwise might go unnoticed.

A Single Episode: Mission Photography and Colonial Politics

The next three photographs document a key political event in the modern history of Madagascar. They feature the same royal figure and, like the pictures of the demonstration in China, they shed light on the colonial politics at work in the places where Western missionaries were investing their resources.

Shown in regal splendor in Photo 4.37, Queen Ranavalona III was the last native monarch of Madagascar. The French occupation of that island nation in 1895 triggered a sequence of events that culminated in 1897 when Ranavalona was deposed and sent into exile in Algeria, where she spent the remainder of her life. To stunning effect, Photos 4.38 and 4.39 capture her final public speech. In the vast gathering shown in Photo 4.38, the queen, surrounded by dignitaries, is barely visible under the canopy on the platform to the left of center. The activity in the open space below and to the right of her, dead center in the composition, appears to be some sort of military display marking the event. Surrounding those two points of interest, a vast assemblage of people covers an enormous expanse, perfectly defining the concept of *multitude*, with every vantage point occupied, including the stairways and balconies of the buildings overlooking the natural amphitheater. The quality of the photograph is sufficiently good that the viewer can easily get lost in the details, but one interpretation that is definitely *not* suggested by this picture is that the people of Madagascar were indifferent to their queen's departure. The following photograph, Photo 4.39, was taken at closer range and from a slightly different angle; it provides a somewhat better view of the platform party. A factual question worth pursuing in the text sources about this period is whether the queen's words (can we learn what she actually said?) or the size of this turnout for her speech, in any way influenced the French decision to formally depose her and send her and her husband (who was also the prime minister) into a safe and distant exile.

These valedictory moments of an indigenous ruler are particularly striking, but in one sense, they are not at all unusual. The photo collections in the IMPA consortium have many pictures of native rulers and dignitaries, often taken just before or just after they were deposed by Western colonial powers. Pictures recording ceremonial public events marking the accession of colonial rule or celebrating its anniversaries are also common, especially in the files of the British missions, but none of these captures the drama of colonial relationships quite as well as the three pictures of Ranavalona.

Photo 4.37   Queen Ranavalona III, Antananarivo, Madagascar, ca. 1890–1895.

SOURCE: © Reproduced by permission of the Norwegian Missionary Society Archive.

With the benefit of hindsight, the final picture (Photo 4.40) that I will offer is also about politics. It freezes a moment just before the missionary movement itself hit a limit, in one place at least. The caption on the picture should be self-explanatory, but one descriptive sentence from the accompanying metadata is useful for grasping the importance of the photo. It reads: "'Waiting for the motor ferry across the Yangtze at Chungking. China Inland Mission truck with the European party of the 49-ers.' The last CIM missionaries to enter China, in 1949, going in." Because we know that 1949 was the year that Mao's forces prevailed and began to expel Western missionaries from the mainland, it is not too difficult to imagine a second photograph, taken shortly after this one, showing the same mission truck reversing course and carrying the missionaries out again.

Photo 4.38   Queen Ranavalona III's last public speech, Andohalo, Antananarivo, Madagascar, 1895.

SOURCE: © Reproduced by permission of the Norwegian Missionary Society Archive.

Photo 4.39   Kabary [speech] of Queen Ranavalona III following French occupation, Andohalo, Antananarivo, Madagascar, ca. 1895.

SOURCE: © Reproduced from London Missionary Society/Council for World Mission Archives.

Concluding Remarks

In viewing these pictures, it is always legitimate, indeed necessary, to ask what the photographers may have had in mind, what they included and what they screened out as they composed their photographs, and what photos they preserved and were prepared to show to various audiences in relation to the ones they might have discarded, destroyed, or put to one side in the collection. In other words, the visual archives of missions must be approached with the same critical scrutiny that is brought to bear on any other organizational record: Why is this document here? Who produced it? What was its intended use? What is *not* here for examination?

With these caveats firmly in mind, what I have sought to show in this brief overview is how historical photographs taken by missionaries constitute a distinct category of information that can be used alongside the more familiar text-based materials that have been the primary stock in trade for scholars. They can lend verisimilitude to written descriptions of occasions and characters, but more important, they are capable not just of confirming but also of challenging our accounts of historical events.

Photo 4.40   Last missionaries to China, 1949.

SOURCE: © Photograph by Ralph Willicome. © Overseas Missionary Fellowship. Reproduced by permission of Overseas Missionary Fellowship.

In the IMPA project, the electronic architecture for scanning, retrieving, and cataloging photographs that is now in place will allow for the expansion of the database—theoretically without limit—so that, in time, it will display greater representation across denominations, geographic regions, and chronological periods than it does at present. Our argument would be that these visual traces of historical change should become a routine and expected part of scholarship about the missionary movement.

Web Resources

BMPIX, the Basel Mission archive in Switzerland: http://www.bmpix.org/
Internet Mission Photography Archive:
    http://www.usc.edu/isd/archives/arc/digarchives/mission/
Dublin Core Metadata Initiative: http://www.dublincore.org/
Moravian Church, (Die Herrnhuter Brüdergemeine): http://www.archiv.ebu.de/
Leipzig Mission (Evangelisch-Lutherisches Missionswerk Leipzig): http://www.lmw-mission.de/e/index.htm
Catholic Foreign Mission Society of America, Inc. (Maryknoll Fathers and Brothers): http://www.maryknoll.org/ABOUTUS/ARCHIV/archiv.htm
Norwegian Missionary Society: http://www.nms.no/
University of London, School of Oriental and African Studies:
    http://www.soas.ac.uk/library/index.cfm?navid=1399
Yale University, Divinity School, Day Missions Library:
    http://www.library.yale.edu/div/identify.html

5

The Failure of
"The President's Choice"

Erina Duganne

*The history of our times and the efforts of this Administration
to meet the challenges of today are graphically expressed in photographs now being made. Photography can show with peculiar
power that government is personal, that we are concerned with
human beings, not statistics.*

President Lyndon Baines Johnson made this statement in a January 9, 1965,
memorandum asking the heads of executive departments and agencies of his
administration to submit by the first of every month the three photographs
"which most powerfully portray the problems of America and the efforts to
meet them."[1] Governmental photographers in each division took the photographs, and to screen their monthly submissions, Johnson appointed a
committee that included photographers Ansel Adams, Walker Evans, and
W. Eugene Smith, as well as Museum of Modern Art (MoMA) Director of
Photography John Szarkowski, who served as the group's executive director.[2] Based on their recommendations, Johnson then selected one photograph every month as "The President's Choice," with the ultimate objective
being their display in an exhibition and a book that would "capture the
spirit of our times."[3]

According to a contemporary reviewer, "The President's Choice" photography program, as well as the general interest in photography by Johnson's administration, "evoked a good bit of hooray and hallelujah among patrons of the photographic arts" (Neubauer, 1965, p. 59).[4] In spite of this initial fervor, the program was discontinued after less than a year; today "The President's Choice" has largely been forgotten.[5] In this chapter, I return to this program but not to restore or even to legitimize it. Instead, I carefully consider archival materials—both text-based and photographs—associated with this program so as to reveal blind spots in widely held assumptions about approaches to 1950s and 1960s U.S. photography and the consequences that these positions had on the selection process for "The President's Choice" nominations.

Selection Process

To unravel what led "The President's Choice" to fail so quickly, I conducted research in the White House Central Files in the LBJ Library in Austin, Texas. There I located two folders relating to the "White House Photography Program," each of which contains a variety of text-based archival materials, including memorandums, letters, and press releases dating from December 1964 through November 1965. Because these documents outline the development, implementation, and ultimately the demise of "The President's Choice," I assumed that they could help me to establish the evaluation criteria used to select "The President's Choice" nominations. I soon discovered, however, that it was not easy to pinpoint what exactly constituted "good" or "effective" photographs and how these were distinguished from "bad" or "inferior" photographs for Johnson and the members of the selection committee.

In his initial memorandum about the program, Johnson asserts that "photography can show with peculiar power that government is personal, that we are concerned with human beings, not statistics."[6] Based on his statement about photography's intrinsic humanism, I assumed that Johnson selected the "The President's Choice" nominations according to their ability to communicate through feeling. Other documents in the file, however, placed the accuracy of this assumption in question. In a letter outlining what the selection committee understood as the mechanics and purposes of "The President's Choice," Szarkowski makes a statement that offers insight into this discrepancy: "Most importantly, this program requires good pictures, not simply good captions. The Committee—and the public—will read the caption only if the picture, as a picture, is compelling."[7] In this passage, Szarkowski asserts that the committee evaluated "The President's Choice" nominations in terms of what lies within the confines of the picture frame and not how effectively the photograph communicated through feeling.

To some, however, the formalist expectations of the selection committee may seem paradoxical. After all, W. Eugene Smith, who frequently immersed himself in the lives of his subjects, understood the communication of feeling as integral to the practice of photography.[8] Such differences about criteria for judging the photographs are by and large suppressed in the archival documents in the "White House Photography Program" folders. Instead, the only evidence detailing the nature of the selection process as well as the reactions of committee members to specific photographs is found in letters written and signed by Szarkowski. Based on these materials, it thus appears that two competing approaches to photography informed the selection process for "The President's Choice." One evaluated the images according to their ability to communicate through feeling while the other valued the formal appeal and self-sufficiency of the photographs. These conflicting approaches are not unique to the archival documents in the LBJ Library; instead, they mirror larger ideological assumptions about U.S. photography during the 1950s and 1960s.

Formalism

A formalist interpretation of photography concerns itself first and foremost with those visual characteristics considered intrinsic to the medium. John Szarkowski laid the groundwork for this formalist agenda in his 1964 exhibition at MoMA entitled *The Photographer's Eye*. In this exhibition, Szarkowski largely changed the approach to photography established by his MoMA predecessor, Edward Steichen, who as photography historian and curator Christopher Phillips (1982) explains in his influential essay, "The Judgment Seat of Photography," valued photography's communicative potential over its formal appeal: "Rather than contest the peripheral status of art photography, [Steichen] was to capitalize on photography's demonstrably central role as a mass medium that dramatically 'interpreted' the world for a national (and international) audience" (p. 45). Phillips justifies this assertion by calling attention to the display of photographs under Steichen in the MoMA galleries, including his 1955 blockbuster exhibition, *The Family of Man*. According to Phillips, Steichen's preference for enlarged prints, usually unframed and mounted on boards, as well as oversized color transparencies and inexpensive prints from color slides promoted "rapid scanning rather than leisurely contemplation" and served to elevate the "designer's hand" as opposed to the "photographer's eye" (p. 49). Through these choices, or, as Phillips maintains, in using a "mass media" approach, Steichen effectively diminished photography's intrinsic formal value.

For Steichen (1960), photography's communicative potential also represented its most important contribution to the field: "We are only beginning to recognize generally and accept the potentialities of photography as an art medium, but as a visual means of mass communication it has become a force and stands without a peer" (p. 137). Yet, in contrast to Phillips's suggestion, Steichen did not adopt a mass media approach solely to lessen photography's aesthetic value or to suppress the photographer's individual vision. What Steichen actually hoped to create through the incorporation of mass media techniques was a more integrated exhibition space in which the audience would identify with the images in *The Family of Man* on an emotional level. Steichen hired Bauhaus-trained architect Paul Rudolph to help him realize this goal:

> In the creation of such an exhibition, resources are brought into play that are not available elsewhere. The contrast in scale of images, the shifting of focal points, the intriguing perspective of long-and-short range visibility with the images to come being glimpsed beyond the images at hand—all these permit the spectator an active participation that no other form of visual communication can give. (Steichen, 1963)

In other words, for Steichen, the importance of photography as mass communication depended on its ability to bring people together as human beings. "The audiences," Steichen (1960) further declares, "not only understand this visual presentation, they also participate in it, and identify themselves with the images, as if in corroboration of the words of a Japanese poet, 'When you look into a mirror, you do not see your reflection, your reflection sees you'" (p. 137).

In contrast to Steichen's goals, Szarkowski's exhibition program at MoMA positioned the medium within a distinctly autonomous aesthetic realm. As Szarkowski (1966) explains in the catalog to *The Photographer's Eye*, "It should be possible to consider the history of the medium in terms of photographers' progressive awareness of characteristics and problems that have seemed inherent in the medium" (p. 7). To emphasize those characteristics unique to photography, Szarkowski organized the pictures in his exhibition under five categories: The Thing Itself, The Detail, The Frame, Time, and Vantage Point. Szarkowski used these five characteristics to construct the discourse of photography as one that is predominately concerned with formalist issues as opposed to the communication of feeling: "The central act of photography, the act of choosing and eliminating, forces a concentration on the picture's edge—the line that separates in from out—and on the shapes that are created by it" (p. 9).[9]

Given Szarkowski's formalist expectations of the medium, it may seem paradoxical that President Johnson invited him to serve as the executive director of "The President's Choice" selection committee or that Szarkowski even agreed to participate. In selecting the committee to screen the selections, however, it appears that Szarkowski's ideological beliefs concerning the medium were left largely unexamined by Johnson's administration; rather, they selected him based largely on the merit of his institutional affiliation and position as director of photography at MoMA. For Szarkowski, on the other hand, accepting this position was consistent with his overall effort to extend his formalist criteria across the range of photography's history, including governmental photographers who worked primarily as photojournalists.

At the same time, photojournalism's explicit ties with the external world may seem incompatible with a formalist approach to photography. In emphasizing the medium's inherent aesthetic properties, however, Szarkowski (1977) never considered photojournalism as a debased art form. Szarkowski instead maintained that photojournalism offered an "especially rewarding area . . . to study photography in its most basic and unadorned form" (p. 81). Szarkowski first explored the essential qualities of photojournalistic images in his 1965 exhibition, *The Photo Essay,* which appeared at MoMA contemporaneously with "The President's Choice." In a wall label for his exhibition, Szarkowski describes a shift that he believed had taken place in the history of the photo essay, whose primary function since World War II had been to tell a story. "Today," as Szarkowski explains, "some essay photographers are questioning the premise of the picture story and suggesting that perhaps the picture should be judged for its intrinsic meaning and not just as one element in a unified statement."[10] Here Szarkowski calls attention to the aesthetic autonomy of photojournalism over its ability to tell a story.

Szarkowski approached the photographs for Johnson's "The President's Choice" program with similar expectations. For instance, in reference to a May 1965 submission by Agency for International Development photographer Jose Carrera Reza, Szarkowski makes the following comment: "This picture has considerable purely visual interest and an unexpected sense of scale which makes it simply fun to look at. If a picture is fun to look at, the person will also read the caption and probably remember it."[11] In this passage, Szarkowski praises Reza's photograph foremost for its intrinsic formal appeal, which he argued exists independent and irrespective of its caption or its ability to tell a story. "There is no equivalent of the syllogism in pictures," Szarkowski (1975) later explains. "The photograph may suggest, but cannot define, intellectual or philosophical or political values. It can only describe appearances" (p. 64). Here Szarkowski again reveals his attempt to position photography within a distinctly aesthetic realm. At the same time, Szarkowski's (1977) clarification does not mean that he understood photographs "as purely abstract constructions that have their meaning enclosed completely within their frame and do not reverberate outside in the rest of the whole world of our knowledge and sensibility" (p. 93). Rather, it was essential to Szarkowski (1978) that associations beyond the frame be entertained only after a photograph's self-sufficiency is established because these connections would ultimately remain speculations and in no way disrupt "the intrinsic or prejudicial capacities of the medium as it is understood at that moment" (pp. 23–24).

Communicating Through Feeling

For Edward Steichen, on the other hand, photography's inherent ability to communicate through feeling represented its most important contribution to the field. This approach to photography had not always been fundamental to Steichen's curatorial or even photographic practice. Steichen began his career working as a painter and pictorialist photographer; he served with Alfred Stieglitz as one of the founders of the Photo-Secession, an artist movement at the turn of the 20th century that mobilized around the aesthetic potential of photography as a legitimate and comparable art form. After participating as a photographer in both World Wars, however, Steichen's approach to the medium changed significantly.

Through his involvement commanding the Photographic Division of the Air Force Service in World War I and the Photographic Division of the U.S. Navy in World War II, Steichen (1963) became aware of photography's power as a form of communication: "I wanted to reach into the world, to participate and communicate, and I felt that I would be able to do this best through photography." During World War I, Steichen photographed the war primarily from an airplane, using the medium as a reconnaissance tool. By World War II, Steichen had learned, as Phillips (1981) explains, "that photography, in addition to serving as a simple recorder of facts and faces, could, in the right hands, serve as powerful instrument for distilling the human meaning of complex events" (p. 28). To convince the Navy of photography's emotional capacity, Steichen encouraged the members of his photographic unit to turn their lenses on the human dimension of the war.

Steichen's newfound humanistic approach to the medium was influenced in particular by photographs taken by members of the Photographic Division of the Farm Security Administration (FSA) during the 1930s. Steichen first encountered FSA photography during the spring of 1938, when he visited the International Photography Exposition in New York City.[12] From these images, Steichen came to understand that the greatest influence of photography was its ability to communicate through feeling. "Look into the faces of the men and the women in these pages," Steichen (1938) writes in a 1938 review of FSA photography in *U.S. Camera Annual*, "Listen to the story they tell and they will leave with you a feeling of a living experience you won't forget" (p. 44).[13] Here Steichen defines FSA photography in terms of its ability to distill the human dimension of an event in a manner that carries emotional resonance for the audience. This enthusiasm for photography's emotional power would continue throughout Steichen's curatorial career at MoMA.

In his approach to "The President's Choice" program, President Johnson seems to align himself more closely with Steichen's humanistic understanding of photography than with Szarkowski's, and by extension the selection committee's, formalist approach to the medium.[14] The refusal of Evans and Smith to vote for any of the submissions sent to the committee in May 1965, only four months after the program's inception, reiterates this bias. So do the submissions for June, which according to Szarkowski, "are *not* what the committee considers distinguished work. They are simply the best that we could find in the total submissions, which were in general very bad indeed."[15] Here Szarkowski suggests that the program collapsed because he and the selection committee members found the submissions lacking in formal aesthetic value. The reason given by Johnson's special consultant, Eric Goldman, for discontinuing "The President's Choice" substantiates this assumption: "The photographs being submitted are simply not of high enough quality."[16]

The weight that Szarkowski and the other committee members placed on the self-sufficiency and visual appeal of the "The President's Choice" photographs that they selected, at expense of their capacity to communicate through feeling, appears to have played a major role in the failure of "The President's Choice." Of course, other circumstances—like the haste with which Johnson devised the program—may have also contributed to its downfall. Overall, however, the text-based archival materials in the White House Photography Program folders suggest that the committee's and Johnson's divergent conceptions of photography seem to be what ultimately led Goldman to inform the appropriate offices and individuals on October 8, 1965, only nine months after its inception, to let "The President's Choice" photography program "die quietly."[17]

President Johnson's general approach to photography supports this reading as well.[18] Ultimately, Johnson cared less about the formal characteristics or aesthetic autonomy of a picture than its ability to communicate through feeling. Johnson's selection of photographer Ken Heyman to illustrate his

1966 book, *This America: A Portrait of a Nation,* provides a case in point. For this book, Johnson employed Heyman, who had previously worked for the United States Information Agency's (USIA) program, the "The Alliance for Progress" (Alianza).[19] The book itself consists of Johnson's text, which editor Jerry Mason paired with 208 photographs selected from the 13,000 that Heyman took while traveling across the United States with a shooting script that Mason had prepared based on Johnson's speeches and other written comments on the Great Society. That the format of *This America* closely resembles the exhibition catalog to Steichen's *The Family of Man* was not a coincidence; Mason also served as editor for that publication.

Although too young to have been included as a photographer in *The Family of Man,* Heyman (1988) has since compared his photographic approach with the type of work associated with that exhibition: "I'm more from the 'Family of Man' school because I think photographs should have an emotional impact: that's how they can make a difference." Heyman's interest in using his photographs to communicate through feeling is also one that Paul Byers addresses in a 1961 *U.S. Camera* article in which he argues that Heyman's photographs "yield more than a lecture in American sociology because it's an elaborate description of human feelings" (p. 88). The human dimension of Heyman's photographs must have also impressed Johnson because, in February 1965, he selected a USIA photograph by Heyman as the first image to earn the title of "The President's Choice."

Nominations

The text-based archival materials in the LBJ Library, together with larger ideological assumptions about the competing approaches to U.S. photography during the 1950s and 1960, all indicated that Johnson's and the selection committee's conflicting expectations about the medium had caused the downfall of "The President's Choice." Yet, on a subsequent trip to the LBJ library, I began to question the accuracy of this hypothesis. Several letters written by Szarkowski to Johnson's special consultant, Eric Goldman, outlining the committee's recommendations note that a selection of photographs had been originally enclosed as attachments.[20] The White House Photography Program folders, however, did not contain any images, and neither did the Audiovisual Archives in the LBJ Library. Where were these images now? A handwritten note on a memorandum to Johnson asking him to name that month's "The President's Choice" offered a clue.[21] The note states that five photographs, including "The President's Choice" nomination had been filed in "oversize." On further sleuthing, I discovered that a total of 69 black and white prints of 11 separate images had been placed on a shelf in the archive for oversized items in 1965 and since forgotten.[22]

The discovery of these photographs was momentous because it forced me to realize a major blind spot in my research. Until this point, I had been relying solely on the text-based archival materials that I found in the LBJ Library as well as larger ideological assumptions about approaches to U.S. photography in the 1950s and 1960s. What was missing from my analysis was a consideration of the images themselves. To rectify this oversight, I first began to look closely at the eight framed prints of the first- and second-place "The President's Choice" nominations. These prints interested me the most because their framing suggested that they had acquired value within the program. Using these photographs as points of reference, I then turned back to the text-based archival materials so as to think about the space in between what these images depict and the discourse around them.

For instance, although Szarkowski also admired Ken Heyman's photographic production and had included 11 of his USIA images in the 1962 exhibition, *Five Unrelated Photographers,* at MoMA, he and the selection committee did not nominate Heyman's photograph of Peruvian children drinking out of tin cups as their first choice (Photo 5.1). Instead, they selected a photograph by Food for Peace photographer Allan Berg that depicts a similar subject, an Ecuadorian child drinking out of a cup, arguing that it was "technically" a better image than the one by Heyman (Photo 5.2).[23]

In his image, Berg depicts a child from such a close proximity that only the cup, part of the child's hand, and her eyes gazing directly at the camera are

Photo 5.1   Peruvian children, submitted by U.S. Information Agency.

SOURCE: Photo by Ken Heyman.

Photo 5.2   Ecuadorian child, submitted by Food for Peace.

SOURCE: Photo by Allan Berg; used with permission.

visible. Heyman, on the other hand, standing at a greater distance from his subjects, depicts a group of children drinking within the context of an interior space. One could argue that for Szarkowski and the selection committee, Berg's severe cropping of the image serves to abstract the child from her or his surrounding context, thereby calling attention to the formal aspects of the picture and obscuring the child's immediate affiliation with the U.S. Food for Peace program. Conversely, in photographing the children from a greater distance, Heyman contextualizes them within their geographic specificity. Even though one may still not know the exact government program with which these children are affiliated, one can at least use the clothing and hats to identify the children as Latin American. This is a detail that Johnson would have certainly wanted to be apparent because of his interest in using "The President's Choice" photographs to communicate "the efforts of his Administration to meet the challenges of today,"[24] which included providing food for children in such underdeveloped countries as Peru.

Heyman's depiction of the children within their surrounding context sacrifices form for clarity. This choice again suggested that Szarkowski's and the committee members' selection criteria depended largely on a photograph's aesthetic autonomy and not on its ability to evoke associations outside of the formal boundary of the frame. The committee's selection for May 1965 further supports this reading. For their nomination, Szarkowski and the committee members chose a photograph by Jean Cote and Robert Moeser that, according to its caption, depicts a catapult officer aboard the USS Ranger CVA-61, signaling the launch of an AI Skyraider while a flight deck crewman mans the console (Photo 5.3). The committee selected this image largely because of its visual power, which Szarkowski defines in terms of "its sense of speed and urgency and competence and strength" and because it gives "an exciting sense of what a modern war plane is about."[25]

The manner in which the photographers have blurred the airplane in the background of the picture and depicted the catapult officer at a moment of contained action instills the picture with the sense of speed and urgency that Szarkowski describes. At the same time, Szarkowski and the committee members do not attribute the competence and strength of the image solely to issues of form. They also credit the image's success to the excitement that its content—a modern war plane—evokes. In making this correlation, however,

Photo 5.3   Catapult officer aboard the USS Ranger CVA-61 signals the launch of an AI Skyraider while a flight deck crewman mans the console.
SOURCE: Photo by Jean Cote and Robert Moeser.

Szarkowski and the selection committee presume that viewers, prior to reading the caption, will automatically recognize the distorted mass in the background of the picture as a modern war plane and instinctively feel a sense of excitement in relation it. Yet, without the caption, there is little in the picture to guarantee that viewers will make this association, much less that this content will actually evoke such prescribed feelings. This discrepancy suggests that Szarkowski's and the selection committee's nominations depended on more than just an image's intrinsic meaning.

Despite its being the first and only image to receive a unanimous vote from the committee, Johnson did not select Cote and Moeser's photograph as the May 1965 "The President's Choice" winner.[26] He instead chose an image by Paul Conklin that depicts Peace Corps volunteer Gail Engles watching children play in Chancay, Peru (Photo 5.4). Conceivably Johnson preferred

Photo 5.4   Peace Corps volunteer Gail Engels, 22, of Queens, NY, is a community development worker in Chancay, Peru.

SOURCE: Photo by Paul Conklin.

Conklin's photograph over that of Cote and Moeser because Conklin, like Heyman, depicts his subject matter in a manner that emphasizes the human meaning of the event in a more straightforward manner. Whereas Cote and Moeser blur most of the subject matter, Conklin renders everything in his picture in clear detail and includes contextual information such as the school in the composition's background. Thus, for Johnson, Conklin's photograph depicted, in human terms that were seemingly more readily apparent than the ones in Cote's and Moser's image, the successful results of his administration's efforts to provide social and economic assistance in Peru.

Two committee members, who voted in favor of Conklin's picture in addition to Cote's and Moeser's photograph, make this association as well: "There is a lot of gaity [sic] and happiness and a nice sense of freedom . . . Not only the children but also the girl seem to be having a very good time and the picture somehow suggests that it is a good thing for everyone concerned that she is there." This account again suggests that the evaluative criteria of the committee members extended beyond issues of form to address photography's communicative potential. At the same time, however, like

Photo 5.5   Concrete and reinforcing rods for a corn silo spin a web-like pattern for progress in northeast Brazil.

SOURCE: Photo by Jose Carrera Reza.

Cote and Moeser's photograph, the committee members also commend Conklin's image for its visual qualities: "[Conklin] has a good eye for the moment when the pattern of the picture seems to express its meaning."[27] Here the members emphasize Conklin's ability to discern that "decisive moment" when, as photographer Henri Cartier-Bresson explains in his 1952 book of the same name, "the significance of an event as well as a precise organization of forms which gave that event its proper expression" come together. It would seem logical that Johnson overlooks this visual aspect, preferring to read Conklin's picture solely in terms of the feelings that he assumes it evokes in relation to the humanitarian efforts of his administration.

Johnson's selection of Reza's image of the concrete and reinforcing rods for a corn silo (Photo 5.5) as the runner-up to Conklin's photograph, however, complicates this logic. This is the same picture that Szarkowski discussed solely in terms of its "purely visual interest . . . which makes it simply fun to look at."[28] Given Johnson's supposed preference for images that represent his administration's personal involvement in issues of human consequence in a clear and self-evident way, this selection appears contradictory. Unlike the pictures by Heyman and Conklin, in which the human dimension of the images is made readily apparent, in Reza's photograph, the concentric ring pattern produced by the concrete and reinforcing rods of the corn silo overshadows the photograph's human subject. This focus serves to draw viewers' attention away from the human element in the photograph and encourages them to read the image in terms of the formal pattern created by the rods. The fact that the photograph provides no contextual information about the Rural Industry Technical Assistance project in northeast Brazil further supports this formalist reading. As a result of the purely visual emphasis of Reza's image, issues of form seem to have also influenced Johnson's selection process. Thus, like Szarkowski and the selection committee, Johnson valued photography both for its formal aesthetic properties and its communicative potential.

Structures of Feeling

These contradictory responses to "The President's Choice" nominations suggest that my initial assumption—that two divergent conceptions of photography had caused the downfall of the program—was incorrect. But, then, what had caused its failure? In my attempt to fit the conflicting approaches to "The President's Choice" selection process into preconceived expectations about 1950s and 1960s U.S. photography, I, much like Johnson and the selection committee, had overdetermined the consequences that these positions have in actual decision-making practices. Thinking through the lens of art history allowed me to reify these conflicting approaches, yet offered me little terminology to address the unpredictable and varied aspects of these interactions, which had begun to emerge as a result of close analysis of the archival images. Turning toward more interdisciplinary fields of study, and in particular, Raymond Williams's oft-cited notion of *structures of feeling,* provided a theoretical flexibility that allowed for greater attention to the complex and at times contradictory dimensions of "The President's Choice" selection process.

According to Williams (1977), a structure of feeling is

> a social experience which is still in *process,* often indeed not yet recognized as social but taken to be private, idiosyncratic, and even isolating, but which in analysis (though rarely otherwise) has its emergent, connecting, and dominant characteristics, indeed its specific hierarchies. These are often more recogniz-able at a later stage, when they have been (as often happens) formalized, clas-sified, and in many cases built into institutions and formations. (p. 132)

In this passage, Williams calls attention to those aspects of social life that are still in the course of being lived and felt, yet despite their ephemerality, remain firmly embedded with the social matrix. "Not feelings against thought," Williams further states, "but thought as felt and feeling as thought: practical consciousness of a present kind, in a living and interre-lating continuity" (p. 132).

Williams's idea—that not all thought processes can be described in terms of conscious and fully formulated ideas and attitudes because they have yet to fully emerge in social life—allowed me to see "The President's Choice" selection process in a different light. In choosing their nominations for "The President's Choice," both the selection committee and Johnson's adminis-tration assume that the meanings of the pictures that they have chosen and the responses associated with them are transparent. For instance, the members of the selection committee presume that the formal interest of the pictures and their effects on viewers can be universally established. The members of Johnson's administration, on the other hand, believe that the amount of information the viewer has about the humanistic aspect of the images and their reactions to this content are both readily apparent and uncomplicated. In actuality, as the failure of "The President's Choice" makes explicit, their meanings are contingent on the subject positions and systems of interpretation embodied in these opposing and at times contra-dictory viewpoints, yet also include those more elusive and ephemeral structures of feelings that Johnson, the selection committee, and viewers brought to bear on them.

In a contemporary review of "The President's Choice" in *Popular Photography,* John Neubauer (1965) addresses this discursive space in between what images depict and what they mean when he argues that it is not the quality of the pictures or the ability of the photographers that caused the program's shortcomings. Instead, Neubauer suggests that the limitation of the program stemmed from the failure of both the selection committee and Johnson's administration to address the complex relationship between their respective assumptions about what these images signify and in turn how these photographs were interpreted. As Neubauer (1965) suggests in his critique of Heyman's photograph of the Peruvian children (see Photo 5.1), "Nothing in the photograph of the Peruvian children drinking milk out of tin cups says the milk was a gift of the United States, or that it was the first milk these children ever tasted . . . Even the best photographs rarely have a built-in caption" (p. 130). Here Neubauer reiterates that the failure of "The President's Choice" program transcended the question of whether photography's aesthetic properties, communicative potential, or both informed the selection process.

In the end, it was not two competing approaches to photography that caused the downfall of "The President's Choice." The program unraveled because both Johnson and the selection committee assumed that what they understood to constitute a "good" or "bad" photograph was both self-evident and universal. Yet, as my close reading of the archival images in conjunction with the text-based documents reveals, the formal and human dimensions of the photographs and the responses that they elicit cannot be so easily established. Instead, the meanings of these images depend as much on the contradictory approaches as on the more elusive and ephemeral structures of feelings that Johnson and the selection committee brought to bear on them. Ultimately, Johnson and the selection committee could never reach a consensus; in assuming that their decision-making process and the nominations that resulted were transparent, they repeatedly overlooked the more varied, unpredictable, and emergent dimensions that also informed their selections.

In falling back on preexisting assumptions about approaches to 1950s and 1960s U.S. photography and relying solely on the text-based archival materials in the LBJ Library, I too had failed to notice these important features in the selection process of "The President's Choice" nominations. It was only by carefully considering the complex and at times contradictory intersections between the text-based documents, the archival images, and ideological assumptions about the history of 1950s and 1960s U.S. photography that these blind spots gradually began to materialize. In our fast-paced and oversaturated visual world, archives and their preservation of what has failed and frequently been forgotten offer important reminders of the need to slow down habits of observation and to rethink long-held systems of belief so that those less fully formulated aspects of everyday life might also begin to emerge.

Notes

1. Memorandum, President Johnson to Heads of Executive Departments and Agencies, 1/9/65, White House Photography Program, Ex PR 6–3, WHCF, Box 236, LBJ Library. This memorandum was released to the public by the Office of the White House Press Secretary on January 13, 1965; it is reprinted in Durniak (1965). For additional information on "The President's Choice" photography program, see Deschin, 1965; Neubauer, 1965; "President Gave," 1965; "Smile Please," 1965.

2. Other members considered for the committee included Edward Steichen, Richard Avedon, Eliot Elisofon, Philippe Halsman, Gene Ostrow, Dorothea Lange, Margaret Bourke-White, and Aaron Siskind.

3. Memorandum, President Johnson to Heads of Executive Departments and Agencies, January 9, 1965.

4. *Popular Photography* ("LBJ Pushes," 1965) also proclaimed: "Photography, as well as Lyndon B. Johnson, won by a landslide in the national elections last November" (p. 58).

5. For instance, I came across "The President's Choice" by happenstance while conducting preliminary research for the Office of Economic Opportunity's 1965 photography exhibition, *Profile of Poverty.*

6. Memorandum, President Johnson to Heads of Executive Departments and Agencies, January 9, 1965.

7. Letter, John Szarkowski to Elton P. Lord, February 5, 1965, White House Photography Program, Ex PR 6–3, WHCF, Box 236, LBJ Library.

8. W. Eugene Smith is known especially for his compassionate approach to photography. For instance, he would spend weeks researching his subjects and then immerse himself in their lives in an effort to most honestly re-create for viewers what his subjects were feeling. For a further discussion of Smith's involvement with his subjects, see Janis and MacNeil, 1977. For more on Smith's working methods, see, Smith, 1980; Smith and Johnson, 1981.

9. For further development of his formalist agenda, see Szarkowski, 1973, 1975, and 1978.

10. Press release, *The Photo Essay,* March 16, 1965, Exhibition Files, Museum of Modern Art Archives, New York.

11. Letter, John Szarkowski to Eric Goldman, May 17, 1965, White House Photography Program, Ex PR 6–3, WHCF, Box 236, LBJ Library.

12. Organized by Willard Morgan, the International Photographic Exposition, which opened in April 1938 at Grand Central Palace in New York City, included about 70 FSA prints. See Hurley, 1972, p. 132.

13. Roy Stryker (1978) reiterates the association of documentary photography with the communication of feeling when he writes in "Documentary Photography," that "a good documentary photograph should not only tell what a place or thing or person *looks* like, but it must also tell the audience what it would *feel* like to be an actual witness to the scene" (p. 1364). For a discussion of this feeling function of documentary in relation to 1930s U.S. culture, see Warren Susman, 1970, and Williams Stott, 1986.

14. The idea that a government-sponsored photography program could bring the nation together as human beings is anticipated by Steichen in his 1962 exhibition *The Bitter Years, 1935–1941: Rural America as Seen by the Photographers of the Farm Security Administration,* which he mounted at MoMA just before relinquishing his directorship position to Szarkowski. See Steichen, 1962 and 1963. Interestingly, Steichen was also one of the individuals on the short list for the selection committee of "The President's Choice."

15. Letter, John Szarkowski to Eric Goldman, July 6, 1965, White House Photography Program, Ex PR 6–3, WHCF, Box 236, LBJ Library.

16. Memorandum, Eric F. Goldman, October 8, 1965, White House Photography Program, Ex PR 6–3, WHCF, Box 236, LBJ Library.

17. Ibid.

18. Johnson's inclusion of 30 photographs, each hung at eye level on a separate gray or beige panel in his White House Festival of the Arts, is one exception. Yet, one could argue that for this event Johnson was more interested in revealing his administration's commitment to and interest in contemporary U.S. art practices, including photography. The promotion of the White House Festival of the Arts, held on June 14, 1965, as showcasing the finest U.S. contemporary art, including prose and poetry, music, drama, motion pictures, dance, jazz, paintings, sculptures, and photography, further supports this argument. See Memorandum, Eric F. Goldman to the President, February 25, 1965, AR/MC 11/23/63–6/4/65, GEN AR 7/26/65, WHCF, Box 2, LBJ Library. Szarkowski, along with Smithsonian curator of photography Eugene Ostroff, and Library of Congress curator of photography, Allan Fern, selected the 30 photographers included in the festival, each of whom was represented by a single work. For a contemporary review of the photography portion of the festival, see Reynolds, 1965.

19. Alianza was a foreign aid program initiated by John F. Kennedy to help underdeveloped countries in Central and South America. As part of his affiliation with this program, Heyman traveled to El Salvador, Panama, Colombia, Peru, and Venezuela from May 10 to July 4, 1962, to document those situations that the Alianza intended to help. Within a year, Heyman returned to photograph the improvement of their situation. Photographs from these trips were exhibited by Szarkowski in his 1962 exhibition, *Five Unrelated Photographers,* at MoMA and have been subsequently published in Ken Heyman and Margaret Mead, 1965 and 1975, and Heyman, 1983.

20. See Letter, John Szarkowski to Eric Goldman, February 25, 1965; Letter, John Szarkowski to Eric Goldman, April 12, 1965; Letter, John Szarkowski to Eric Goldman, May 17, 1965, White House Photography Program, Ex PR 6–3, WHCF, Box 236, LBJ Library.

21. See Memorandum, Jack Valenti to Mr. President, May 22, 1965, White House Photography Program, Ex PR 6–3, WHCF, Box 236, LBJ Library.

22. Since their rediscovery, the photographic prints have been cataloged and transferred to the Audiovisual Archives in the LBJ Library.

23. See Memorandum, Eric F. Goldman to Jack Valenti, January 30, 1965, White House Photography Program, Ex PR 6–3, WHCF, Box 236, LBJ Library.

24. Memorandum, President Johnson to Heads of Executive Departments and Agencies, January 9, 1965.

25. Letter, John Szarkowski to Eric Goldman, May 17, 1965.

26. The only image that both the committee and Johnson voted for unanimously for the "The President's Choice" was a portrait by Staff Sergeant Steven Stibbens of Master Sergeant Evans H. Johnson, who was serving as a U.S. Army Special Forces adviser to the Montagnard tribesmen in Vietnam.

27. Letter, John Szarkowski to Eric Goldman, May 17, 1965.

28. ibid.

References

Byers, P. (1961). Ken Heyman. In T. Maloney (Ed.), *U.S. Camera '62*. New York: US Camera Publishing.

Cartier-Bresson, H. (1952). *The decisive moment*. New York: Simon & Schuster.

Deschin, J. (1965, January 24). Shows at five galleries. *The New York Times*, p. X19.

Durniak, J. (1965, April). The president as picture editor. *Popular Photography*, p. 46.

Heyman, K. (1983). *The world's family* New York: Putnam.

Heyman, K. (1988). *Hipshot*. New York: Aperture.

Heyman, K., & Mead, M. (1965). *Family*. New York: Macmillan.

Heyman, K., & Mead, M. (1975). *World enough: Rethinking the future*. Boston: Little, Brown.

Hurley, F. J. (1972). *Portrait of a decade: Roy Stryker and the development of documentary photography in the thirties*. Baton Rouge: Louisiana State University Press.

Janis, E. P., & MacNeil, W. (Eds.). (1977). W. Eugene Smith, In *Photography within the humanities* (pp. 97–109). Danbury, NH: Addison House.

LBJ pushes photography in his first 365 days. (1965, November). *Popular Photography, 57*, 58.

Neubauer, J. (1965, November). The president's choice: Photography can show. . . . that government is personal. *Popular Photography*, p. 57.

Phillips, C. (1981). *Steichen at war*. New York: Portland House.

Phillips, C. (1982, Autumn). The judgment seat of photography. *October 22*, pp. 27–63.

President gave retroactive pay. (1965, January 14). *The New York Times,* p. 38.

Reynolds, C. (1965, November). White House presents photography as art. *Popular Photography, 57,* 58.

Smile please. (1965, February 16). *The Wall Street Journal,* p. 14.

Smith, W. E. (1980). *W. Eugene Smith: Early work.* Tucson, AZ: Center for Creative Photography.

Smith, W. E., & Johnson, W. (1981). *W. Eugene Smith: Master of the photographic essay.* Millerton, NY: Aperture.

Steichen, E. (1938). The F.S.A. photographers. In T. J. Maloney (Ed.), *U.S. Camera Annual 1939.* New York: Morrow.

Steichen, E. (1960). On photography. *Dædalus, 89*(1).

Steichen, E. (Ed.). (1962). *The bitter years, 1935–1941: Rural America as seen by the photographers of the Farm Security Administration.* New York: Museum of Modern Art.

Steichen, E. (1963). *A life in photography.* Garden City, NY: Doubleday.

Stott, W. (1986). *Documentary expression and thirties America* (Reprint). Chicago: University of Chicago Press.

Stryker, R. (1978). Documentary photography. In A. Feininger (Ed.), *The complete photographer.* Englewood Cliffs, NJ: Prentice Hall.

Susman, W. (1970). The thirties. In S. Coben & L. Ratner (Eds.), *The development of an American culture* (pp. 179–218). Englewood Cliffs, NJ: Prentice Hall.

Szarkowski, J. (1966). *The photographer's eye.* New York: Museum of Modern Art.

Szarkowski, J. (1973). *Looking at photographs.* New York: Museum of Modern Art.

Szarkowski, J. (1975, April 13). A different kind of art. *The New York Times Magazine,* pp. 64–68.

Szarkowski, J. (1977). John Szarkowski. In E. P. Janis & W. MacNeil (Eds.), *Photography within the humanities.* Danbury, NH: Addison House.

Szarkowski, J. (1978). *Mirrors and windows: American photography since 1960.* New York: Museum of Modern Art.

Williams, R. (1977). *Marxism and literature.* Oxford, UK: Oxford University Press.

6

Using Photography in Studies of Immigrant Communities

Reflecting Across Projects and Populations

Steven J. Gold

For the last 20-some years, I have been involved in studies of immigrant and ethnic communities. At the time I began research in this area, I was already familiar with visual sociology and believed that the use of photography could contribute much to research on immigration. However, there were few sources of information that could direct me toward integrating visuals into sociological research. Through a trial and error process, I eventually developed a series of techniques to achieve this end. In retrospect, I realize that I learned as much from the social interactions involved with taking photographs, showing images to respondents, and sharing prints with colleagues and students as I did from analyzing what is shown in the images themselves. The purpose of this chapter is to share some of these techniques with those who wish to incorporate visual methods and data into their own studies.

Integrating Visuals Into Social Research

In the last two decades, a considerable body of literature has been published that offers a variety of theoretical and practical suggestions about how to incorporate visuals into social research. However, no single approach has emerged as being appropriate for all of the myriad activities with which sociologists are involved (Banks, 2001; Becker, 1986; Prosser, 1998; Rose, 2001; Wagner, 2002). A major debate within this scholarship concerns if the visual should be treated as the primary object of analysis or if images should be used as one of many tools available for the investigation of social life.

One body of work contends that images should be the central object of study and focus of investigation. For example, Ball and Smith (1992) seek to make visuals "a serious source of data worthy of analysis" (p. 14), while Emmison and Smith (2000) hope to "position visual research as a central theme of investigations into society and culture" (p. x). Erving Goffman's *Gender Advertisements* (1979), which relies on the analysis of hundreds of magazine clippings, is held up as an exemplar of this orientation (Emmison & Smith, 2000).

Proponents of this method berate the use of images as illustrations that depict visually what is already described in the text (Hammond, 1998). For example, Ball and Smith (1992) criticize the use of photographs and film footage to illustrate ethnographic work.

> We have argued that as part of ethnographic reports, photographs are largely ancillary to the principal analytic purposes of the work. They are usually presented as a descriptive resource rather than a visual topic of inquiry.
>
> Here as is so often the case . . . pictures serve a simply decorative and illustrative function. (pp. 11–12)

Studies reflecting this approach offer convincing evidence of the value of visually based scholarship. Paradoxically however, by demanding that visuals be placed at the center of social research, this scheme may actually discourage a broader body of investigators from incorporating visual elements into their projects. Because relatively few sociological issues are fundamentally visual, those whose research concerns nonvisual topics and requires the analysis of nonvisual data may get the impression that incorporating photographs into their projects is "purely illustrative or documentary" and, hence, an inadequate application of visual methods (Emmison & Smith, 2000, p. 55).

An alternative approach rests on the idea that images can be effectively integrated with other forms of information to improve sociological work, even if analysis of the visuals is not the central focus. In such cases, photos are treated not solely as sources of data, but also as tools that facilitate the process of research more generally. They help to establish rapport with respondents, contextualize and lend specificity to the subject matter in question, and humanize the portrayal of respondents. In addition, the inclusion of images can encourage students and colleagues to join the analytical enterprise, and it makes presentations more accessible to diverse audiences (Collier & Collier 1986; Grady, 1996; Harper, 1987; Vergara, 1997).

In a recent article on the use of visual evidence in sociological analysis, Howard Becker (2002) refers to this use of visuals as he describes Berger and Mohr's (1975) *A Seventh Man,* a study of migrant laborers in Western Europe. Becker contends that even though the accompanying images are uncaptioned, the article provides enough information (ethnographic, statistical, and historical) about the experience of these workers to permit readers to interpret what is shown. Becker further asserts that this mode of presentation yields a more active, personal, and engaging experience than if images and text were explicitly integrated by the authors.

The work of ethnographic filmmakers offers another model for incorporating images into fieldwork projects (Barbash & Taylor, 1997). For filmmakers, a good deal of knowledge and analysis about the group, community, or phenomenon in question has already been generated prior to the initiation of filming. Images are used as a means of illustrating important themes, relationships, and processes associated with the subject of study or to reflect on the endeavor of documentary making itself (Minh-Ha, 1992). Filmmakers edit footage, audio, and narration into a sequence that they can share with an audience. Such documentary footage is not raw data, nor is it analyzed to generate findings. However, neither is it superfluous in the ways that Ball and Smith condemn. Instead, as Barbash and Taylor (1997) assert in their guide to ethnographic filmmaking, "The act of filming is often likened by anthropologists to the documentation or demonstration of research that precedes and determines it" (p. 70). In other words, these scholars' approach to ethnographic filmmaking involves the portrayal and exploration of themes identified during earlier research. Prior fieldwork and analysis, thus, permits the arrangement of images and concepts into a coherent presentation.

By adopting an approach that emphasizes the integration of visual and nonvisual data into broader sociological work (as opposed to demanding a visual sociology that deals solely with visual topics), this technique offers the many benefits of visual sociology to a broad community of students and colleagues. In applying it, perhaps we can make visual sociology a less marginal and more mainstream practice. This will benefit not only those of us with personal commitments to visual sociology, but the broader discipline as well.

Four Uses of Photography in Immigration Research

Ethnographic investigations are commonly used to interrogate social life and to reflect on the applicability of theoretical formulations to real-world settings (Burawoy, 1991). Many of the most influential of these reveal the complex and often unexpected ways that people cope with the situations that they confront. Drawing from this tradition, I suggest that photographic methods and visual data can contribute to the refinement of general propositions about the behavior of immigrant and ethnic groups as they adapt to new environments. In the following section, I briefly describe four ways that photography assisted me in studies of Soviet Jewish, Vietnamese, Israeli, and Arab immigrant communities (Gold, 1992, 1995a, 2002a, 2002b). These include gaining orientation, developing rapport, communicating with respondents via e–mailed images, and improving analysis.

Gaining Orientation

When starting a field study, photographs are useful for recording information about people, locations, and events of interest. For example, photographs can document what environments look like, how they provide a context in which groups interact, and who is present at events. The resulting images can be reviewed to assist in recording, coding, and analysis of fieldnotes (Collier, 1967; Suchar, 1997).

As Stinchcombe (1984) notes, as an academic discipline, sociology tends to value parsimonious and abstract findings that describe social relationships without having to deal with the full range of complexity associated with real people and situations. The most prestigious forms of social research are based on methods like library research, surveys, and analysis of official statistics, which keep investigators distant from the people, processes, and settings that they claim to study (Blumer, 1969; Harper, 1987; Stinchcombe, 1984). Even ethnographic data are often collected through gatekeepers and spokespersons in office settings or focus groups distant from the places where the social relations of greatest sociological significance take place. Moreover, in describing what they have discovered, social scientists too often rely on academic abstractions—about which they know a great deal—rather than situational knowledge associated with the setting at hand—about which they know much less (Harper, 1987). When social scientists describe an occupation as "service work," they gloss over what it is like to actually perform the job; when they refer to social relations as "embedded in networks," they add little to a more general understanding of the deep and intricate relationships on which communities are based. These scholastic tendencies discourage sociologists from acquiring direct knowledge about real people and settings.

Through my experience of using and teaching visual sociology, I have found that the need to create photographs in research settings can provide a corrective to academic distancing by demanding that researchers get involved with the people and settings that are their objects of study to a degree that exceeds what is generally applied in other methods.[1] For example, Vergara's (1997) photographic explorations of inner-city environments—based on years of immersion within them—offers a more detailed, phenomenologically rich, and arguably more powerful account of life in urban America than is available in more traditional approaches to the topic.

I have worked to apply this procedure in my research on migrant communities. Accordingly, whenever I could, I moved out of the air-conditioned offices of restaurants and factories into kitchens, shop floors, and warehouses. To chronicle religious communities, I often returned to research settings following interviews to observe and photograph holiday celebrations. I have also attended festivals, classes, weddings, baby showers, and political demonstrations. In this way, the act of making photographs both required and encouraged me to confront individuals and aspects of the social world from which I might have otherwise remained at a distance. My need to get near was further reinforced by my reliance on wide-angle lenses, which require close proximity to work effectively (Becker, 1986; Gold, 1995c). The resulting interactions and images enhanced my own insight and my ability to share findings with colleagues.

Developing Rapport

Making and sharing photographs can be helpful in generating rapport with respondents. As John Collier, Jr., pointed out in *Visual Anthropology* (1967), many individuals and groups who are unfamiliar with the goals and intentions of social science researchers *can* comprehend the purposes of photographers. In this way, making photographs gives a fieldworker a basis for meeting and interacting with those present in the location of research. The initial interaction leads to another: return visits when photographs are presented to participants.

I often begin interviews by showing respondents a series of pictures that I have taken in the course of studying their communities. (See Photo 6.1.) This allows me to quickly and specifically demonstrate my familiarity with the subject and environment of research. I believe that this grounding often enhances the quality of the interviews that follow. For example, at the start of a fieldwork trip among Israeli emigrants in London, I presented a slide

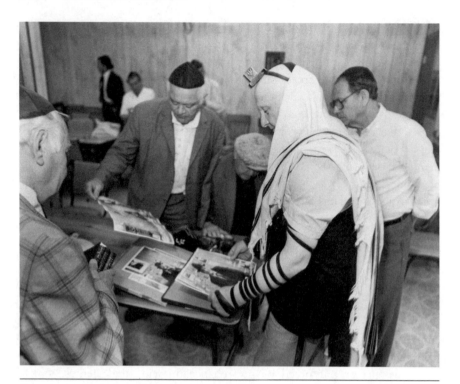

Photo 6.1   Soviet Jews look at photographs that I had taken of their community. Showing photographs to respondents generates rapport. In addition, the comments they made while looking at prints provided me with a lot of insight into respondents' knowledge of and opinions about members in their communities.

talk on Israelis in the United States to several members of the community at a meeting that had been arranged by a local colleague. Over the course of a week, I interviewed a number of the people who had attended my talk. This presentation offered an excellent introduction and facilitated the interviews that followed.

In many cases, the rapport that is established by showing photographs to members of migrant communities can be treated as a form of a photo elicitation interview (Harper, 2002). As respondents view images of their community, their comments can be very informative. Such reflections have provided me with significant insight into migrants' views of their broader community and how specific events and people are regarded.

In addition, respondents' reactions suggest their impressions of and familiarity with various personalities, strategies, locations, and subgroups within their population. For example, migrants' often cynical comments about other members of their communities shown in photographs played an important role in making me realize that in contrast to academic assertions about pervasive coethnic solidarity, migrant populations are often highly segmented and stratified (Gold, 1992; also discussed later in this chapter).

Whenever possible, I give copies of images to the people I photograph. Not only does this allow me to honor the respondents' willingness to be photographed, it also provides for additional rapport-building interactions and establishes an opportunity for informal photo elicitation. When individuals are shown pictures of themselves, highly specific comments are sometimes elicited. Such was the case when members of a Vietnamese family poignantly reflected on their experience of downward mobility—from relative affluence in the country of origin to their current austere circumstances in the United States.

E-mailing Images (and Other Benefits of Digital Photography)

In the last few years, photography, and with it visual sociology, have been transformed by digital technologies. Younger scholars whose involvement in photography doesn't predate the digital revolution, as well as veteran image makers who quickly made the changeover, have few complaints about computer-based imaging. However, a fraction of visual sociologists prefer film cameras and find many flaws with the new techniques. Some bemoan the fact that once readily available support equipment, such as darkrooms, slide projectors, and copy stands, has become as scarce as typewriters, and they resent having to purchase and master costly new tools when they were perfectly satisfied with those already on hand.

Moreover, advocates of film cameras point to the medium's superiority for work involving low light and wide angle lenses; they value the archival quality of negatives, Kodachrome slides, and silver prints and point to the difficulty involved in doing long-term visual fieldwork in remote locations that lack access to battery chargers and computers. Many film-based photographers would prefer to rely on hard-earned darkroom skills to manipulate images rather than having to master a complex computer program like Photoshop to accomplish the same results. Finally, some devotees of film worry that the easy manipulation of digitized images makes the use of photographic evidence more suspect than when using film-based imaging.

This is not the place to resolve all of the debates about film versus digital photography as tools for visual sociology; however, it is important to acknowledge that digital has important advantages as well as liabilities. For one, because there is no need to develop film or prints, images can be viewed instantly on the camera's LED, or very soon after they are taken on a laptop computer. Enlarging, reproducing, and arranging photographs, as well as adding text, are done with ease, and results can be shared via PowerPoint and over the internet.

Digital technology allows photographers to create numerous images with less effort and far less cost than is the case with film-based photography. For example—a postage-stamp-sized, one gigabyte media card (the digital equivalent of film)—can store more than 500 high-quality images, permitting a photographer to shoot roughly 14 times the number of exposures contained on a standard roll of 35mm film, all without having to stop to reload the camera or lug boxes of light and x-ray sensitive film. Finally, while the cost of digital cameras and accessories is consistently going down, their quality and versatility continues to increase.

One of digital photography's greatest advantages for visual sociology lies in its ability to expand paths of connection with respondents. I realized this as I photographed an Arab American community festival in 2005 (Gold, 2002a). (See Photo 6.2.) While I had done this kind of photography for years at various events, I had not used a digital camera in the past. As I normally do, I introduced myself to participants, spoke with them, asked for permission to take a picture, and then got their address so that I could send a print. In the past, this interaction was not complete for a week or so, during which time I would develop negatives, make prints, and send each one to the person whom I had photographed. With digital, I collected the subjects' e-mail addresses. Not

Photo 6.2   Dearborn Arab International Festival, 2005.

having to develop the images, I was able to deliver images immediately after the event. This rapid turn-around, coupled with a general access to e-mail among members of the community I researched, allowed me to establish communication with several of the people whom I had photographed.

These connections permitted me to then correspond with people I met in more immediate and visual ways. Accordingly, I became much more aware of their organizations' activities, and two of the photographs that I took during the festival wound up being published in community publications, which I now read regularly to keep informed of the community's activities. (See Photo 6.3.) In this way, digital photography and e-mail allowed me to extend rapport with, learn about, and contribute to a community in a

Photo 6.3   Image of Arab-American Anti-Discrimination Committee staff members taken by the author during fieldwork at the Dearborn Arab International Festival, 2005. The photo was published in the June 25–July 1, 2005, issue of the Arab-American News after the author sent it to the organization's e-mail address. The ability to quickly send images via e-mail is a valuable rapport-generating advantage of digital photography for visual sociologists.

manner superior to that which I had used during years of previous experience with film cameras.

Analysis

Most fieldwork methodologies encourage researchers to engage in a sequential process of collecting, coding, and analyzing data; memo writing; and revisiting field settings to check their observations, refine findings, and create higher-level generalizations (Berg, 2001; Emerson, Fretz, & Shaw, 1995; Strauss, 1987; Whyte, 1984). Visual sociologists have understood how visual information, whether film-based or digital, can be useful in this kind of research, and they have developed a body of literature that describes ways in which photographs can be incorporated (Gold, 1995c; Harper, 1987; Suchar, 1997).

Suchar (1997) draws on what he calls Becker's (1986) *interrogatory principle,* whereby images are used to help answer sociological questions suggested by literature review and previous fieldwork. The resulting photos are then analyzed in light of other data to generate supplementary questions. Repeating this cycle allows a researcher to incorporate additional evidence (photographic and otherwise) and produce findings.

Case Applications

The discussion that follows demonstrates some of the ways that I have used photography within three topics that are of general interest to scholars of international migration—migrant communities, ethnic economies, and the place of gender in migration processes.

Communities

Studies of immigrant communities associated with *ethnic mobilization* theory suggest that in the modern era, major benefits are garnered by populations who organize on a broad, groupwide, or international scale (Shanahan & Olzak, 2002). Consequently, local forms of organization and group solidarity are likely to be superseded by group-level patterns. "Modernization . . . first eliminates collective action on the basis of small-scale and local cleavages" (Nielsen, 1985, p. 147).

However, many recent immigrant and refugee populations are marked by diversity in terms of background, interests, experiences, identities, and patterns of resettlement. For them, ethnic identification and community formation tend to take place within subgroups that share commonalties rather than at the level of the entire population (Gold, 1992, 1995a, 2002b; Kim, 1981; Light, Sabagh, Bozorgmehr, & Der-Martirosian, 1994; Menjivar, 2000). Hence, scholars of ethnic and minority groups seek to understand the prevailing forms of group solidarity that exist within various populations. Do small networks predominate? Are broad-based collectives more common? Or is a combination of both forms prevalent? Finally, what group characteristics and contexts are associated with segmented and inclusive solidarity?

My research with photographs informed this debate. I found that Soviet Jews, Vietnamese, and Israelis cooperate among themselves and with other ethnic groups as well. However, various subgroups of these immigrant populations (based on common background, outlook, and orientation) have more extensively developed forms of cooperation than these ethnic communities as a whole.

Photos 6.4, 6.5, and 6.6 of these various communities reveal diversity in social orientations and access to resources even within a single migrant community. The existence of various subgroups suggests diverse orientations and patterns of association and cooperation. Social capital is shared among those bonded by common social features.

I discerned this as I showed photographs that I had taken in the course of fieldwork to other members of the same ethnic groups. I initially expected respondents to take pride in the upward mobility and organizational accomplishments of their successful countrymen. However, respondents were often unimpressed by the achievements of elite co-nationals. Instead, they

Photo 6.4   Soviet Jewish doctors' association banquet.

Photo 6.5   A Vietnamese American runs for political office, Orange County, California, 1994.

Photo 6.6   Israeli Independence Day Festival, San Fernando Valley, California, 1994.

expressed feelings of alienation from those shown in my photos and described the people as self-serving. As suggested by photo-based interviews and other evidence, the strongest ties, at least among these populations, tended to be maintained among those subgroups and networks already sharing high levels of social capital. While group members expressed a desire to develop groupwide alliances, these were hard to establish and maintain (Gold, 1992, 1995a, 2002b).

Coethnic and Outgroup Labor

Since the 1960s, sociologists have revised their understanding of the place of ethnicity in social and economic life. Prior to that time, social theorists asserted that as societies became more and more advanced, ascriptive characteristics—race, gender, religion, and ethnicity—would be of diminishing economic, social, and political importance; instead, societies would become increasingly organized on the basis of skills. However, since the 1960s, a broad range of scholars have come to understand that ethnic-based ties and resources continue to be vitally important in shaping economic life and access to resources (Bonacich & Modell, 1980; Light & Gold, 2000; Portes & Rumbaut, 1996).

While appreciating the importance of ethnicity in economic life, much literature on the topic has been concerned with the forms of connection, integration, and solidarity that occur *within* a single ethnic group. Portes and Bach (1985) show how Cuban entrepreneurs work together and hire recently arrived coethnics to maintain a powerful ethnic economy in Miami, one that offers coethnics better earnings than generally available to Cubans who find jobs in the larger economy. Kim (1981) and Min (1996) make a similar argument about Korean Americans' economic pursuits. However, in recent years, a number of scholars have noted the ways in which ethnic entrepreneurs take advantage of their connections with other ethnic populations, institutions, and social developments to create jobs, successfully manage businesses, and increase earnings.

Through fieldwork, I found that many migrant groups have a desire to help their countrymen and women by providing jobs and advice. Loyalty alone, however, is a poor basis for running a business. A deeper look reveals that the issue of coethnic employment is a complex one. Among Soviet Jews, Vietnamese, and Israelis, the desire to hire coethnics is often constrained by economic realties involving the costs and accessibility of coethnic workers versus other potential employees who are available in the labor market.

Drawing from Becker's (1986) suggestion to pose sociological questions that can be addressed visually, I asked who is employed in ethnic businesses and what is the relationship between employers and workers. As I observed, photographed, and discussed this question, I developed a better understanding of it. (See Photos 6.7, 6.8, 6.9, and 6.12.)

During interviews, members of all three groups said it was easier to communicate with coethnics, compared to out-group members, and described coethnics as more resourceful, knowledgeable, predictable, and, sometimes, trustworthy. At the same time, they also mentioned the disadvantages.[2] For example, as a result of coethnic expectations, business owners claimed that such workers demanded privileges (including preferential treatment and higher wages) not extended to out-group members. A London-based Israeli real estate broker who formerly ran a restaurant described why she avoided co-national employees:

> I had two chefs—[a man] from Thailand and an Israeli woman—and their atti-tude was completely different. She was always moody, having a long face. I needed to constantly pacify her. On the other hand, with him, I had no prob-lems whatsoever. He recognized who is the boss, and complied with my demands. With her, I needed to plan ahead every conversation. (Gold, 2002b, pp. 73–74)

In the course of observing and photographing Soviet Jewish, Vietnamese, and Israeli businesses, I consistently noticed Latinos and members of other groups as employees. (See Photos 6.8 and 6.12.) This finding contrasted dra-matically with the prevailing image of coethnic cooperation. The consistency of this observation prompted me to look closer, to ask questions about out-group labor, and to collect more photographic and other kinds of informa-tion about inter- and intraethnic economic cooperation.

Through this approach, I found that another reason entrepreneurs have for avoiding coethnics is that coethnic workers are generally more likely than out-group members to use their employment experience as an apprenticeship that provides them with the knowledge, connections, and capital needed to start their own businesses at a later date. This practice is very common among populations with high rates of self-employment and can be a source of considerable consternation because employers realize that they are training today's coethnic employee to be tomorrow's competitor (Light & Gold, 2000). Because immigrant business resources and strategies have their origins in shared communal sources, the potential for coethnic competition is considerable. Accordingly, Soviet Jewish, Vietnamese, and Israeli entrepre-neurs are generally concerned with competition control.

These migrant entrepreneurs found out-group labor to be beneficial in running ethnic businesses. Rather than employing coethnics, they increas-ingly relied on Mexican, Chicano, and Central American workers. A Chinese-Vietnamese journalist who had extensive contacts in the Southern California business community explained why many coethnic businesses employed Latinos: "Mexican, no green card, so you pay cheap. I pay you $5 an hour, but I pay Mexican $3 an hour. Mexicans are strong, and if I need to fire him,

Photo 6.7   Soviet Jewish enclave in Brighton Beach, Brooklyn, New York.

Photo 6.8   Sign seeking sewing machine operators in the Los Angeles garment district. Errors in Spanish suggest that someone not themselves fluent in Spanish is intentionally seeking Latino workers.

Photo 6.9   Israeli mini-mall in North Hollywood, California. Like other entrepreneurs in Southern California, many Israeli business owners employ Latino laborers to work in their shops. A similar pattern is evident among some of the laborers employed in the Soviet Jewish enclave of Brighton Beach in Brooklyn, New York, as shown in Photo 6.7.

he just goes." Reliance on Latino workers had become so common that during visits to the Los Angeles garment district, I frequently observed and photographed signs in grammatically flawed Spanish, suggesting that Latino workers were sought by non-coethnic employers. (See Photo 6.8.) The use of photography helped me notice, document, and explore the use of out-group labor in ethnic businesses. In so doing, I was moved to challenge widely held assertions regarding the role of coethnic cooperation in making these enterprises viable. In recent years, several scholars have published studies validating my findings as they describe the employment of one migrant group by another. My research, influenced by photography, played a role in contributing to this new approach (Chin, 2001; Kim, 1999; Lee, 2000). In turn, this growing body of work is clarifying our understanding of ethnic economies.

Gender

Popular debate often emphasizes family values and gender roles as being central to migrant groups' social and economic fate (Sowell, 1981). However, relatively little systematic research has been devoted to examining the gender patterns of migrant families. As a consequence, many assertions regarding the role of gender in migrants' adaptation overemphasize the effect of invariant group culture on outcomes while disregarding contextual effects. Consider the example of Korean women's behavior. Korean women have an extremely low rate of labor force participation in Korea, but a high one in the United States (Min, 1998). Aphorisms about "Korean family values" are thus incapable of accounting for such a dramatic transformation in family arrangements. Alternatively, the importance of a group's experience and context must be considered.

Instead of relying on assertions of cultural determinism to account for gendered patterns among migrant groups, another approach stresses the skills and outlooks shared by members of an ethnic group: the tool kit of experience-based symbols, stories, rituals, and worldviews that people may use in varying configurations to direct action and solve different kinds of problems they confront (Swidler, 1986, p. 273). A growing number of scholars have found this approach to be helpful in understanding the complex patterns of gender that exist within migrant populations (Fernández-Kelly & Garcia, 1990; Gabaccia, 1994; Hondagneu-Sotelo, 1994; Kibria, 1993). While acknowledging that gender norms exist among migrants (and indeed all social groups), scholars find that most cultures include contradictory prescriptions about gender (e.g., women should stay at home; parents need to work to support their children) and, moreover, norms are interpreted according to immediate concerns. Whatever their cultural preferences, women, men, and families generally make decisions about working, caring for children, gaining education, involving themselves in community organizations, and other issues according to context.

Among Soviet Jewish, Vietnamese, and Israeli immigrants, I observed diverse approaches with regard to gender, reflecting circumstances. Photographic evidence documents the context-driven diversity in the gender arrangements maintained within these populations. Such evidence provides a useful corrective to blanket generalizations about the supposed gender orientations of various nationalities. In addition, an examination of who appears in photographs highlights how gender patterns were implicated in my own fieldwork interactions with respondents. Vietnamese refugees reveal probably the most multiform array of gender arrangements, reflecting generational, cultural, economic, and class diversity within their larger population and the myriad circumstances they confront in adapting to new environments. (See Photos 6.10, 6.11, and 6.12.)

For example, members of the same network of recently arrived Vietnamese families with whom I conducted fieldwork in Oakland, California, during the early 1980s maintained very different gendered relations with me. During two years of weekly visits, the La family, made up of two brothers, a sister, and two male cousins, never introduced me to the female member of the household, even though the men often described her and showed me examples of her schoolwork. My relations were exclusively with males.

In contrast, visits with the Dinh household, which included a married couple, male and female cousins, and a young daughter, always included both male and females. In addition, the Dinhs introduced me to several male and female friends and relatives who were not part of the household. This

Photo 6.10   Recently arrived Vietnamese men hold a party in a cramped apartment in downtown Oakland, California.

Photo 6.11   Vietnamese refugees protest against the government of Vietnam. Political leadership for such events is generally organized by men.

Photo 6.12   Vietnamese female employer and a Latino worker.

example demonstrates that two families who shared common nationality, social network, location, and refugee status maintained distinctly different patterns of gendered sociability (Gold, 1992).

While diversity was evident among these populations, gender arrangements were not simply random. For example, among the Vietnamese, women were heavily involved in entrepreneurship, with men often attempting to establish high-prestige careers in existing firms or the nonprofit sector. This was most evident among high-status refugees, men who had been in the military or government prior to entering the United States and who sought to take on activist roles within the refugee community. (See Photo 6.11.) These men sometimes found positions in the refugee resettlement system (Gold, 1992). Vietnamese women explained that they readily entered self-employment because in Vietnam, small business is understood to be an extension of domestic duties and also because shortages of men during the war years yielded an increased demand for women's labor. Over time, women sometimes became more successful breadwinners than men (Kibria, 1993). However, depending on their resources, opportunities, and needs, women too took bureaucratic positions while men became entrepreneurs. For example, in Photo 6.10, taken at a Vietnamese party, male guests (myself included) and their male hosts sat around the tablecloth and were served by women (including residents and guests) who congregated and ate in the kitchen. In contrast, at a workplace setting, a Vietnamese woman manager maintains an assertive stance as she instructs a male employee. (See Photo 6.12.)

Israelis followed an opposite pattern with regard to gender. Men revealed very high rates of self-employment—most of the self-employed Israelis who work in places such the ethnic mini-mall shown in Photo 6.9 are men. Their substantial earnings permitted their wives to maintain lower rates of labor force participation.

For their part, Israeli women often engaged in social networking to acquire assistance for the domestic activities with which they were charged, to develop a social life, and to provide Israeli-style cultural and linguistic activities for their children. A considerable fraction of Israeli women have training and skills in areas relevant to community work—teaching, social work, and the like. Consequently, they drew on these skills in delivering services to their community and to native-born co-religionists, as well. (See Photo 6.13.) Even Israeli immigrant women with income-generating careers were involved in community work—as journalists, teachers, real estate saleswomen, and the like (Gold, 1995b, 2002b). Moreover, many suggested that networking provided them with a degree of empowerment and access to resources whether or not they worked for pay. Because Israeli migrant women were so extensively involved in activism, they were my key communal contacts, and I employed several as research assistants during a decade of fieldwork research on their group (Gold, 2002b).

Photo 6.13   Israeli women who publish a community newspaper in London.

Finally, having grown up in the former Soviet system that mandated employment of both women and men and provided education in technical and professional fields for both genders, Soviet Jewish men and women alike focused on paid employment, often in technical and professional fields, as illustrated in a mixed gender Russian doctors' association. (See Photo 6.4.) Furthermore, members of this group were often less oriented toward communal activism than many other migrant populations, largely because they are unfamiliar with it. (Prior to the 1990s, organizational life in the Soviet Union took place only under government control.) Accordingly, among Soviet Jews, neither gender manifests a significant propensity toward activism, whereas both women and men are involved in work (Gold, 1995a, 2003). Some forms of communal activism and leadership within this population are furnished by the Orthodox Jewish Chabad movement, within which male rabbis take dominant roles (Gold, 1995a). Like the Soviet Jews, a fraction of the Israeli emigrant population is also involved in gendered religious activities, in which adult women and men interact and pray separately. (See Photo 6.1.)

Despite these patterns of gendered adjustment, each group showed a considerable degree of variation in its gender arrangements, with both men and women engaging in domestic care, income generation, and communal activism. Photographic documentation of such diverse strategies, in combination with evidence acquired through conventional methodology, suggests that migrant families' gender arrangements reflect practical concerns as much as they do idealized notions about how women and men should behave.

While I obtained many benefits from using images in my research, photography was not always an asset. On the contrary, it was sometimes an obstacle. For example, certain respondents made it clear that I should limit my photography to special occasions. Another impediment to the collection and use of visual documentation occurs when social norms rule it out. Religious Jews prohibit the use of cameras during the Sabbath and on certain religious holidays, thus making some of the most significant communal events for both Soviet Jews and Israelis off limits, methodologically, from a technique that I had used to document and explore other aspects of their group life. Finally, viewers of photographs sometimes draw their own conclusions about what is shown, thus weakening their acceptance of the analytic frame that I had developed. Photographs showing posters of partially clad women on the walls of a refugee family's apartment caused some viewers to assume that the male head of household, who was actually very supportive of his wife and daughter, was a lecherous sexist.[3] Similarly, the presence of collectively purchased TV and stereo equipment shown in a refugee family's apartment gave some viewers the incorrect impression that the poverty-stricken household was relatively affluent.

Conclusion

When integrated with other research techniques, photography has contributed richness and nuance to my studies of migrant adaptation. Admittedly, many of the social patterns that I discuss could not have been discovered through the use of photography alone. However, the incorporation and analysis of visual information helped me to learn more about the groups in question and also to connect my observations with existing sociological knowledge.

Showing photographs to respondents facilitated rapport and often yielded insightful comments about the nature of the communities in question. The need to take photographs encouraged me to approach, observe, and think about the social world in a much more focused and empirically based manner than would have been the case had I not used photography. E-mailed images helped me expand my relations with members of a community that I studied. Photographs provided me with an additional form of evidence that I used to confirm, refine, or question existing sociological knowledge. Photographs allowed me to illustrate the diversity of behavior patterns that exist within groups and social categories, thus challenging overly general characterizations of groups. Finally, photographs offered a means of sharing analysis and research findings with community members, students, and colleagues.

My use of photography as one of many tools for the exploration of social issues may not satisfy those who seek to develop a fully visual social science, nor is it always beneficial for building rapport or informing audiences. However, these techniques do offer means of including a visual dimension into the investigation of a wide range of topics and circumstances.

Notes

1. Research manuals encourage fieldworkers to get close to subjects and observe activities firsthand. However, many recent ethnographic works rely on formal interviews as their primary method.

2. Workers often sought to avoid coethnic employers as well in order to obtain better wages, benefits, and working conditions (Gold, 2002b; Light & Gold, 2000).

3. To avoid confusing readers, a book publisher cropped the offending pinups from a photograph of a refugee family, thus deleting important visual information about this environment.

References

Ball, M. S., & Smith, G. W. H. (1992). *Analyzing visual data* (Qualitative Research Methods, No. 24). Newbury Park, CA: Sage.

Banks, M. (2001). *Visual methods in social research.* Thousand Oaks, CA: Sage.

Barbash, I., & Taylor, L. (1997). *Cross-cultural filmmaking: A handbook for making documentary and ethnographic films and videos.* Berkeley: University of California Press.

Becker, H. S. (1986). *Doing things together.* Evanston, IL: Northwestern University Press.

Becker, H. S. (2002). Visual evidence: A seventh man, the specified generalization, and the work of the reader. *Visual Studies, 17*(1), 3–11.

Berg, B. L. (2001). *Qualitative research methods for the social sciences* (5th ed.). Boston: Allyn & Bacon.

Berger, J., & Mohr, J. (1975). *A seventh man.* London: Writers and Readers Publishing Cooperative.

Blumer, H. (1969). *Symbolic interactionism.* Englewood Cliffs, NJ: Prentice Hall.

Bonacich, E., & Modell, J. (1980). *The economic basis of ethnic solidarity: Small business in the Japanese American community.* Berkeley: University of California Press.

Burawoy, M. (1991). The extended case method. In M. Burawoy, A. Burton, A. A. Ferguson, & R. Fox (Eds.), *Ethnography unbound: Power and resistance in the modern metropolis* (pp. 271–287). Berkeley: University of California Press.

Chin, M. M. (2001). When coethnic assets become liabilities: Mexican, Ecuadorian, and Chinese garment workers in New York City. In H. R. Cordero-Gizmán, R. C. Smith, & R. Grosfoguel (Eds.), *Migration, transnationalization, and race in a changing New York* (pp. 279–299). Philadelphia: Temple University Press.

Collier, J., Jr. (1967). *Visual anthropology.* New York: Holt, Rinehart and Winston.

Collier, J., Jr., & Collier, M. (1986). *Visual anthropology* (revised and expanded edition). Albuquerque: University of New Mexico Press.

Emerson, R. M., Fretz, R. I., & Shaw, L. L. (1995). *Writing ethnographic field notes.* Chicago: University of Chicago Press.

Emmison, M., & Smith, P. (2000). *Researching the visual.* Thousand Oaks, CA: Sage.

Fernández-Kelly, M. P., & García, A. M. (1990). Power surrendered, power restored: The politics of work and family among Hispanic garment workers in California and Florida. In L. A. Tilly & P. Gurin (Eds.), *Women, politics, and change* (pp. 130–149). New York: Russell Sage.

Gabaccia, D. (1994). *From the other side: Women, gender, and immigrant life in the U.S., 1820–1990.* Bloomington and Indianapolis: Indiana University Press.

Goffman, E. (1979). *Gender advertisements.* New York: Harper & Row.

Gold, S. (1992). *Refugee communities: A comparative field study.* Newbury Park, CA: Sage.

Gold, S. (1995a). *From the workers' state to the golden state: Jews from the former Soviet Union in California.* Boston: Allyn & Bacon.

Gold, S. (1995b). Gender and social capital among Israeli immigrants in Los Angeles. *Diaspora, 4*(3), 267–301.

Gold, S. (1995c). New York/L.A.: A visual comparison of public life in two cities. *Visual Sociology, 10*(1/2), 85–105.

Gold, S. (2002a). The Arab-American community in Detroit, Michigan. *Contexts, 1*(2), 48–55.

Gold, S. (2002b). *The Israeli Diaspora.* London and Seattle: Routledge and University of Washington Press.

Gold, S. (2003). Israeli and Russian Jews: Gendered perspectives on settlement and return migration. In P. Hondagneu-Sotelo (Ed.), *Gender and U.S. immigration: Contemporary trends.* Berkeley: University of California Press.

Grady, J. (1996). The scope of visual sociology. *Visual Sociology, 11*(2), 10–24.

Hammond, J. D. (1998). Photography and the "natives": Examining the hidden curriculum of photographs in introductory anthropology texts. *Visual Sociology, 13*(2), 57–73.

Harper, D. (1987). *Working knowledge: Skill and community in a small shop.* Chicago: University of Chicago Press.

Harper, D. (2002). Talking about pictures: A case for photo elicitation. *Visual Studies, 17*(1), 13–26.

Hondagneu-Sotelo, P. (1994). *Gendered transitions: Mexican experiences of immigration.* Berkeley: University of California Press.

Kibria, N. (1993). *Family tightrope: The changing lives of Vietnamese Americans.* Princeton, NJ: Princeton University Press.

Kim, D. Y. (1999). Beyond coethnic solidarity: Mexican and Ecuadorian employment in Korean-owned businesses in New York City. *Ethnic and Racial Studies, 22,* 581–605.

Kim, I. (1981). *New urban immigrants: The Korean community in New York.* Princeton, NJ: Princeton University Press.

Lee, J. (2000). Immigrant and African American competition: Jewish, Korean, and African American entrepreneurs. In N. Foner, R. G. Rumbaut, & S. J. Gold (Eds.), *Immigration research for a new century: Multidisciplinary perspectives* (pp. 322–344). New York: Russell Sage Foundation.

Light, I., & Gold. S. J. (2000). *Ethnic economies.* San Diego: Academic Press.

Light, I., Sabagh, G., Bozorgmehr, M., & Der-Martirosian, C. (1994). Beyond the ethnic enclave economy. *Social Problems, 41,* 65–80.

Menjivar, C. (2000). *Fragmented ties: Salvadoran immigrant networks in America.* Berkeley: University of California Press.

Min, P.-G. (1996). *Caught in the middle: Korean communities in New York and Los Angeles.* Berkeley: University of California Press.

Min, P.-G. (1998). *Changes and conflicts: Korean immigrant families in New York.* Boston: Allyn & Bacon.

Minh-Ha, T. (1992). *Framer framed.* New York: Routledge.

Nielsen, F. (1985). Towards a theory of ethnic solidarity in modern societies. *American Sociological Review, 50*(2), 133–149.

Portes, A., & Bach, R. (1985). *Latin journey: Cuban and Mexican immigrants in the United States.* Berkeley: University of California Press.

Portes, A., & Rumbaut, R. G. (1996). *Immigrant America: A portrait* (2nd ed.). Berkeley: University of California Press.

Prosser, J. (1998). *Image-based research: A sourcebook for qualitative researchers.* London: Falmer Press.

Rose, G. (2001). *Visual methodologies.* Thousand Oaks, CA: Sage

Shanahan, S., & Olzak, S. (2002). Immigration and conflict in the United States. In P.-G. Min (Ed.), *Mass migration to the United States: Classical and contemporary periods* (pp. 99–133). Walnut Creek, CA: Alta Mira Press.

Sowell, T. P. (1981). *Ethnic America.* New York: Basic Books.

Stinchcombe, A. L. (1984). The origins of sociology as a discipline. *Acta Sociologica,* *27*(1), 51–61.

Strauss, A. L. (1987). *Qualitative analysis for social scientists.* Cambridge, UK: Cambridge University Press.

Suchar, C. S. (1997). Grounding visual sociology research in shooting scripts. *Qualitative Sociology, 20*(1), 33–55.

Swidler, A. (1986). Culture in action. *American Sociological Review, 51*(2), 273–286.

Vergara, C. J. (1997). *The new American ghetto.* New Brunswick, NJ: Rutgers University Press.

Wagner, J. (Ed). (2002). Contrasting images, complementary trajectories: Sociology, visual sociology, and visual research. *Visual Studies, 17*(2), 160–171.

Whyte, W. F. (1984). *Learning from the field: A guide from experience.* Beverly Hills, CA: Sage.

7

Inner-City Children in Sharper Focus

Sociology of Childhood and Photo Elicitation Interviews

Marisol Clark-Ibáñez

Ten-year old Nanci sat on a stack of tightly packed clothing wrapped in opaque plastic near the front of a small, dimly lit warehouse. Her father worked in the back, ironing and assembling clothing. The darkness seemed to cool down the place on this hot summer Saturday in downtown Los Angeles. He came out occasionally to check on us, offering a tired smile and a nod of his head.

Nanci's thick chestnut-colored braids fell around her round face; this is the style she wore everyday for school. She excitedly looked over the photographs I had developed for her, exclaiming "oh no!" "cool!" and "hmmm" as she surveyed her own handiwork.

We were about to begin our photo elicitation interview. I settled onto my own bench of clothing to begin the session. I asked her to tell me which were her favorite images.

Nanci explained to me, "This isn't my favorite outfit, but it's the best photograph, like, in terms of the lights." She handed over the 3 by 5 picture.

I nodded my head in agreement, "Yeah, you're right. The lighting is good." I added slyly, "Nanci, you never told me about this!"

She giggled proudly, "Yeah, I do this a couple times a month. I'm pretty good!"

I knew Nanci as a fourth grade student at a charter school that emphasized high academic standards. Only after coordinating the time and place for her interview did I realize she was the daughter of a garment worker and that she sometimes worked with her dad in a warehouse. Now, after seeing the photos that Nanci took, I realized she was also a mariachi singer.

In her favorite picture, Nanci is dressed in a black suede *traje* or suit with silver *greca* (stylized floral embroidery) sewn up and down the outside of her pants legs and on the front opening of her jacket. Her black and silver *moño* (tie) puffed onto her chest complemented her large silver hoop earrings and framed her brightly painted red lips and black-lined eyes. Except for her makeup and her *banda* (sash) made of sparkly silver cloth, she wore the masculine costume, foregoing the fitted long skirt and cinched-waist jacket women typically wear.

Nanci's story illustrates the benefits and insights that I was hoping to discover in my photo elicitation study. First, the photo elicitation methodology allowed students to show me aspects of their lives that might have otherwise been hidden from an adult researcher like myself. I will spend much of this chapter elaborating on these aspects of photo elicitation. Second, photo elicitation helped me to uncover some of the institutional practices that might have served to perpetuate educational inequalities that might have otherwise not been revealed by just examining the school setting. I will briefly explain this here, as it will also illuminate the genesis of my study.

Nanci was an average student at a charter school in South Central Los Angeles. She had a sweet disposition and did her work but did not garner any special attention from the teacher or school officials. When I learned that she was an accomplished mariachi singer, I could not help but wonder why this extracurricular skill did not translate into valuable cultural capital and a better social ranking at school. I asked her teacher about it. Her teacher knew about Nanci's performances but thought her parents used Nanci for additional income. Rather than encouraging these performances, her parents should concentrate on her academic progress, Nanci's teacher felt. The teacher's judgment potentially cost Nanci any rewards, such as kudos given to students who play institutionally valued instruments, such as the violin or piano. For the study of schooling I was conducting at the time, the teacher's perspective on Nanci's extracurricular activities provided me with valuable insight to understand how the school's achievement ideology functioned (Clark-Ibáñez, 2004). However, I thought there was more to Nanci's story: It reflected a new and rich perspective about the complexity of inner-city children's lives. Without reviewing those photographs with Nanci on that hot summer day, I might never have seen this other world, segregated (and devalued) in her inner-city classroom.

How do we understand children sociologically? Previous research has discussed kids as *tabula rasa*, negating their agency (Jenks, 1996). However, I approach the study of inner-city children and their social worlds with the new sociology of childhood, a perspective that tries to understand children as active, creative, and important actors in their own right (Corsaro, 1997; Mayhall, 2002). This chapter explains how the use of photo elicitation interviews became critical to my understanding of kids in poverty and the way they viewed their own lives.

The Study

My current study of inner-city children emerged from my previous ethnographic study on inner-city schools (Clark-Ibáñez, 2004). When I began soliciting volunteers to participate in my study, I had already fostered relationships with the children through intensive participant observation in their classrooms for almost a full academic year. Through that year, I had established relationships with the kids and their families outside of the school setting as well. With parental permission, I took some students on weekend outings—we went to the beach or movies, drove through exclusive neighborhoods in Los Angeles (girls wanted to find actor Leo DiCaprio's house), and went to eat at fast-food restaurants. I also chatted with parents about school, life, diet, and work. I helped Spanish speakers fill out forms in English and accompanied teachers on student home visits. In short, I became immersed in the students' school and social lives for almost an academic year before I began the photography project.

Through my ethnographic fieldwork, I realized that many children had richly complex home lives, and I wanted to understand how this impacted their school lives. Nanci's case is just one example. Yet, once I began reading about the topics of children and poverty, I noticed gaps in the literature that did not capture the realities of the kids' social world outside of school—realities such as familial responsibilities, play, or peers.

Shortcomings in the Sociology of Childhood

Studies of children have several crucial shortcomings. They mainly tell about white, middle-class childhood because many times, these are the children to whom researchers have access (Adler & Adler, 1998). They study children in the aggregate and consider the effects of independent variables to understand children's experiences and likely outcomes. They study children in relation to other entities—motherhood, schooling, immigration, welfare system, racial segregation, and so on. They typically do not examine children's own lived experiences.

With the above factors at play, the literature does not address the subjective questions of what it is like to be poor, a minority, and a kid. A small group of publications, such as those that emerged from the California Childhoods project (directed by Catherine Cooper and Barrie Thorne) and Annette Lareau's (2003) *Unequal Childhoods*, provide insightful analysis into the lives of poor, working class, and minority children. Yet, in most of the current literature, multidimensional answers are largely missing because they tend only to highlight alarming (and real) issues such as the effects of violence, experiences related to schooling, or descriptions of abject poverty. Is this all there is to being poor and a kid?

Admittedly, several of my young participants recognized the local drug dealer's car; this curtailed their ability to play outside when the car stopped for a long period of time near their homes. I am not suggesting that researchers should downplay the stark realities of these kids' lives. Yet, my study revealed that tree houses, Barbies, and Tupac Shakur (hip hop artist) posters were just as relevant to children and their daily lives. Researchers have not been able to capture the quotidian aspect of their lives. By missing how kids negotiate mainstream media and material culture, studies create a static and staid frame of inner-city childhoods. Inner-city childhoods are framed as unidirectionally shaped by outside forces, disregarding the ways in which kids are shaping, creating, and negotiating aspects of their childhood experiences in an inner-city community.

In response to this gap, a growing number of researchers, such as Barrie Thorne, William Corsaro, and Jans Qvtrup, conceptualize children as collectively participating in society. To further elaborate this theoretical and analytical framework, it is useful to incorporate a methodology, such as photo elicitation, that allows researchers to explore and better understand the texture and complexity of inner-city kids' lives.

The Method: Choices and Children in Photo Elicitation

As I read the literature in search of this textured approach to children's lives, I also read more about photo elicitation as a methodology, and I thought this would be an ideal way to capture the tangible and intangible aspects of children's lives. In photo elicitation, the researcher introduces photographs to the interview context as a way to generate responses beyond the language-based conventional interview protocols. This approach is based on assumptions about the role and utility of photographs in prompting reflections that words alone cannot. Photo elicitation interviews, for example, can "mine deeper shafts into a different part of human consciousness than do words-alone interviews" (Harper, 2002, p. 23). Photographs can generate data illuminating a subject that otherwise may be invisible to the researcher but blatantly apparent to the interviewee (Schwartz, 1989).

There are a variety of approaches to conducting photo elicitation interviews. One of the first decisions that researchers must make is who will take the photographs.[1] Some researchers opt to take photographs themselves and present the images they captured to the research participants. This option allows the researcher to frame, select, develop, organize, and present the images to the interviewees based on their own research questions. For example, Harper (2001) used aerial views of farmland and historical photographs to interview farmers about their identity and community. (See Harper, 1987, and Schwartz, 1992, as additional examples.)

Using researcher-produced photographs is an excellent way to conduct theory-driven research. Toting a camera can help researchers better interact with the people they are studying (Collier, 1967; Schwartz, 1989), although it can take time (Shanklin, 1979). Once granted access, researcher-photographers may capture taken-for-granted aspects of the subjects' community or life that prompt discussion. In some cases, the interviewees alert the researcher to omissions and questions that later can be included in the interview protocol. Yet, photo elicitation in which the researcher makes the images may be limited by the researchers' interests and miss an essential aspect of the research setting that is meaningful to the participants.

In addition to the intrinsic biases of research questions, researchers must also be cautious of the tendency to capture the "visually arresting" images (e.g., homeless person asleep near a school entrance) rather than what might be meaningful for the interview subjects (Orellana, 1999). In documenting visual descriptions of South Central Los Angeles for my study, I noted my tendency to include images that, as an outsider, I found unique or beautiful (e.g., see Photos 7.1 and 7.2). However, for the children in my study, these images were unnoticed and "natural" elements of their environment; they lacked the significant meanings I may have imputed to them. For these reasons, I would not recommend the researcher-photographer approach for researching with children.

Given my framework conceptualizing children as active agents in their own right, I used a more inductive research approach where the researcher asks interview subjects to take their own photos to be used later as interview

Photo 7.1   Pizza delivery man on bicycle.

SOURCE: Used with permission.

Photo 7.2   Virgen de Guadalupe mural on meat store wall.

SOURCE: Used with permission.

stimuli. This is called an *autodriven* photo elicitation (Clark, 1999). Cindy Dell Clark reports that photographs taken by children captured and introduced content area that from an adult viewpoint might have been poorly understood (or even overlooked). I have found that, when adapted for the purpose of interviewing children, the autodriven photo elicitation becomes an ideal methodology to engage young people.

Previous researchers have outlined the limitations and problems of research with children (Adler & Adler, 1998; Thorne, 1993). Clark (1999) observes that researchers must have patience or sensitivity to work with children's pace, style, and playfulness. Conventional interviews are especially problematic for children. Clark (1999, p. 38) summarizes the following four challenges associated with interviewing children: children's level of linguistic communication, their cognitive development, the question and answer setting, and the accentuated power dynamics of the adult interviewing a child. Photos lessen some of the awkwardness of interviews because there is something to focus on, especially if the interviewee takes the photographs: They are familiar with the material.

Photo elicitation nicely intervenes along each of these challenges of conventional interviewing. First, in terms of linguistics, photo elicitation lets the children set the linguistic level in accord with their ability. The children decide what they want to say and how to do so. The researcher typically does not have a structured or complex interview schedule but rather lets the photographs and child's insights lead the way for conversation and sharing.

Second, in photo elicitation, children's cognitive development is matched with the type of information that may be elicited. Photography stimulates kids' memories in ways that are different from verbal-based interviews— ways that are potentially unknown to the researcher. Using photos can improve the interview experience with children by providing them with a clear, tangible, yet nonlinguistic prompt.

Third, because children lead the interview, the potentially awkward social setting created in the question and answer context all but vanishes. In particular, children may believe that if someone poses a question (especially an adult), there is a "correct" answer. I found that children were a bit confused when I asked them to tell me about their photographs, as if they had expected a more conventional interview. As illustrated in Nanci's interview, I usually found that asking an open-ended question—for example, Which one was your favorite?—was a good way to begin the photo elicitation session. Yet, once I made it clear that I wanted to know what they thought of their own photographs, they barely needed any probing at all.

Finally, photo elicitation disrupts some of the power dynamics involved with regular interviews. This is especially relevant in the cases where there are acute status, age, class, gender, or racial power differences (see Clark, 1999, and Harper, 1987, as examples). In my study, for example, when one of my participants, Silvia, went to Oregon for the summer to work in the fields with her relatives, she brought along her camera. For our interview that fall, I met Silvia at her home. She lived on a busy intersection in South Central Los Angeles and in front of an enormous electrical energy plant. Her mother hung back in the kitchen, and her little sister and brother sat in the living room with us, curious but quiet, during the interview. Image after image, Silvia became the expert. She explained how various kinds of farm machinery work, how tomatoes are grown and harvested, and how her relatives live (see Photo 7.3)—all topics, despite growing up in an agricultural area, that I knew nothing about and would not have been able to ask about in our interview had it not been for the visual data that Silvia provided. Photo elicitation can be a powerful tool to simultaneously gather data and empower the interviewee.

Photo 7.3   Silvia's aunt and farm machinery.

SOURCE: Used with permission.

While it resolves the methodological challenges of working with children that Clark (1999) points out, photo elicitation has its own complications, which must be taken into consideration when working with children. For example, when the interviewees produce the images, researchers should be aware of differing definitions of what belongs in a photograph.

In my study, Victoria and her mother clashed over the concept of photographic content: Her mother thought what Victoria *should* use the camera to produce "important" images of her family and *not* the images she did produce of her friends and their clubhouse. In another example, Carla took photographs of her mother in front of the washer and dryer; during our interview, she revealed that her mother wanted her to take these. If children are producing images, researchers must understand that family dynamics of power and authority may affect their ability to take the photographs of their own choosing or to finish the project. In addition, these family interactions become another source of data. I learned about the household dynamics of the children's families and their effects on school assignments or homework.

The literature does not discuss children's inappropriate use of the camera. For example, in my study, Stanford's mother informed me that she caught him taking photographs of his naked sister, and so she destroyed the camera.[2] Photo elicitation allows the researcher into the interviewee's home and life through photographs in different ways and with different results than when the researcher is physically present. Because of this, photo elicitation practitioners grapple with issues of confidentiality and ethics on a case-by-case basis.

Photo elicitation is a powerful method, yet researchers must be cautious and thoughtful of their specific population's needs and capacities, especially in research with children. The choices and strategies that play to the strengths of children and the strengths of the method should be considered. With this in mind, the autodriven approach to photo elicitation can be an appropriate and successful methodology for studies of childhood or projects involving children.

Logistics of Photo Elicitation Interviews

Selecting photo elicitation for its methodological benefits within the interview process raises a new set of logistical considerations. Researchers must consider the overall financial cost, coordination of camera dissemination and retrieval, and time spent developing the photographs and conducting the interview. In terms of access, institutional support or insider connections are common prerequisites for conducting photo elicitation interviews (e.g., hospital in Clark, 1999; school in Clark-Ibáñez, 2004; community center in Orellana, 1999; kin in Schwartz, 1992). For interviewees, the addition of photographs may mean an additional layer of intimacy compared with regular face-to-face interviews; as a result, the researcher may find it harder to obtain permission from institutions or to recruit interviewees. However, unlike the researcher-photographer model, the potential for the interviewees to own a camera and the novelty of taking photographs for an outsider can help researchers overcome barriers to soliciting interviewees.

In my study, it took the last 2 months of the school year to obtain permission from parents, the school, and children.[3] Several parents helped me craft a permission form that would be clearly understood by other parents and that addressed issues such as costs, care of equipment, time commitment, reciprocation, and intended follow-up. I gave the following written instructions to the children who participated in the project:

> **What you'll do:** Take pictures of the people and the things that are the most important to you (e.g., family members, favorite places, toys—it's up to you!). This is a FREE project—it will not cost you or your parents anything.
>
> - This camera belongs to you! Remember to keep it out of the sun.
> - I will pick up the camera when you are done taking the pictures. I think a week should be enough time, but let me know if you need more time.
> - After the photos are developed, I will bring you the photos.
> - We will take some time to talk about the photos you took.
> - Call me with any questions: [my phone number]
> - Have fun!!

Reflecting on my study, I would now inform the children that they have the right to withdraw any photographs that they do not want to discuss. I learned this going through the photo elicitation process. When interviewees see the images, they may regret having taken some of them; if the researcher has already viewed them, this cannot be remedied. Therefore, the researcher should not view the photographs until the interviewee has had time to look them over and remove unwanted ones. Of course, the interviewees should be told in advance that this is the process.

Parents talked with me after school or called me at home to discuss the "camera project." Some wanted to be clear about the monetary costs to them (none), and others expressed anxiety about giving their children a camera for fear they would lose it. I explained to them that the children would be given "disposable" or single-use cameras, and I would have a few extras in case some children lost theirs. (I bought the cameras wholesale for $5 each.)

I gave the kids their cameras as soon as I received their signed permission slips. Although most children had never taken a photograph, they understood the basic principles of operating a camera and required little instruction. Most children completed the project within a week of receiving their camera. I developed double copies of their film at the local drugstore (about $8 per camera). Once the film was developed, I arranged an interview time and day with the child.

Viewing photographs gave other family members an incentive to be present; frequently, parents and siblings took part in the interview. Initially, I thought the participants might be shy about sharing their photographs in front of others, but most had arranged the interviews to include their families. This was no small feat because most parents worked two or three jobs each: many times, they alternated shifts so that someone could be home with the children. As I will discuss later, photographs elicited extended personal narratives that illuminate the viewers' lives and experiences, especially when viewed in a group setting (Schwartz, 1989).

The interviews lasted from a half-hour to 2 hours. Fifty-five children participated in the project, and 47 completed interviews. I spent three summer months exclusively conducting photo elicitation and then returned to Los Angeles for the rest of the interviews in the subsequent year. Most interviews took place in participants' living rooms, at the kitchen table, or on the front porch and in the backyard when it was too hot inside. I also conducted several interviews on Saturdays inside warehouses in the Los Angeles garment district, where kids helped their parents.

Making Sense of Image and Text

I am in the midst of coding the 959 images by using a semigrounded theory approach to see what categories emerge. I will also transcribe and code the kids' interviews to hear how they talk about their photographs. In my view, there is nothing inherently interesting about photographs; rather, photographs act as a medium of communication between researcher and subject. The photographs do not necessarily represent empirical truths or reality. In this sense, photographs used in photo elicitation have a dual purpose. Researchers can use photographs as a tool to expand on questions, and simultaneously, subjects can use photographs to provide a unique way to communicate dimensions of their lives.

The photo elicitation method can present a challenge of coding words *and* images.[4] Analysis may be difficult if the researcher must sift through the data from a lively group who viewed and referred to multiple photographs. People may talk over each other, it may be hard to identify which individuals are talking, or conversation may significantly shift themes. Careful and patient listening to the data, as required in other qualitative methods, is key in photo elicitation. The same attention to detail is required of the photographs. I numbered each photograph before the interview so that I could refer to the number throughout the taped conversation. This allowed me to identify the photographs by my cues on the audiotaping during the data analysis stage.

For initially understanding the visual data, I found it useful to draw on Doug Harper's (2002) three uses of photographs in photo elicitation. First, I used photographs as visual inventories of objects, people, and artifacts. Second, photographs depict events that were a part of collective or institutional paths (e.g., photographs of schools or images of events that occurred earlier in the lifetime of the subjects). Third, photos are intimate dimensions of the social. For example, photos of family or other intimate social groups, images of one's own body, and photos that connect oneself to society, culture, or history. It is important to add that a single roll of film may display multiple uses. For example, a child in my study took photos of her refrigerator and Barbies (inventory), her afterschool program building (institution), and portraits of herself and her sisters (social). After categorizing the images, I then could begin coding based on substantive issues, such as gender. I found that the significance of these images reflecting the textured lives of the children in this project arose at the intersection of these various levels of meanings and utility. While I favor the interpretive meanings of images throughout this chapter and the way that children can speak to and through them, I am not disregarding the empirical potential of photography as documentation discussed here. In fact, in this project, the two processes work hand in hand.

Visualizing the Texture of Inner-City Childhood

The kids' photographs and interviews revealed the day-to-day experiences of low-income urban children. The preliminary data presented in this chapter show the myriad experiences that shape these children's lives. My research gives priority to the voices and images of inner-city children and, thus, captures a complex social world that is deeper than images that are frequently used to characterize the inner city in popular media, such as gang activity, drive-bys, run-down schools, and cramped living conditions. Using photo elicitation was crucial to accessing the children's perspective about specific issues and experiences and uncovering their worldview in general. Photo elicitation, as a method, is good at giving children agency because the images and explanations mainly come from the kids themselves; this responds to the call from sociologists to allow for agency when studying children (Mayhall, 2002).

First, contrary to popular media, the children's photographs reveal more intimate and reflexive aspects of what we consider trappings of middle-class childhood. Students showed me their photos of the artifacts meaningful to them, such as soccer trophies, pop star fan books, and doll collection (see Photos 7.4, 7.5, and 7.6). While these artifacts could be found in middle-class homes, if you look more closely, they reflect indicators of poverty. The

Barbie dolls shown here were bought at garage sales and the "99 Cent Store," and the fan books were checked out of the library. Look more closely at twins Lucia and Mariana's backdrop (Photo 7.7). Because there are so many people living in their home, they prop up mattresses against the wall during the day and lay them out on the floor as bedding by night.

Second, autodriven photographs showed me students' interpretation of material reality. For example, they inventoried any "big ticket items" they owned, such as a computer, Nintendo, or a television. The most common reason they gave for photographing these items was so that they would have a memory of it in case it was stolen or taken away. Indeed, within one year, several children did experience robberies of the very things they captured on film. However, most students did not own expensive items. After I developed the film and saw the items, I presumed the kids would discuss them with pride of ownership. Their tone as they described the items, however, was a melancholy pride: happy they owned it but anticipating its loss. This shows the importance of photo elicitation because the method allowed for the children to express *their* understanding of what constituted a potential everyday threat. For me, the images of everyday threat were the boarded-up illegally occupied homes, the bars on the windows and doors, and the constant police helicopter activity. For the kids, threat was symbolized in a more personal, intimate way.

Photo 7.4   James's trophies.

SOURCE: Used with permission.

Photo 7.5   Natalia's fan books.

SOURCE: Used with permission.

Photo 7.6   Maria Sonia's Barbies.

SOURCE: Used with permission.

Photo 7.7   Twins Lucia and Mariana's stuffed animals.

SOURCE: Used with permission.

Third, the kids took the most photographs of aspects of their social lives such as their friends, pets, and family parties (see Photos 7.10 through 7.15). To me, the images of the social contrasted with the image of the inner city in the popular media, as well as the academic perceptions of depression, fear, and fatalism in this environment. When listening to the kids explain these social photographs, I realized the power of the photographs to reveal much more about their lives. For example, one of my first interviews was with Janice, who took 38 photos of her new kitten (for an example, see Photo 7.16). I admit I dreaded this interview. What would we discuss besides her *gatito*? Janice still attended the school in my first study but had moved mid-year to a slightly better-off community. For Janice, moving to a new community and not yet knowing anyone were factors in her strong attachment to her kitten. What became more important (and interesting) was the conversation about how her parents let her have the kitten after moving from Watts to Oak Park. For example, Janice explained that her family's slightly improved economic situation made it possible for her to have a kitten. Also, the images of the kitten sparked Janice's memory of the pets she had in México, eliciting a detailed discussion about her immigrant journey from Mexico to Los Angeles.

Photo 7.8   Ricky's computer.

SOURCE: Used with permission.

Photo 7.9   Antwon's television.

SOURCE: Used with permission.

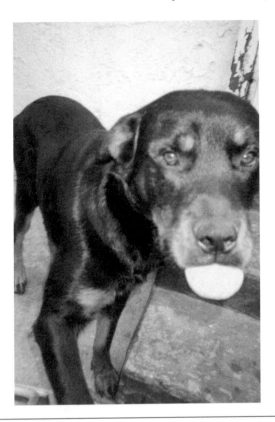

Photo 7.10   Tommy's dog.

SOURCE: Used with permission.

Fourth, I am finding a gender difference in the position from which the photos were taken. Compared to boys, more girls take photos of the outdoors from inside. Boys as subjects of photographs and as photographers are more likely to be outside the home. Note how David has taken his photograph from the street (see Photo 7.17). Contrast this to the images from Jasmine, Julia, and Mercedes (see Photos 7.18 through 7.20)—all taken from within their homes. In the fourth girl's photograph (Photo 7.21), Pati's perspective is from within the home's second story. I could have simply coded the images themselves—without the kids' explanations—to come to this conclusion. Yet, the interviews offered deeper insight about how girls and boys experience the special environment.

For example, Melissa showed me the photograph of a gigantic tree across the street, which she had taken from her front door (see Photo 7.22). She commented that it was her favorite tree. I asked her why. She explained,

Photo 7.11   Sergio's siblings.

SOURCE: Used with permission.

Photo 7.12   Lorena's family cookout.

SOURCE: Used with permission.

Photo 7.13   Melodie's friends.

SOURCE: Used with permission.

Photo 7.14   Fernanda's birds.

SOURCE: Used with permission.

Photo 7.15   Phillip's family party.

SOURCE: Used with permission.

Photo 7.16   Janice's *gatito*.

SOURCE: Used with permission.

Photo 7.17   David's photograph from the street.

SOURCE: Used with permission.

with tears filling her eyes, that she can only look at it and never really be near it. I probed, wanting to know why she couldn't cross the street. She told me that her dad makes her stay in the house and told her she would be deported to México if she is caught by *la migra* (Spanish slang for the Immigration and Naturalization Service [INS]). Indeed, INS vans did troll the community. With a rush of words, Melissa revealed that she was not documented, and neither was her mom, 20-year-old brother, or 16-year old sister. They all had to work so they needed to risk leaving the house. Melissa stayed at home alone until 8 or 9 P.M. each night. Thus, the tree was not just a tree (just as the kitten wasn't just a kitten) but rather a symbol of Melissa's immigration status, which restricted her movement. As in Melissa's case, immigration status may make a difference, but the trend to photograph from indoors held true for documented Latinas *and* African American girls, neither of whom have immigration issues.

In contrast, my photo elicitation interview with Toño confirmed that boys were "out and about" more than girls; he and his family provided insight about their experiences in the neighborhood. Toño took photos of his family in portrait and in action (e.g., his brother on a skateboard), his neighborhood, his afterschool care, and his favorite games in his room. As the family and I sat around the dining room table, the content of the photos spurred

Photo 7.18   Jasmine's friends getting relief from the summer heat in the backyard.

SOURCE: Used with permission.

Photo 7.19   Julia's little sisters in the front yard.

SOURCE: Used with permission.

Photo 7.20   Mercedes has her friends pose in her backyard.

SOURCE: Used with permission.

Photo 7.21   Pati's view from the second story of her home.

SOURCE: Used with permission.

Photo 7.22   Melissa's tree.

SOURCE: Used with permission.

much conversation about the meaning of each artifact or action. What also occurred, especially when his father sat down at the table, was discussion of the graffiti (and the gangs it belonged to) that showed up in the background of the photos taken outside of the house and the day workers who also appeared in the photos taken outside (for an example, see Photo 7.23). Each family member who joined the conversation had a particular perspective and reality concerning these details that were inadvertently included in Toño's photos.

After viewing the photos, the family began to discuss the hardship of being *sin documentos* (undocumented or illegally in the United States) and finding work, as well as the trouble of having the gang members use their front driveway as a hangout. Relational and contextualized meanings emerged from the interview that may not have without the photographs. In this same interview, I was so focused on the "boys outside" photographs, that I missed the significance of the graffiti "tagging" of gang names and symbols (e.g., Grape Street High Rollers) in the background on which the other family members immediately focused. This early interview alerted me to other details that I might have otherwise considered background.

Photo 7.23   Toño's outside.

SOURCE: Used with permission.

Finally, the collaborative aspect of the photo elicitation interviews revealed dynamics in familial relationships. Many of my interviews with the children included their families and sometimes even their neighbors and friends. Sometimes, as in Toño's case, the family sessions were characterized by stories and insights building on one another. However, in other collaborative sessions, family tensions became apparent. Mostly, the kids and parents clashed over what the kids are doing when the parents are at work. For example, Melodie's mother laughed yet expressed dismay at hearing her daughter characterize the front yard tree as her "tree house" (no actual house is there, but she and her friends hung out in the tree limbs). She seemed somewhat embarrassed that she did not know the range of her daughter's play area because she was always working.

A clear conflict emerged with Victoria, a light-skinned, bright Latina and her mother. Victoria took her assignment very seriously and documented her social world in detail. She took photos of a secret club house, friends who dressed up for the "photo shoot," her little sister's chalk artwork, and the "blue line" train (taken by daylight) in front of her house that wakes her up at night (see Photo 7.24). In her lively interview, Victoria explained her photos and their meaning with passion. Her mother, who occasionally passed through the living room where Victoria and I sat for the interview, told her daughter that she was upset and "embarrassed" that Victoria did not take pictures of her own mother and father and "wasted" photos on her friends. Victoria countered that her mom goes to school and works two jobs; because she does not see her mother except at night and she could not figure out how to do the flash on her camera, she couldn't take her mother's photo. Her mother asked me for another camera so that Victoria could take photos on their next family trip to Water World (see Photo 7.25). I agreed and gave them another disposable camera, and later, I conducted a second interview. In this case, the content of Victoria's first set of photos painted the creative and rich social life that Victoria, her sister, and their friends created when not in school. In addition, the conversation around the content also yielded data about Victoria's family dynamics.

In conclusion, while the categorical substantive findings are the stuff of sociological research, the process by which these emerge is where I found some of the most nuanced and intimate insights about inner-city childhoods. As I conducted interviews with children in South Central, I found that the data generated from photo elicitation interviews went beyond the normal scope of regular words-alone interviews. Photographs seem to allow the interviewees to reflect on related but indirect associations with the photographs themselves. In group settings, photographs serve to illustrate multiple meanings for the participants and sometimes reveal tensions among them. The most common experience conducting photo elicitation was that photographs spurred meaning that otherwise might have remained dormant in a face-to-face interview. The images may not contain new information but can trigger meaning for the interviewee (Collier, 1967; Schwartz, 1989). Although I have just begun to code the photographs and interviews to examine inner-city childhood, the data provide a rich perspective of "growing up poor" from the kids' own visual and verbal expressions, which go beyond solely pessimistic visions of urban blight yet are simultaneously shaped by urban poverty.

Rethinking Childhood

Theories on children currently examine the death (and for some the post mortem) of childhood. Researchers of this ilk examine (1) the effect of consumerism and electronic media, along with the corporations that produce these products and (2) the lack of "play" due to parental overscheduling of kids (Buckingham, 2000; Steinberg & Kincheloe, 1997). The kids in my study did take photos of consumer artifacts (e.g., Nintendo), yet when discussing their significance, it was clear that these products did not take an

Photo 7.24   Victoria with best friends on first attempt at project.

SOURCE: Used with permission.

Photo 7.25   Mother-approved photograph of Victoria and friends at Water World.

SOURCE: Used with permission.

overwhelming role in or have a brain-numbing affect on their lives. Also, my participants showed through their photos that they have plenty of time to play. This gap (where empirical reality does not support theory) points to possible class or racial bias in the current theories that try to understand the nature of childhood. Whose childhood died? Researchers first must be able to understand the diversity of childhoods before declaring their death.

Using photo elicitation was crucial to accessing the children's perspective about specific issues and experiences and uncovering their worldview in general. Photo elicitation, used with other qualitative methodologies such as interviews or participant observations, can illuminate dynamics and insights not otherwise found through other methodological approaches. In addition, photo elicitation empowers the interviewees to teach the researcher about aspects of their social world otherwise ignored or taken for granted. When he introduced the methodology, John Collier (1967) wrote, "no type of fieldwork requires better rapport" (p. 51). I would argue that no type of fieldwork yields richer data.

Sociology of childhood scholars urge researchers not to view children as passive recipients of larger cultural processes and constraints. Photo elicitation can help address this concern. Jon Wagner (1979) writes that such methodology can benefit "social scientists interested in examining the connection between people's lives and the social and economic structures of the larger world" (p. 18). Indeed, the photographs of inner-city children reflected institutional, structural, and community understandings of their every day life. But more than that, photographs reveal the highly textured ways in which children negotiate these spaces and somehow once again become kids before our eyes.

When my interview with Nanci was finished, she kept her copy of the photographs and returned to work with her father. That day, I had another interview with one of her classmates, whom I was meeting in a nearby laundromat. As I drove away from downtown, I wondered about Nanci's life and future. Through looking at the corpus of photographs these children took, a part of me understands the kids' creativity and resiliency. Nanci embodies what is fascinating about children in the inner city. Through her images, she captured the intersection of play, work, culture, and dreams for a better future. The sociologist in me cannot ignore the structural inequalities and institutional processes that will shape their lives. However, at least in Nanci's case, I can report today, several years after the completion of my study, that she is still doing OK in school, still lives in South Central Los Angeles, and is still singing (see Photo 7.26).

Photo 7.26   Nanci the mariachi singer.

SOURCE: Used with permission.

Notes

1. Researchers also use historical photographs or the interviewees' family photo albums as interview stimuli.

2. This is the only time such an incident occurred in my study. However, students revealed that they took surprise photographs of their mothers, siblings, or friends. Thus, sometimes the cameras were being used for pranks and not for their intended use.

3. I obtained permission from the institutional review board at my home university to include the use of videos in the classroom and photography with the children. The review process took 6 months to complete. I wrote the board-required letter to the children and parents in my study in Spanish and English. Once in the field, I realized that parents did not understand the content of the official letter so with the help of several parents, I rewrote the letter maintaining its spirit but simplifying its language. I believed I would have done more of a disservice to the

parents and violated the true goal of institutional review by giving them a letter they did not completely understand.

4. See Wagner (1979, chapter 10) for a terrific discussion of avoiding production and analysis errors using photo elicitation.

References

Adler, P., & Adler, P. (1998). *Peer power: Preadolescent culture and identity.* New Brunswick, NJ: Rutgers University Press.

Buckingham, D. (2000). *After the death of childhood: Growing up in the age of electronic media.* Cambridge, UK: Polity Press.

Clark, C. D. (1999). The autodriven interview: A photographic viewfinder into children's experiences. *Visual Sociology, 14,* 39–50.

Clark-Ibáñez, M. (2004). Lessons in inequality: A comparative study of two urban schools. *Dissertation Abstracts International A: The Humanities and Social Sciences, 64*(7), 2650-A.

Collier, J., Jr. (1967). *Visual anthropology: Photography as a research method.* Beverly Hills, CA: Sage.

Corsaro, W. (1997). *The sociology of childhood.* Thousand Oaks, CA: Pine Forge Press.

Harper, D. (1987). *Working knowledge: Skill and community in a small shop.* Chicago: University of Chicago Press.

Harper, D. (2001). *Changing works: Vision of lost agricultures.* Chicago: University of Chicago Press.

Harper, D. (2002). Talking about pictures: a case for photo elicitation. *Visual Studies, 17*(1), 13–26.

Jenks, C. (1996). *Childhood.* London: Routledge.

Lareau, A. (2003). *Unequal childhoods: Class, race, and family life.* Berkeley: University of California Press.

Mayhall, B. (2002). *Towards a sociology for childhood: Thinking from children's lives.* Maidenhead, UK: Open University Press.

Orellana, M. F. (1999). Space and place in an urban landscape: Learning from children's views of their social world. *Visual Sociology, 14,* 73–89.

Schwartz, D. (1989). Visual ethnography: Using photography in qualitative research. *Qualitative Sociology, 12*(2), 119–153.

Schwartz, D. (1992). *Wacoma twilight: Generations on the farm.* Washington, DC: Smithsonian Press.

Shanklin, E. (1979). When a good social role is worth a thousand pictures. In J. Wagner (Ed.), *Images of information* (pp. 139–157). Beverly Hills, CA: Sage.

Steinberg, S., & Kincheloe, J. (1997). *Kinderculture: The corporate construction of childhood.* Boulder, CO: Westview.

Thorne, B. (1993). *Gender play: Girls and boys in school.* New Brunswick, NJ: Rutgers University Press

Wagner, J. (1979). Avoiding error. In J. Wagner (Ed.), *Images of information* (pp. 147–159). Beverly Hills, CA: Sage.

8

When Words Are Not Enough

Eliciting Children's Experiences of Buddhist Monastic Life Through Photographs[1]

Jeffrey Samuels

One of the challenges an ethnographer commonly faces is arriving at questions and issues that are meaningful to the interviewees. Initially, field research begins with a set of questions that a researcher finds interesting and for which he or she wishes to find answers. Even though the questions posed by the ethnographer might elicit responses from the interviewees, the ethnographer must remain *en garde* that the questions themselves are not too detached from the everyday world of those interviewed. Bridging the worlds of the subjects and the researcher requires the ethnographer to reflect continually on the validity and relevance of questions to a given context. In addition, the ethnographer needs to assess, from time to time, whether his or her choice of field methods is appropriate for addressing the questions underlying the inquiry and if the methods employed in data analysis are appropriate.

My first attempts with photo elicitation occurred during the summer of 2003 and built on my earlier work on the monastic training of young novices in contemporary Sri Lanka (Samuels, 2004, 2005). After completing my PhD dissertation in 2002, I became particularly interested in locating a place for the emotions and an emotional experience of Buddhism in the lives of young ordinands and novices. Two larger questions guiding my interests were: What constitutes an emotionally satisfying experience of Buddhism? How are the young novices taught to bring about those experiences for Buddhist lay people? The topic and questions were largely derived from my own observation of earlier ethnographic works on Sri Lankan monasticism, which have tended to favor the head rather than the heart. The incongruity between previous ethnographic studies and my own observations led me to ponder new questions as well as different methods for collecting data.

In this chapter, I reflect on one of several methods I employed during my field research with child Buddhist novices in Sri Lanka during the summers of 2003 and 2004: asking research subjects to take photographs on various aspects of their lives as monastics and inserting those photographs into the interview process. This particular method is referred to, in the field of visual studies, as autodriven photo elicitation. In the remainder of this article, I will evaluate and reflect on my experiments with photo elicitation by addressing three interrelated areas: (1) the field methods and procedures I employed in both 2003 and 2004, (2) the theoretical insights I arrived at as a result of using autodriven photo elicitation, and (3) my own reflections about the benefits and limitations of photo elicitation, particularly in relation to the connection made between seeing, memory, and knowing.

Autodriven Photo Elicitation: Background, Field Sites, and Procedures

Photo elicitation as a field method is certainly not new. Numerous studies have used photographs to elicit information from research subjects. One early case study of photo elicitation is John Collier's (1957) work examining mental health in Canada, particularly how families adapt to ethnically diverse people. In that study, Collier found that by inserting photographs into the interview process, he was able to "relieve the strain of being questioned" (p. 849) and, thus, garner much more concrete information from his interviewees. Since Collier's study, other researchers have used photo elicitation in conducting fieldwork, many of them also assessing the benefits and shortcomings of this particular research tool.

The majority of studies using photo elicitation inserted into the interview photographs that were taken by people other than the interviewees. My choice to insert photographs taken by the subjects themselves—*autodriven,* as it is known in the field of visual studies—is based on my belief that photographs taken by the research subjects themselves are likely to reflect more accurately their world, and thus, using them is better suited to bridging the culturally distinct worlds of the researcher and the researched. Although photographs taken by the interviewer certainly have the potential to elicit reactions and responses from interviewees, it has been argued (Beyers, 1966; Cavin, 1994; Clark, 1999; Heisley & Levy, 1991) that using the subjects' own photographs in the interview process gives primacy to their world and provides a greater opportunity for research subjects to create their own sense of meaning and disclose it to the researcher.[3]

Field Sites

The temple where I conducted the first set of photo-elicited interviews is located in the hill country of Sri Lanka, about 15 kilometers outside of the city of Kandy. The temple itself is a training center for Buddhist novices. During the summer of 2003, 52 novices between the ages of 7 and 19 were living in the temple. Of the novices living there at the time, I had interviewed 25 during the research I conducted 3 years earlier.

During the summer of 2004, I returned to Sri Lanka to conduct further interviews with ordinands and novices. In addition to carrying out semistructured interviews with the interviewees, I continued my experiments with autodriven photo elicitation. In 2004, I was able to complete photo-elicited interviews with 15 novices and ordinands. Some of those interviewed were living in the temple where I had conducted research the year before (main temple); others were at two smaller nearby branch temples. All three temples were located in the district of Kandy in upcountry Sri Lanka.

The novices I interviewed during both summers came from a variety of regions in Sri Lanka, the majority of them from the northern district of Anuradhapura, the upcountry district of Matale, and the southeastern district of Ampara. Like many other temples in Sri Lanka, the temples where I completed my research were run by head monks (Sinhala: *nāyaka*). The main temple, which housed the greatest number of novices and ordinands at the time (65 in 2004), had a deputy head monk (Sinhala: *anunāyaka*) as well.

Field Methods and Procedures

The first set of photo-elicited interviews I conducted took place over a 2-month period during the summer of 2003. Admittedly, the decision to use photo elicitation as a field method was a last-minute one, decided over a conversation with Greg Stanczak during a conference we attended in

Philadelphia. During that conference, Greg and I began thinking through a series of topics or a script that I would ask young ordinands and novices to photograph. Prior to leaving Philadelphia for Sri Lanka, I stopped off at a downtown pharmacy, where I purchased 10 auto-focus, auto-exposure mult use cameras with built-in flashes. I also purchased 20 rolls of 200 ASA film.

Although I had previous experience interviewing children, this would be my very first attempt at autodriven photo elicitation as a field method. My familiarity with this particular research method was limited to a simple understanding that I would ask interviewees to photograph a variety of top-ics and, after developing the film, would interview them by inserting their own photographs into the interview process.

On arriving in Sri Lanka, I immediately began sharing this new research method with my research assistant. After discussing my interests at great length, we began revising the original script in hopes of making it more meaningful to the interviewees and better attuned to the topic of the emo-tions. After some deliberation, a final script of 11 topics was created: Take a photograph of (1) a good/perfect/ideal (*yahapat*) monk, (2) something beautiful, (3) an important temple activity, (4) what is important to you as a monastic, (5) what is difficult about being a monastic, (6) what makes you happy as a monastic, (7) what is good about being a monastic, (8) something that captures the essence of Buddhism, (9) what you think is sinful or unmer-itorious (Sinhala: *pavak*), (10) something that is meritorious (Sinhala: *pinak*), and (11) anything you like. These topics stemmed from my previous research in Sri Lanka and included both specific subjects (e.g., take a picture of a perfect monk) and more general topics (e.g., take a picture of something beautiful or take a picture of anything you want). After deciding on the script, we printed a list of the 11 topics in Sinhala. The printed sheets were given to the research subjects at the same time they were given cameras.

Before setting off to Sri Lanka in 2003, I had planned to conduct photo-elicited interviews with all 52 novices living in the temple. With each novice taking 11 photographs, I hoped to share each roll of film (24 exposures) among two different interviewees, the second one working on the assign-ment only after the first monastic had taken all 11 photographs. However, due to various problems encountered that summer (e.g., the cameras locking up, novices opening the camera prior to completing the assignment, novices forgetting to turn on the flash while shooting indoors, novices taking several weeks to shoot all 11 photographs, and so on), only 16 monastics were able to complete the assignment satisfactorily over the 2-month period. As a result of my own time constraints, I was only able to complete full interviews with nine novices, four of whom I had interviewed 3 years previously (Silananda, Dhirananda, Jinaratna, Tanhankara) and five of whom I had not met earlier (Medhankara, Dhammapala, Piyananda, Sumedha, Anomasiri).[4]

Prior to handing out cameras to the novices, I chatted informally with them about their lives in the monastery. With the novices I had not met previously, I introduced myself and completed two initial interviews in which I asked them about the number of people in their families, their home village, their schooling prior to becoming a novice, their parents' professions, and the way in which they became connected to the temple where I was conducting research. With the novices I had met previously, I chatted informally with them about their lives and experiences during the past 3 years.

Before taking part in the assignment, I procured written assent from each novice. I also obtained consent from the head monk—who is considered to be the novices' legal guardian—to interview each novice. I then briefly explained the project privately to each novice. I purposefully did not divulge much, fearing that any in-depth explanation of the project would influence the novices' choice of what to photograph. I also explained about how to use the camera, told each novice that he could take as much time as needed, and mentioned that I would be making an extra copy of the pictures and would be giving the copies to each of them only after everyone else had completed the assignment. Finally, I made clear to each monastic that I did not want them to share their ideas or choices of photographs with the others.

Once the film was developed and the photographs printed, each novice was interviewed separately in a private room. Prior to beginning each interview, I asked the novices to identify and match each photograph to its topic (i.e., which was the photograph of the perfect monk, something beautiful, and so on). Once all of the photographs were identified, I started the interview, beginning with the 1st topic and ending with the 11th topic (i.e., anything you want). As we began looking at each photograph, I prompted the novices to discuss each picture by simply saying, "Tell me about this photograph." While the openness of the question was sometimes met with a baffling look and a "what do you want me to tell you?" response, the more open-ended approach tended to elicit, after an initial hesitation on the side of the novices, very focused and detailed descriptions. I tried to do as little as possible in guiding the interviews. If ideas were raised that required further elaboration, I asked the novices about them (e.g., what do you mean by X?) before moving on to the next photograph. In some instances, I encouraged the novices to expand on their descriptions by saying "Is that so!"

Although most of this chapter focuses on the outcomes of the photo-elicited interviews conducted in 2003, I will also make reference to another set of photo-elicited interviews I conducted in 2004. Unlike my impromptu decision to use photo elicitation in my field research in 2003, I embarked on the 2004 project with much more forethought and background in visual studies. Prior to leaving for Sri Lanka, I began weighing the option of not using a detailed script. As my research continued to center on an emotional and aesthetical experience of Buddhism among child monastics, I decided simply to ask the novices to take photographs of 10 things that they liked ("Photograph 10 things that attracts your heart/mind [*hita ädagannavā*]").[5] This more open-ended or scriptless approach resulted from reading a draft of Marisol Clark-Ibáñez's (2004) study of elementary school children in which she asked children simply "to take photographs of what is important to them" (p. 1508), as well as from considering Cindy Clark's (1999) point that the ethnographer should strive to capture "the active involvement of children as arbiters of their own experience" (p. 39).

During the summer of 2004, I handed out cameras to the novices only after conducting an informal interview in which I caught up with them and discussed the project (for those interviewed previously) or in which I explained the project after gathering information from them about their families, their schooling as lay boys, and their connection to the temple (for those not previously interviewed). The novices were also told that they would receive copies of the photographs once I completed the assignment with all the others. They were asked not to share their thoughts or ideas with their fellow monastics.

As in 2003, each novice was interviewed privately. Before beginning the photo-elicited interviews, each monastic was given the chance to look through all of his photographs and to put the pictures in whatever order he preferred. As before, discussions about each photograph began by me saying, "Tell me about this photograph." When the photograph did not elicit a very detailed response, I added, "What is it about this photograph that attracted your heart/mind?"

Having provided a brief outline of the field sites and research procedures, I will now discuss some of the insights that resulted from using autodriven photo elicitation. In doing so, I will focus my attention on how this field method led me to reassess my own understandings of what constitutes an important temple activity and who constitutes a good or ideal monastic. That discussion will be followed with a more sustained reflection on the benefits and limitations of photo elicitation, especially comparing shooting scripts and scriptless shooting.

Theoretical Insights: Body, Emotions, and Community

The photo-elicited interviews were markedly different from the word-only interviews I conducted from 1998 to 2000. Besides being much richer in content and detail (a point to which I will return), the photo-elicited interviews forced a reconsideration of several of my own previously held assumptions about monastic life. Indeed, as a result of foregrounding the world of child monastics over my own preconceived ideas about Buddhist monastic culture, photo elicitation became a useful tool to access new sets of meanings and understandings. In the remainder of this section, I will focus on two ways in which autodriven photo elicitation contributed to and led to a reassessment of my own understanding of monastic life. In doing so, I will mainly limit my discussion to the interview material elicited from two particular scripts used in 2003: (1) take a photograph of an important temple activity and (2) take a photograph of a good/ideal/perfect monk.

Breaking Frames: From Meditation to Sweeping

While conducting research in Sri Lanka from 1998 to 2000, I spent much of my time observing the many temple activities in which the novices were involved. Having begun my ethnographic research after reading numerous anthropological accounts of Buddhism in South and Southeast Asia, I was particularly interested in the roles that rituals play in the socialization of young ordinands and novices—especially the activities of worshipping the Buddha (*Buddhapūjā*), worshipping the previous Buddhas and the tree under which the Buddha attained enlightenment (*bodhipūjā*), meditating, performing protection rituals (*pirit*), preaching (*baṇa*), and conducting funeral rituals (*paṅsukula*). Perceiving my keen interest in these particular temple duties, which I believed at the time to be central to monastic life, many young novices began offering their own reflections on these particular activities.

Despite my conversations with the novices, I failed to acknowledge at the time that my concerns and interests were partially based on my own Western assumptions about Buddhist monastic culture, particularly my understandings of what constitutes important temple activities. It was only when I returned from the field that I began to understand how my own ideas, interpretations, and biases impinged on the data I had collected. Even though many novices graciously responded to my questions and research interests, I later determined that the very questions I asked (and the responses I received) often had more to do with my own understandings of Buddhist monastic life than with the everyday lives of Buddhist novices in 20th- and 21st-century Sri Lanka.

Allowing novices the occasion to take pictures of what *they* considered an important temple duty had a profound effect on what Douglas Harper called *breaking frames*. In a recent study of rural American farmers, Harper (2002) sought to elicit information from them about the phenomenology of farming by inserting photographs that he had taken into the interview process.

What he found initially, however, was that the photographs did not elicit responses from the research subjects because the photos "looked essentially like the illustrations in the many farm magazines found in the house and shop" (p. 20). As such, the photographs were unable, in the words of Harper, to "*break the frame* of farmers' normal views; they did not lead to a reflective stance vis-à-vis the taken-for-granted aspects of work and community" (p. 20). To break the farmers' frame, Harper inserted aerial and historical photographs, which enabled the farmers to think about and communicate farm strategies in a much more meaningful way by evoking "aspects of the past that have a great deal of significance in the context of farming's continuing evolution" (p. 20).

Aiding the interviewees in reflecting on their lives and community and in communicating their ideas to the researcher is, no doubt, one of the benefits of photo elicitation as a research method. However, in situations where the worlds of the researcher and the researched are culturally distinct, the goal of choosing an appropriate field method, it seems, should be less about breaking the subjects' frame to elicit more detailed descriptions; instead, the goal, as Harper himself notes, is to bridge the world of the researcher and the researched, a process that requires the researcher's own frames of reference to be broken or impinged on by the frames of the research subjects.

While inserting photographs into the interviews process often elicits more information from research subjects, I found that one of the most fruitful benefits of *autodriven* photo elicitation is that it led to a breaking of my own frames.[6] For example, had I used *my own* photographs to explore the place and roles of temple duties and rituals in the lives of young monastics, I would have inserted photographs of what *I* considered key temple duties: worshipping the Buddha, learning in monastic schools, receiving advice from the head monk, and so on.[7] By allowing novices to take their own photographs in 2003 of what *they* considered important temple activities, I was able to privilege to a greater degree the world of the interviewee. Put somewhat differently, by focusing attention on the interviewees' worlds, particularly on their roles as Buddhist novices,[8] autodriven photo elicitation was able, in the words of Cindy Clark (1999, p. 43), to capture and introduce content areas that had previously been outside of my own purview.

Even though several novices took pictures of other monastics receiving advice from the head monk and worshipping the Buddha in the evening as important temple activities, two thirds of the novices interviewed in 2003 took photographs of a monastic or several monastics sweeping.[9] The photo-elicited interviews I conducted with these novices about their photographs of monastics sweeping pointed, moreover, to very different understandings of monastic training and what constitutes ideal monastic-lay relations.

Photo 8.1   Jinaratna's photograph of an important temple activity.

SOURCE: © Used with permission.

Discussing with me the photograph (Photo 8.1) he took of another novice sweeping the building that houses the Buddha (*buduge*), Jinaratna said,

> As a monk, temple activities have to be done. There are many temple activities that have to be done. Sweeping is one of them. It is important. There are several places that need to be swept. Sweeping in the *vihārage* (i.e., the place where the statue of the Buddha is kept) is more important. It is more powerful/potent (*balavat*). When we go there, the statue of Lord Buddha can be seen. Many people visit this place. Sweeping in this place is what is needed the most.

Although it is not uncommon to see novices and monks sweeping the temple grounds, particularly during the morning and evening hours, Jinaratna's photo-elicited interview suggests that a gradation of sweeping exists. As certain parts of the temple are regarded to be particularly powerful (e.g., the tree of enlightenment [*bōdhiya*], the reliquary mound [*caitya*], and the building that houses images of the Buddha [*buduge*]), sweeping in those areas is regarded to be not only more important, but also a more powerful way to accrue spiritual merit. Moreover, in his response, Jinaratna also alludes to the role that sweeping plays in maintaining harmonious relationships with the temple's lay population, a point to which I will return.

When I asked another novice, Piyananda, about the photograph (Photo 8.2) he took of the deputy head monk sweeping around the *buduge,* he explained,

Photo 8.2   Piyananda's photograph of an important temple activity.

SOURCE: © Used with permission.

People look at the temple thinking that a temple is a place where Lord Buddha is kept. Lord Buddha is a teacher and the founder of the religion. Because he is there, the temple should be kept clean. People come to the temple often. It is not like other places. . . . Lord Buddha and his relic came to clean places. So, if the place is clean like that, relics may come.

For both novices, sweeping the temple—particularly the places in and surrounding the building that houses images of the Buddha (*buduge*)—is a temple activity that not only must be done but that demonstrates their own personal respect and reverence to the Buddha as a teacher and the religion's founder. With their photographs in hand, the two novices spoke about gradations in acquiring merit and about how a pleasing monastic environment ensures harmonious relationships between lay and monastic communities. This last point was made by yet another novice, Anomasiri, who discussed his photograph (Photo 8.3) as follows:

If the *buduge* (i.e., building where the statue of the Buddha is kept) is not swept, then the lay donors would think "there are 40 or 50 young novices

Photo 8.3   Anomasiri's photograph of an important temple activity.

SOURCE: © Used with permission.

living here. We provide alms food for them. We give them other things, too. These young novices are lazy." Thinking that, lay people would feel disgusted (*kalakireneva*) as they don't even like to keep their own homes dirty. The places around the *buduge,* the Bo tree (i.e., tree of enlightenment), the preaching hall (*dharma salava*), and alms-giving hall (i.e., *dana salava*) are not like the other places in a temple. They should be kept clean. When these places are dirty, people will not like to come to the temple.

Unlike most discussions of ideal lay-monastic relationships, in which monastics are portrayed as providing the laity with religious teachings, social counseling, education, rituals, and the opportunity to make merit in exchange for the laity's offerings of food, clothing, shelter, and medicine, the photo-elicited interviews pointed to somewhat different understandings of monastic roles and duties. For Anomasiri, lay people do not merely flock to the temple out of their own greed for spiritual merit; rather, their continued patronage is based, partially at least, on the temple's cleanliness or on a particular aesthetic experience. Such connections between aesthetics and merit or, in Sinhalese, between pleasing or attracting the heart/mind and making merit challenged my earlier assumptions about merit making in contemporary Sri Lanka.[10]

Cindy Clark (1999), in her study assessing the benefits and limitations of autodriven photo elicitation among children, has argued that "research methods need to capture children's active role in the social order . . . [and the] active involvement of children as arbiters of their own experience" (p. 39). What I found particularly worthwhile about autodriven photo elicitation is that it increased the likelihood for interviewees to take greater part in constructing meaning and expressing their personal perspectives. For instance, when I asked Dhirananda to tell me about his photograph taken of a novice sweeping around the *buduge* (Photo 8.4), he began discussing how novices are able to acquire merit from sweeping as well as how sweeping and purifying the heart/mind are closely related:

As a monk, this is the work from which we can always get merit. Here, this can be a type of meditation. We meditate to become enlightened and to remove defilements. Sweeping is also a meditation to remove the rubbish (*kunu*) in the heart/mind (*hita*). Here, removing rubbish from the compound is like removing the impurities from the heart/mind. On the other hand, it is a cleaning of the compound where lord Buddha's temple (*ge*) is situated. Therefore, it is most important temple duty. Every monk must do it.

When I prompted him by saying "really?" he continued,

Photo 8.4   Dhirananda's photograph of an important temple activity.

SOURCE: © Used with permission.

We listen to sermons to remove the greed, hatred, and delusion that are in our *hita*s. In a similar way, cleaning the compound means cleaning of the impurities in the heart/mind. At the same time, we can focus our heart/mind toward the rubbish while cleaning. It is like a form of meditation.

With his photograph in hand, Dhirananda was able to illustrate well and clearly express certain ideas that were, by and large, absent from the many word-only interviews I conducted 3 years earlier. While it may certainly be the case that the connection that Dhirananda drew between sweeping the temple and purifying one's heart/mind came from one of the nightly advice sessions of the head monk or from reading stories about the disciples of the Buddha, Dhirananda's photograph nonetheless provided him with an opportunity to think through and express this important relationship he made between his own external activities and his internal states.

The Perfect Monk: From Abstract Ideas to Concrete Reality

Another area in which autodriven photo elicitation provided the interviewees with a chance to reflect on and share their own thoughts and experiences as novices concerns ideas about ideal monks, appropriate roles, and responsibilities incumbent on members of the Buddhist monastic community or *sangha*.

During the research I conducted with child novices from 1998 to 2000, I was interested in how novices understood what is demanded of them as members of *sangha*. At that time, I dealt with the topic by asking novices, in semistructured interviews, to describe a good/ideal/virtuous monastic (Sinhala: *yahapat bhikṣuvak*). After later comparing the material collected from word-only interviews with that elicited from inserting photographs, I found that the former interview method tended to elicit only succinct and abstract depictions of who constitutes a perfect monastic: for example, those who follow the monastic behavioral code (*Vinaya*), those who fulfill the religious needs of the laity, and those who are concerned with higher aims and purposes (such as enlightenment or *nirvāna*). More specifically, replies to my question, "How would you describe a good/ideal (*yahapat*) monk?" included

"An ideal monk is one who serves others" (Tanhankara)

"One who protects his morality (*sil*) and serves the laity" (Dhirananda)

"The monk who can do religious activities" (Somananda)

"One who works toward higher aims without breaking his morality (*sil*)" (Silananda)

"One who has good qualities and does not take drugs or drink alcohol" (Jinaratna)

Looking back over the data collected from word-only interviews, I also found that most follow-up questions at the time largely failed to elicit information that was personally meaningful.

In contrast to those word-only interviews, discussions centering on the novices' photographs of a perfect monk tended to invoke responses that were not only more lengthy but also markedly different in content and tone. Rather than merely communicating one or two abstract qualities, the novices' photo-elicited responses were more descriptive and, more important, personally relevant. This point is perhaps best illustrated in Dhirananda's discussion of the photograph he had taken of the temple's deputy head monk:

As an elder brother, he shows us wonderful affection. He shows us the path we should follow. He helps us in our studies. He associates with us like a friend. He attracts the heart/mind (*lengatu*). He is a great teacher. Unlike other teachers, he never hits us if we fall asleep in class. When he teaches us, he shows interest in us and wants us to learn. He even gives us money if we need it. When our parents come, he treats all of them equally and treats them very well by giving them tea and food. He is very clean.

Unlike the response that Dhirananda gave in 1999—"One who protects his morality (*sil*) and serves the laity"—his photo-elicited description resulted in the collection of, in the words of Deborah Heisley and Sidney Levy (1991), "enriched qualitative information concerning events as informants perceive them" (p. 257). Rather than being based on abstract qualities such as protecting his morality and serving the laity, Dhirananda's photograph of the deputy head monk provided him with an opening to express and interpret his own individual experiences as a Buddhist novice undergoing training in 21st-century Sri Lanka.

Similar qualitative responses were culled from other novices. Silananda's description of the photograph (Photo 8.5) he had taken of an excellent monk was also quite telling:

Thinking that this monk is excellent, I took this photograph. In the photograph, he shows restraint. He is dressed in a way that is well-suited for a monk and well-suited for our particular monastic lineage. He is calm. When people see him, their hearts become attracted to him.

Following up his response with a simple "really?" provided sufficient impetus for him to continue:

Lord Buddha's disciples have put on the robe in a way that covers both their shoulders. His bowl is there. He has a Palmyra-leaf umbrella. He is complete. This is the full garb of a monk much like the soldier with a gun and uniform ready to go for a war. Since there are no shortcomings in his appearance, the people's *hita*s become attracted to him.

Silananda's photo-elicited interview led him to make a fascinating connection between a monk armed with an umbrella and a uniformed soldier armed with a gun. Unlike the abstract description he gave 3 years earlier—one "who works toward higher aims without breaking his morality (*sil*)"—Silananda's photograph also resulted in a more salient discussion of monastic behavior, monastic appearance, and the roles that monastic appearance and demeanor play in establishing suitable connections with the laity.

Like Dhirananda and Silananda, Anomasiri used his photograph as an opening to discuss qualities of an ideal monastic that were much more relevant to his life as a Buddhist novice:

Photo 8.5   Silananda's photograph of an excellent monk.

SOURCE: © Used with permission.

The head monk looks after us. He is compassionate. He gives everything he has to us youngsters. He treats both the older novices and younger novices the same. He is happy with the younger ones. He explains to us what is good and what is bad. He is very good at preaching. He is good to us. His expectation is to teach us and make us good people.

When I asked Anomasiri to clarify what he meant by "preaching well," he added,

He preaches in a very beautiful way. The listeners like to hear him preach. People come from far-away places to invite him to preach. Even though there are other temples that are closer, people come here to invite him. . . . If there is some merit-making ceremony, he preaches in a way that is appropriate for the situation and appropriate for the particular place. . . . Also, his voice is very beautiful. He pronounces the words well. He also walks in a beautiful way. Seeing that, people become pleased. He is very friendly with the lay people. He knows how to associate well with any type of person.

By granting interviewees an increased voice and a greater authority to interpret their own personal experiences as Buddhist novices, photo-elicited interviews resulted in the collection of field data that were personally relevant and meaningful. Rather than merely describing abstract qualities, the novices touched on such qualities as being affectionate, being friendly, preaching and walking in a beautiful manner, and having a pleasing voice.

Implied in the responses evoked from the photo-elicited interviews with Dhirananda and Silananda is a whole emotional dimension of Buddhist monasticism that had been somewhat absent from the interviews I conducted previously. Even though I was able to tap into the emotional lives of Buddhist novices during my earlier research, those discussions were largely confined to the novices' descriptions of their lives at home. When conversations turned to their experiences as members of a Buddhist monastic community, their responses became much more cerebral and, to varying degrees, devoid of emotion.

As a result of "reaching deeper centers of reaction," photographs, in the words of John Collier (1957), have a capacity to trigger "spontaneous revelations of a highly-charged emotional nature" (p. 858; see also Collier and Collier, 1986). Indeed, the potential for an image to tap into the emotional life of the interviewee was made evident in a number of interviews conducted with several novices. When I asked Dhirananda to tell me about the photograph he took of a perfect monk (Photo 8.6), he mentioned how a perfect monk is affectionate, friendly, compassionate, loyal, generous, and even clean. When I asked him about what he meant by clean, he briefly defined *clean* as not having a single stone in his room and then added,

His *hita* is not divided. There is no hatred in his *hita*. . . . He looks after us like a mother. He cooks when the food we receive from lay people is not enough. He even spends his salary on our meals. He never gets angry if we take anything that belongs to him. . . . If the head monk is not here, he looks after us very well. If the head monk is not here, he gives us medicine. Like the head monk, he is affectionate to us. He is concerned about the development of the temple, even more than his own family. . . . He treats everyone equally. He is not angry. He has no hatred. He never keeps hatred in his *hita*. . . . He smiles with us. He helps us in a wonderful way to do our studies. Even though I have not asked him for money, I know he would give me some if I asked him. He

Photo 8.6   Dhirananda's photograph of a perfect monk.

SOURCE: © Used with permission.

would even give us his own food. I don't know his personal life but as I see him, he is a monk who keeps the precepts. He knows how to preach to lay people. He is well-respected by lay people. . . . He is humble. He is not cunning. He is honest. He is not angry. . . . He is not greedy. . . . We can associate with him as if he were our mother, father, brother, or friend. We don't have mothers [who live close by]. He is there. We don't have fathers. He is there. We don't have brothers. He is there. We don't have friends. He is there. We can associate with him in many different ways. Recently, the father of a novice living here had an accident. He [i.e., the deputy head monk] was the one who took the father to the hospital, gave him food and other necessary things. He gave him money to go back home. He is ready to provide help to us, to the temple, and to the village in any way possible. With all these qualities, he is a perfect monk.

Rather than merely describing an ideal monastic as one who "protects his morality (*sil*) and serves the laity," Dhirananda gave a more emotionally grounded response as he described the photograph of the deputy head monk. In marked contrast to the word-only interviews I conducted with him in 1999, the photo-elicited interview led to a sharing of information about monks, monastic roles, and temple responsibilities that was concrete, personally relevant and meaningful, and not emotionally removed or disconnected.

Seeing and Knowing: Reflections on Autodriven Photo Elicitation in Facilitating Rapport

In evaluating my own experiences, I discovered that this particular field method yields numerous benefits. First, I found that novices exhibited a much greater interest in taking part in my research, particularly younger novices for whom participation meant their first chance to hold and use a camera. Having a camera in their possession during the days or weeks that it took them to complete the assignment appeared to increase the novices' social standing, especially among their peers.

Photo elicitation also allowed me to establish a quicker rapport with novices, thus facilitating discussions on substantial issues.[11] Indeed, after learning about the assignment from their peers, a number of novices I had not met previously began to approach me and ask to take part in the assignment. When I mentioned that their participation meant that they would have to speak to me about their family life and the factors leading up to their decision to become a novice, several of them immediately sat down in front of me, indicating their readiness for me to begin the interview process. Like Collier, I also found that inserting the novices' photographs into the interview process deflected any uneasiness about the interview process, while at the same time, readily captured the interviewees' attention.

Seeing and Remembering: The Benefits of Using the Subjects' Photographs

One pioneering work that used photo elicitation is John Collier's (1957) study of mental health in Canada. In comparing the data collected from word-only interviews with the data from photo-elicited interviews, Collier found that the "photographic interview got considerably more concrete information" (p. 849) from the interviewees, as the photographs functioned to sharpen the interviewee's memory. Similarly, John Berger (1992) discussed the relationship between memory and seeing when he wrote,

The thrill found in a photograph comes from the onrush of memory. This is obvious when it's a picture of something we once knew. That house we lived in. Mother when young. . . . Memory is a strange faculty. The sharper and more isolated the stimulus memory receives, the more it remembers. (p. 192)[12]

The relationship that Collier and Berger draw between memory and seeing *something we once knew* is yet another reason why autodriven photo elicitation (rather than photo elicitation) provides the interviewees with an even greater opportunity to reflect, recollect, and describe. I found that the photo-elicited interviews were, on the whole, much longer and more encompassing; indeed, most of the interviews lasted well over one hour, and several interviews took almost 2 hours (spread over two interviews) to complete. In numerous instances, discussing the first photograph (a perfect monk) lasted between 15 and 30 minutes alone. Whereas I found that the novices' attention waned after about 45 minutes of word-only interviews, the photographs appeared to capture the novices' attention and keep it affixed to the interview for as much as 90 minutes.

My conversations with the novices about their reactions to the *autodriven* photo elicitation interviews point further to the photographs' ability to create meaning and spark memories. When I asked Silananda about what he thought of the assignment, he replied,

If we look at a photograph taken by someone else, then we would simply see the photograph and think "this is a reliquary mound (*caitya*)," and "this is a Bo tree." However, these photographs have a lot of meaning (*artha*) and value for us now because we had to think about it. Through looking at the photographs together, you too come to understand our own attitudes and behavior (*ākalpa*).[13]

It was the forethought that Silananda put into the assignment that made his photographs more meaningful to him as well as better suited for transmitting his thoughts to others. While it may certainly be true, as Dona Schwartz (1989) has pointed out, that "meaning is actively constructed, not passively received" (p. 120) in the viewing process, it also appears to be the case that for Silananda and several other novices, meaning was actively constructed in the very act of thinking about what to photograph as well as while taking the actual pictures.[14]

Other novices raised similar points about their experiences with autodriven photo elicitation. When I asked one about the differences he perceived between photo-elicited and word-only interviews, he explained, "The photographs are like a mirror for us. We can learn a lot of things by discussing the photographs. It is easier to speak while holding the pictures in our hand and while looking at the pictures. We can explain more when the pictures are close at hand."[15] For him, knowing and thinking are not merely mental processes; feeling (holding the pictures) and seeing (looking at the pictures) are intimately connected to remembering, learning, and expressing. Indeed, taking photographs and later discussing them with me enabled many novices to recall, in greater depth, their own ideas; it also provided many novices with the occasion to construct meaning in a manner that was much more personally significant. This point was, perhaps, most poignantly made in my postinterview discussion with Sumedha. Asked to reflect on the use of photographs in the interview process, Sumedha said,

> With the pictures, my ideas come out much more easily than without the pictures. Pictures include my feelings too. . . . In terms of the pictures, there are a lot of things that come with the photographs—feelings, ideas that this is good, this is not good, and so on. More ideas come.

Scriptless Shooting: Breaking All Frames

One point I raised when discussing the photographs of an important temple duty is how the autodriven approach led to a breaking of my own frame of reference. Making specific reference to how my own views about what constituted important temple duties shaped the questions I asked and responses I received during the word-only interviews conducted from 1998–2000, I suggested that the autodriven method is particularly effective in eliciting responses that are more relevant and meaningful to the interviewees themselves.

Even though I found autodriven photo elicitation to be an effective field method and an important complement to word-only interviews, I nonetheless reevaluated my decision to use scripts once I returned from Sri Lanka in 2003. Indeed, after reading through Marisol Clark-Ibáñez's (2004) study of elementary school children, in which she asked children simply "to take photographs of what is important to them" (p. 1508), I began to suspect that my script, while somewhat privileging the world of the Buddhist novices, nonetheless still favored my world over theirs. After I returned, I asked myself: What does the script I provided the novices say about my own assumptions of Buddhist monasticism? Does employing such a script hamper, even implicitly, my own desire to treat children as active arbiters of their own experience? As a result of these questions, I decided to carry out another round of autodriven photo-elicited interviews in 2004.

Taking my cue from Clark-Ibáñez and Cindy Clark, I decided that rather than give the novices a script to photograph, I would simply ask them to take 10 photographs of anything that they like (literally, anything that attracts their heart/mind). Once they completed the assignment, I asked each novice to look over all the photographs he had taken and to order them in any way he deemed fit. After asking the novice if he was ready to begin, I took the first photograph from his pile, and I asked him to tell me about the photograph.

Although the photographs elicited lengthy responses from several interviewees, most novices were much less able to articulate their own thoughts behind why they took each photograph and what attracted their heart/mind to their photograph. For instance, when I asked Buddharakkhita why he took a photograph of himself standing on the roof of the living quarters, he simply replied, "I had no photographs that belonged to me. I wanted to take my own photographs. So, I took this one." When I asked him what attracted his heart/mind to that particular image, he succinctly replied, "I wanted to show it to my mother." Further questioning failed to elicit additional responses from him.

I decided to help the interview process along by moving to his next image: lay people performing a Buddhist ritual in the temple's assembly hall. When I asked him to tell me about the photograph, he responded, "It is a photograph of lay people performing a *bodhipūjā* ritual in the assembly hall (*dharmasālāva*)." I prodded him further by asking, again, what was it about the photograph that attracted his heart/mind. His only response was, "I had an idea to take this photograph." I asked him why. He did not respond.

Further attempts at eliciting responses from Buddharakkhita failed. Moreover, photo-elicited interviews with almost two thirds of the other novices yielded similar results. Why was this so? What was it about scriptless photo elicitation that led to this outcome? While I have been unable to pinpoint a single reason why scriptless photo elicitation resulted in an increased reticence from the novices, I found two possible causes that may have contributed to such a drastic difference: that the novices did not perform the assignment with the degree of foresight and reflection that was required when they had a script and, equally significant, that I as an interviewer lacked the sufficient background to ask thought-provoking questions outside of the field of Buddhist studies.

Related to the first cause, I immediately recollected Silananda's reflection on the photo elicitation assignment, particularly his comment about how the "photographs have a lot of meaning (*artha*) and value for us now because we had to think about it." While it may certainly be the case that some of the novices put forethought into the scriptless assignment, its very open-ended nature made it much easier to take photographs simply because one wanted to have a particular memory, hoped to send the photograph home, or thought that something was beautiful. In that regard, my attempt to ask questions that sought to locate some underlying cause for the photograph and to relate that cause to their experiences as Buddhist novices failed to elicit the types of responses I collected during the previous summer.

Intimately related to that reason was my own inability to ask questions that were relevant to the novices' own world. As a historian of religion focused on the field of Buddhist studies, I came to Sri Lanka with the background to approach many issues that center on Buddhist training, ideal monastic relationships, monastic recruitment, and Buddhist rituals. As many of the photographs taken in 2004 had little or nothing to do with these topics, I was unable to formulate questions that elicited the quality of responses I received in 2003. Although I continually tried to relate their photographs to their experiences as Buddhist novices living in contemporary Sri Lanka, those attempts were unsuccessful largely because, I believe, I failed to recognize at the time that their photographs had less to do with Buddhism and more to do with being a preadolescent or adolescent away from home for the first time.

Conclusion

My initial and subsequent experiments with autodriven photo elicitation point to its numerous benefits as a field method. Unlike word-only interviews I conducted with the young novices from 1998 to 2000, the autodriven photo-elicited interviews conducted in 2003 resulted in a greater interest to take part in the study on the part of the novices, and enabled me to establish a rapport with the novices much more quickly. In most cases, inserting photographs into the interview process deflected any feelings of discomfort about the interview process while, at the same time, captured the interviewees' attention much more easily and for a longer period of time.

In addition, the autodriven photo-elicited interviews resulted in a collection of data that was much more detailed and, I believe, more meaningful to the interviewees. The novices' responses to the photographs were far from succinct and abstract; indeed, the responses centered on concepts, ideas, and experiences that had a much greater relevance to their lives as novices undergoing training in contemporary Sri Lanka. The data collected from the photo-elicited interviews also included a much greater range of emotions, often centering on the feelings, likes, and dislikes of the interviewees.

My experiments with the autodriven approach to photo elicitation was based on my desire to bridge two culturally distinct worlds. While inserting my own photographs into the interview process may have prompted the novices to give encyclopedic responses, reflecting back on my own conceptions of what constitutes ideal monastics, temple activities, and religious rituals reveals an important benefit of the autodriven approach: providing the interviewees with the opportunity to present their own worlds by becoming arbiters of their own experiences and actively involved in the construction of meaning.

Indeed, the openness of the autodriven method led me to reevaluate my own assumptions and conceptions about monastic life in Sri Lanka. Despite the fact that I arrived in Sri Lanka in 2003 with a list of topics that I wanted the novices to photograph, I was nonetheless able to bridge two culturally distinct worlds or, more accurately, to allow the novices' world to infringe on my own world. While the scripts I asked them to shoot may, to some degree, have prevented a total bracketing of my own perspectives and understandings, my attempts with scriptless shooting in 2004 proved largely ineffective in eliciting responses that had relevance to my research interests or to the field of Buddhist studies altogether. In that regard, my own limitations as a field researcher specializing in Buddhist monastic culture became even more apparent with the sheer open-endedness of the second assignment.

Along with the effectiveness of script-based autodriven photo elicitation, some problems and limitations need to be acknowledged. The first issue concerns my time constraints. I had expected the novices to take 2 or 3 days to complete the assignment; most novices took more than a week. Furthermore, my wish to divide each roll of film between two novices meant that it would be almost 3 weeks, in some cases a whole month, before I was able to conduct the interviews. Other problems I encountered with the cameras—novices opening the cameras and exposing the film, the cameras locking up, and novices forgetting to use the flash while shooting indoors—further hindered my ability to conduct photo-elicited interviews. Indeed, although I had intended to have all 52 novices participate in the assignment, I was only able to complete the assignment (photographs and full interviews) with nine novices over a two-month period in 2003.

Although it is a powerful tool for eliciting information from informants, photo elicitation needs to be combined with other methods, such as formal and informal interviews as well as detailed observations and accounts of monastic life. Photo elicitation is undoubtedly an important field method, but it is not, in the words of Collier (1957, p. 858) "an infallible technique."

Notes

1. I would like to thank Greg Stanczak for reading through an earlier version of this chapter and making helpful suggestions on how it may be improved. The research conducted during the summer of 2003 was funded by a Junior Faculty Scholarship from Western Kentucky University. Research conducted in 2004 was funded by The Spiritual Transformation Scientific Research Program, sponsored by the Metanexus Institute on Religion and Science, with the generous support of the John Templeton Foundation. Any errors, editorial or otherwise, are solely my responsibility.

2. Recent works that have reflected on the use of photography in fieldwork are Becker (1974 and 1986), Caldarola (1985), Collier and Collier (1986), Heisley and Levy (1991), Kenney (1993), Butler (1994), Cavin (1994), Suchar (1997), and Clark (1999), to name only a few. Douglas Harper (2002), in an important study of the history and development of this research method, explores the range of topics that have been investigated through photo elicitation.

3. This notion of constructing meaning is discussed in Beyers (1966) when he characterizes photographs as containing the raw material for the construction of meaning. Clark (1999) makes a similar point when discussing her choice to use autodriven photo elicitation. She writes, "The autodrive technique—because of its ability to portray behaviors in context, as well as to explore the meaning of those behaviors to the actors—allowed children to visually show and tell aspects of their lives that were important to them" (p. 40).

4. All the names used have been changed.

5. The actual assignment was phrased as, "Take 10 pictures of people or things or places that attract your heart. What you take is entirely up to you. You can take 10 pictures in any way that you would like." As I will discuss in the following section, this emic notion of "attracting the heart/mind" resulted from the photo-elicited interviews of the previous summer's research on emotions and Buddhist monastic culture.

6. John Berger and Jean Mohr (1982, pp. 17–37) also discuss the need for the subject to choose which photograph is appropriate or not appropriate in the construction of a photo essay.

7. The photographs I would have taken are partially based on what I believed symbolized the different (or exotic) lives of monastics. Jay Ruby (1976) raises this concern about the use of photography in anthropological research when he writes,

When an anthropologist takes pictures in the field he most closely resembles someone from his culture on vacation. . . . While on vacation or in the field, the camera is taken everywhere. The experience is exotic and to be recorded visually so that it can be remembered and shared with others who were not there. . . . The selection of subject matter for the anthropologist is not based on his particular research problem but rather on the dictum that, "A good photographic record is an essential part of every kind of anthropological field work." (p. 12; see also Ruby, 1973)

Even though Ruby (1976) warns the ethnographer by saying that the researcher must at least entertain "the possibility that the pictures these people take will be more a reflection of our culture than theirs" (p. 13), my own experiments with autodriven photo elicitation point to the fact that, in general, this method gives primacy to the subjects' world of ideas and meaning. For instance, one topic that the novices were asked to photograph was of something beautiful. While some novices, as might be expected, did photograph a Buddha image, a number of novices took photographs that were quite unexpected: a race car, a flowering tree, and the mountains.

8. This tendency for word-only interviews to concentrate attention on the researcher's own questions and concerns is discussed in Charles Briggs's (1986) *Learning How to Ask,* where he writes,

> By participating in an interview, both parties are implicitly agreeing to abide by certain communicative norms. The interview moves the roles that each normally occupies in life into the background and structures the encounter with respect to the roles of interviewer and interviewee. Attention is concentrated on the topics introduced by the researcher's questions. (p. 2f)

9. In the earlier research that I conducted in Sri Lanka, only 2 out of 38 novices brought up the issue of sweeping when I asked them about the factors that helped them learn about their status and roles as monastics; the full purport of what they were saying eluded me at the time.

10. Ideas surrounding merit (*puñña*) and the role that the heart/mind plays in merit making are published in Samuels (in press).

11. Lenora Butler (1994) also discusses this benefit in her article on the use of photographs as a stimuli to discussion.

12. Collier (1957) makes a similar point when he writes, "It appeared that photographs stimulated a restoration of expression. The imagery opened doors of memory and released emotions about forgotten circumstances" (p. 853).

13. This novice's comment echoes well with another point that John Berger makes (1980) in his discussion of the private photograph, when he writes that "such a photograph remains surrounded by the meaning from which it was severed. . . . The photograph is a memento from a life being lived" (p. 52).

14. For the novices, the photographs had a centering function that helped them focus their ideas and attention. The role of seeing is similar to the process of meditating on an image of a Buddha, which allows monks to build a bridge between their own lives and the life of the Buddha (Swearer, 2003).

15. Other novices drew a similar connection between photographs and their heart/mind as well as a the ability of a photograph to transmit their thoughts to others. According to one such novice,

> You are able to learn about our ideas more when we you look at the photographs. By looking at the photographs, you are able to come to know about what our ideas/thoughts are in our heart: how we act, how we think, how we speak. Those things can easily be known. You can come to know what is in my heart.

References

Becker, H. S. (1974). Photography and sociology. *Studies in the Anthropology of Visual Communication, 1*(2), 3–26.

Becker, H. S. (1986). *Doing things together: Selected papers.* Evanston, IL: Northwestern University Press.

Berger, J. (1980). *About looking.* New York: Pantheon Books.

Berger, J. (1992). *Keeping a rendezvous.* New York: Vintage International.

Berger, J., & Mohr, J. (1982). *Another way of telling.* New York: Pantheon Books.

Beyers, P. (1966). Cameras don't take pictures. *Columbia University Forum, 9,* 27–31.

Briggs, C. L. (1986). *Learning how to ask: A sociolinguistic appraisal of the role of the interview in social science research.* Cambridge, UK: Cambridge University Press.

Butler, L. F. (1994). Autodrive in qualitative research: Cracking the ice with young respondents. *Canadian Journal of Marketing Research, 13,* 71–74.

Caldarola, V. (1985). Visual contexts: A photographic research method in anthropology. *Studies in Visual Communication, 11*(3), 33–53.

Cavin, E. (1994). In search of the viewfinder: A study of a child's perspective. *Visual Sociology, 9*(1), 27–41.

Clark, C. D. (1999). The autodriven interview: A photographic viewfinder into children's experience. *Visual Sociology, 14*(1/2), 39–50.

Clark-Ibáñez, M. (2004, August). Framing the social world with photo-elicitation interviews. *American Behavioral Scientist, 47*(12), 1507–1527.

Collier, J. (1957). Photography in anthropology: A report on two experiments. *American Anthropologist, 59,* 843–859.

Collier, J. J., & Collier, M. (1986). *Visual anthropology: Photography as a research method.* Albuquerque: University of New Mexico Press.

Harper, D. (2002). Talking about pictures: A case for photo elicitation. *Visual Studies, 17*(1), 13–26.

Heisley, D. D., & Levy, S. J. (1991). Autodriving: A photoelicitation technique. *Journal of Consumer Research, 18,* 257–272.

Kenney, K. (1993). Using self-portrait photographs to understand self-concepts of Chinese and American university students. *Visual Anthropology, 5,* 245–269.

Ruby, J. (1973). Up the Zambesi with notebook and camera or being an anthropologist without doing anthropology . . . with pictures. *Savicom Newsletter, 4*(3), 12–14.

Ruby, J. (1976). In a pic's eye: Interpretive strategies for deriving significance and meaning from photographs. *Afterimage, 3*(9), 5–7.

Samuels, J. (2004). Toward an action-oriented pedagogy: Buddhist texts and monastic education in contemporary Sri Lanka. *Journal of the American Academy of Religion, 72*(4), 955–971.

Samuels, J. (2005). Texts memorized, texts performed: A reconsideration of the role of *Paritta* in Sri Lankan monastic education. *Journal of the International Association of Buddhist Studies, 28*(2), 339–367.

Samuels, J. (in press). Is merit in the milk-powder? The pursuit of *Puñña* in contemporary Sri Lanka. *Contemporary Buddhism.*

Schwartz, D. (1989). Visual ethnography: Using photography in qualitative research. *Qualitative Sociology, 12*(2), 119–154.

Suchar, C. S. (1997). Grounding visual sociology research in shooting scripts. *Qualitative Sociology, 20*(1), 33–55.

Swearer, D. K. (2003). In the presence of the Buddha. In A. M. Blackburn & J. Samuels (Eds.), *Approaching the Dhamma: Buddhist texts and practices in South and Southeast Asia* (pp. 91–104). Seattle, WA: BPS Pariyatti Editions.

9

Signs of Resistance

Marking Public Space Through a Renewed Cultural Activism

Emmanuel A. David

For several years prior to the catastrophic events surrounding Hurricane Katrina, New Orleans was the site of an ongoing tension between artist-activists, progressives, and revolutionaries and what some might call an anti-graffiti vigilante. Fred Radtke, president and founder of Operation Clean Sweep, Inc., a nonprofit anti-graffiti organization, vowed that his group would remove graffiti within 7 days after it was reported to a 24-hour a day hotline. Radtke reported that graffiti had dropped 65% in New Orleans, and more specifically, 85% in the French Quarter ("Pride Reflected," 2002). Earlier cleanup campaigns in the city involved New Orleans public housing residents and were funded by the city and the U.S. Department of Housing and Urban Development. Unlike these "beautification programs," which turned communities into "beehives of productive summer activity" ("Residents Key," 2002), Radtke single-handedly created a group of community advocates to enforce a zero tolerance policy for graffiti, often with the help of members of the City Council and the local police districts ("Crusading Graffiti-Busters," 2002).

In various arenas of the public sphere, Radtke is known by his proper name. However, at the (sub-)cultural level in which he is in competitive

Photo 9.1   Traces of the Gray Ghost in the French Quarter

dialogue with artist-activists, Radtke is also infamously known as the "Gray Ghost" because of his practice of indiscriminately covering all types of graffiti with gray paint, regardless of the color of the surface behind it. If indeed, there was a reduction in graffiti in New Orleans during his campaign, as Radtke reported, there most certainly was a proliferation of another type of pervasive markings on the city streets. For a time, monotone gray squares speckled the colorful walls of the French Quarter and lined the historic avenues throughout the city (see Photo 9.1). If you ever travel to New Orleans, you may see widespread traces of the notorious Gray Ghost on walls of several streets, which remain after the Hurricane Katrina flooding and cleanup.

Even though many residents, business owners, and politicians commended Radtke's efforts, including former President Bill Clinton and former Mayor Marc Morial ("N.O. Man," 2002), some citizens were upset about the approach to the graffiti problem, contending that the "Band-Aid solution of one fanatical volunteer" actually accelerated the rate of graffiti instead of decreasing it" ("Gray Paint," 2000). In addition, scholars on cultures of graffiti argue that youth cultures create new spaces of pleasure by evading the authority's efforts to suppress their activities (Ferrell, 1997). For example, stencils depicting a portrait and the words, "I LOVE FRED," began appearing on the streets in direct response to the eradication efforts (see Photo 9.2).

Even more, cultural responses to Radtke also emerged on the streets of New Orleans in the form of political stickers posted on stop signs that read, "Fred Radtke: Stop the Gray Ghost." These glossy stickers revealed direct resistance to the name of the symbolic authority in both its forms, real and fictitious; a subject who is silencing expressions on the street with a bucket of gray paint and producing an acceleration of political action and agitation.

Despite the efforts to eradicate graffiti through intensified civic and (il)legal avenues of social control, these fascinating examples of symbolic exchanges on the street reveal the productive as well as repressive nature of policing subcultural practices. Policing of cultural activity is potentially

Photo 9.2   I LOVE FRED on Baronne Street.

productive in the sense that it opens up possibilities for new forms of discourse and new displays of cultural and political resistance.

Adding to discussions on the nature of power, Foucault (1977/1980) posits,

> There are no relations of power without resistances; the latter are all the more real and effective because they are formed right at the point where relations of power are exercised; resistance to power does not have to come from elsewhere to be real, nor is it inexorably frustrated through being the compatriot of power. It exists all the more by being in the same place as power; hence, like power, resistance is multiple and can be integrated in global strategies. (p. 142)

I use Foucault's words alongside the whole complex of mediated social interactions between the Gray Ghost and artist-activists, progressives, and revolutionaries in New Orleans as a point of departure to develop a notion of visual resistance that can be integrated into discussions of sociocultural agitations and relations of power. In this sense, policing graffiti is not a unidirectional display of power that is independent of forms of resistance. Instead, the examples provided here demonstrate how relations of power and resistance tend to operate and circulate through the streets in an endless cycle of markings and cover-ups. In this chapter, I use visual and ethnographic methods to document and discuss various exchanges on the streets of New Orleans between 2001 and 2004. This research explores the mediated dialogues that exhibit the intersection between power and resistance and, ultimately, the productive nature of social control. In what I will call visual resistance strategies, the artist-activists transform the street space into an alternative cultural space for political dissent and engage in conversations on the street with other activists and also with structures of power and authority. Through visual resistance strategies, activists engage in a conversation of signs in an innovative and radical pursuit of democratic participation in cultural areas saturated with discursive power.

Research Goals and Methodology

I have been car-free for several years, and this entire research project was conducted while traveling the streets of New Orleans by bicycle. This urban mobility accomplished with two wheels enabled new ways of seeing the city and, by extension, new ways of knowing the social world. This method of travel enabled a way of experiencing a city by moving through it. It was in this movement-oriented experience that I first encountered the strangely intriguing images on the walls of Baronne Street in New Orleans' central business district. Luckily, on that day I had my camera in my bag.

Amazed by the complex political commentary and extraordinary detail of the visuals, my first impulse was to document and preserve the images as I saw them on that day. I was motivated by an overwhelming suspicion that the images and messages would undoubtedly be covered or removed in the immediate future. Because of the political content of the messages and the city's zero tolerance policy on graffiti, which treats these artistic and political expressions as criminal practices, the visual sentiments I observed were vulnerable to being erased.

So I pulled out my camera and photographed the political graffiti, moving between long shots to capture the breadth of the image and close-ups to capture the details. By photographing the images, I fixed what might otherwise be fleeting phenomena: cultural products weathered by exposure to the elements or removed by individual or institutional forces. It was only later that I tried to make sense of these fleeting cultural expressions that often reveal the political sentiments of the time and location; some of them are included in this chapter.

At the time, several neighborhoods in New Orleans were experiencing rapid redevelopment through urban renaissance projects. Just a few miles away, a Wal-Mart Superstore was meeting intense opposition by citizens and preservationists as developers tried to secure a space within the historic Lower Garden District. In the area surrounding the proposed building site, artist-activists launched a major canvassing campaign that commented on the negative impacts that an entity like Wal-Mart would have on neighborhood cultures and local economies. In addition to economic shifts in the city, politicians and state officials were launching a campaign for the second war on Iraq. Again, the streets were canvassed with political posters as part of the local anti-war movements.

What began as a small project to document the political images on those blocks turned into a case study of visuals on Barrone Street, and it also led to an exploratory study of political images and the Gray Ghost cover-ups in several other New Orleans neighborhoods. Shortly after developing this first roll of film, I became much more attuned to similar markings throughout the city. As I passed by on the street, I noticed that in some places, the markings were removed completely, and in others, the markings were transformed almost daily.

I began seeking out graffiti on public streets and creating an archive of poster art and political images, as well as the monotone gray squares indicating the Gray Ghost's eradicating efforts—an archive that now is composed of hundreds of images. I used 35 mm and digital photography as the method of data collection. Because of my method of travel, the amount of research equipment I could carry was limited to the space available in my bag. This constraint usually meant that I traveled with only one camera at a time, but on rare occasions, I carried multiple cameras. Because of the ephemeral nature of the data, I used whichever camera was with me at the time. In the event that I did not have a camera with me, I noted the location in notebooks, on scrap paper, even on my own skin, and I returned as soon as possible to document the images. If I was far from home and without a camera when I came across the markings, I would go as far as finding a local drugstore to purchase a disposable camera.

Most of the time, the images were still there when I returned. However, on several occasions, the posters had been ripped down or the markings painted over between the time I first saw them and the time I returned with a camera. In the most extreme case, I saw a street-level billboard that had been transformed with several layers of mounted posters. This cultural practice, often referred to as *culture jamming,* is well documented by Naomi Klein (2000). I rode to my home less than a mile and a half away to retrieve my camera and returned within half an hour. To my surprise, the images were covered by a new billboard advertisement. The glue was still wet and running down the wall when I arrived. I include this narrative description to highlight the fleeting nature of this cultural resistance.

Because of the speed and portability of the camera, I find photography to be the most useful form of collecting these cultural artifacts because it enables me to document the expressions and transgressions before they disappear. The research instruments consisted of 35 mm and digital cameras, and my own interpretive experiences of the settings were documented in fieldnotes and memos. Using my access to a university darkroom, I printed the images myself to stay as close as possible to the images. However, because of issues of economy, several of the images were machine printed at a local lab or left in digital form. After completing my university degree and subsequently relinquishing my darkroom access, I had all other images machine printed. I noticed differences in the individual photographs based on the type of film and camera used. I lost rich colors when I shot in black and white, and I would often return to the field setting with different cameras and film to capture those differences.

Throughout the analysis of visual resistance, I arranged the content of various political slogans, images, and texts in much the same way as a literary scholar might study genres. Through this sorting practice, I searched for themes within the content, topical areas, style, and authorship. In addition to focusing on content, I focused on forms, practices, and techniques employed in the execution of the sign in the resistance movements. While interpreting the photographs of visual resistance practices, I also contextualized the work by noting the surrounding cultural and geographic spaces in which the agitations occurred while historicizing the images and texts within sociopolitical climates.

Anonymous postings, illegible scribbles, and nameless graphics on street surfaces pose several methodological considerations that make studying these transgressive practices both challenging and exciting. The interactions among those in resistance subcultures, as well as their interactions with structures of authority, are often invisible (Ferrell, 1996). I describe a few dimensions that characterize a political subculture of artist-activists employing these practices by means of describing the messages left visible. In other words, the conversations and social interactions taking place on the street are often mediated; the dialogue is stretched out over time and space, and it takes place through the symbols, markings, and images left on the surfaces.

Rather than focusing solely on human subjects, this research employs an ethnography of images, as illustrated in cultural criminology studies of urban graffiti subcultures (Ferrell, 1996, 1999). Using photography along with fieldnotes to describe and contextualize research settings, Jeff Ferrell explores *intertexual dynamics* and subcultural styles, codes, and shared meanings through an examination of freight train graffiti. Ferrell (1996) writes, "In just two years of research I have photographed many hundred examples of such graffiti throughout the western and midwestern United States, and watched as fast-moving trains have carried many thousands more beyond my photographic reach" (p. 238). Using visual data and ethnographic descriptions, Ferrell's work highlights the local production of many graffiti images but situates them within a *context of dislocation,* in which the images are constantly shifting in relation to other images. Drawing heavily on postmodern and anarchist theoretical assumptions, Ferrell's (1996) work engages the playful mobility of the freight train graffiti, which "capture[s] particular patterns of meaning and style, but in doing so follow[s] no set temporal or geographic order" (p. 240).

Once again, moving away from direct fieldwork with human subjects to the mediated symbolic exchange, researchers can use the visual method to understand social relationships discursively through an *ethnography of images.* Consistent with a grounded theory method and the process of open coding (Glaser & Strauss, 1967; Strauss & Corbin, 1998), where data collection and analysis occur simultaneously, my first theoretical orientations emerged from the initial data. The visual resistance confronts political issues that could be organized under a variety of categories and concepts. I initially organized the images under a geographic schema divided into local issues, regional issues, and global issues. As I continued with this exploratory and interpretive project, I found that this thematic categorization was inadequate because the discrete categories mask the interrelationship and movement between the themes. Even more, the artist-activists blur these spatialized boundaries of classification when the signs of visual resistance are absorbed into the digital arena. Through the interplay between high technology and low technology communication, local issues become global issues, global issues become localized, and regional boundaries collapse and expand into both local and global categories of analysis. Finally, I conclude this chapter by discussing how visual research has the potential to disrupt the disciplinary boundaries of mainstream sociological knowledge production and how this research itself is a form of visual resistance against structures of disciplinary boundaries. More specifically, in light of the focus of this edited collection, I will demonstrate the utility of visual research methods in understanding parts of everyday life by fixing fleeting moments and mediated interactions to reveal deep social and structural arrangements.

Developing a Concept of Visual Resistance

From the beginning of this project, I searched for language to describe the complex phenomena without drawing on terms that invoked a moral evaluation of the practice as inherently problematic. This process proved to be extraordinarily difficult. As I sifted through images, I tried to make sense of these cultural expressions using the term *graffiti*. But as I continued to study these expressions, and also during conversations with many others about this project, I began to see how the term graffiti is problematic. Despite research that shows the productive effects of graffiti subcultures for creating relationships and identities among practitioners through shared values and understandings of style, graffiti itself has a long history of being understood as deviant and criminal (Ferrell, 1995). Choosing to label these works as graffiti risks trivializing the complicated relationships that exist between criminal/state, victim/offender, and public/private, thus reducing subjects of study to relationships of binary opposites and masking the ways in which these terms are often mutually supportive, codependent, and contingent.

After discarding the use of *graffiti* as a working definition for studying these expressions, I tried to employ the term *street art*. Street art has a more positive connotation and seems more likely to get an approving nod than the practice of graffiti. However, I now find the phrase problematic as well because it seems to aestheticize these actions and political expressions, when the phrase might be better reserved for legitimized artistic expressions such as community murals or city-sponsored artwork. The content on Baronne Street is uneasy, politicized, disrupting. The act itself can be understood as a violent form of resistance against legitimate spatial relations. It is here that I found the phrase *visual resistance* more useful than either the term *graffiti* or the term *street art*.

In using the phrase *visual resistance*, I seek to move beyond discussions of the criminalized practice of graffiti, which is often associated with deviance and delinquency and thus is rigorously policed by the state, community activists, and neighborhood associations. Instead, I look at the discursive functions of practices of visual resistance at the very sites where power exists.

Visual resistance seems to speak to the spirit of these expressions on the street, both in the content of the messages and in the acts of transforming and challenging the meanings of the street spaces within relations of power. I use the term to express any human transformation of a surface, such as written or sprayed graffiti, painting, line drawings, stickers, T-shirts, cartoons, stencils, and mounted posters. This is not meant to be an all-inclusive list of visual resistance expressions. Rather, I provide these examples to show a few of the many possible resistance techniques that are not included in a more narrow definition such as *street art* or *political graffiti* and that emerge within relations of power. Future research can locate other forms of visual resistance in places and relations where the visual is used as a disciplinary technique of social control.

Visual resistance is situated at the intersection between the action as a cultural practice of disseminating expressions of dissent; the resulting cultural, material, and symbolic products; and the efforts to police these practices. In other words, visual resistance exists in the milieu of institutional and individual power and social control. Even though the visual resistance may have been displayed on private property, I use the term *public space* because anyone on a public street has visual access to the expression. Unlike political commentary that enters museums or private galleries, visual resistance on public streets sidesteps certain cultural gatekeepers, such as curators or gallery owners, who often regulate the distribution of other artistic expressions.

The regulation of visual resistance as an illegitimate and illegal practice functions within the cultural boundaries of deviance and the legal definitions of state intervention. As stated in other research, graffiti as a cultural practice is often considered a criminal practice, most often by structures of authority that criminalize alternative spaces to perpetuate systems of domination and to maintain mainstream cultural boundaries (Ferrell, 1997). In other words, because of the cultural dimension of these political, social, and identity-based expressions, I will continually refer to these techniques of communication as *resistance* rather than *art* or *crime,* although I recognize the act of vandalism involved. It may be true that resisters thrive under conditions of intense surveillance and social control and that the whole apparatus of state intervention may intensify the practices described here. However, proposing new language to describe the practices at the level of discourse undermines the state's power in criminalizing the cultural practices by showing that it is precisely at the moments of exerting control that these visual resisters thrive.

In the spirit of Ferrell, I assert that visual resistance in the city actually contributes to the production of new spaces, as well as new cultural meanings and social interactions, through the transformation of surfaces often assumed as static. Not only is visual resistance a marking of space, it is a marking *against* certain spatial relations. In this sense, visual resistance is functional in several ways. The resistance occurs in both the form and content of the message itself, challenging explicitly a variety of social-political powers and legal structures.

Drawing on interpretive traditions, visual resistance also functions at the cultural level by disrupting, negotiating, challenging, and contesting any stable meanings and understandings of the city street. We often see architecture as just buildings, and although we often view these walls simply as structural constraints, visual resistance encourages us to recognize the interpretive process involved in our understanding of the city streets and the extent to which we reinforce these understandings of space in everyday life. When the wall becomes a text that must be read and then interpreted, the meaning of the surface is continuously (re)constructed and maintained. Thus, our efforts to understand the relationship between (criminalized) social actors, structures of power, and their relationships to the street must take into account how the meanings are changed, challenged, reinforced, and negotiated through a process of interpretation.

Before moving into the specific ways in which visual resistance functions in this case, a discussion of the preliminary theoretical orientations will help ground my argument.

Cultural/Interactionist Criminology

The artist-activist, operating as an individual or as part of a collective, can use the street as a canvas, a forum, and a tool for social change. As mentioned earlier, because of the cultural dimension to these political, social, and identity-based expressions, I will continually refer to these techniques of communication as resistance in the company of power, rather than as art or crime. Like cultural practices such as street art and graffiti, visual resistance is often considered a criminal practice, most often by structures of authority that criminalize alternative spaces to perpetuate systems of domination and maintain mainstream boundaries (Ferrell, 1997). The regulation of visual resistance as an illegitimate and illegal practice is a function that falls within the cultural boundaries of deviance and the legal definitions of state intervention. Just as deviance is a characteristic conferred on a behavior rather than a property inherent to the behavior (Erikson, 1966), crime is a function of the state and as a result, the "criminality of crime is defined by law" (Black, 1983, p. 42).

Many scholars have been engaging in this conversation in the area of cultural criminology. In developing a *cultural criminology,* Jeff Ferrell and Clinton Sanders (1995) demonstrate that

> shared symbolism and mediated meaning, subcultural style and collective imagery, define the nature of crime, criminality, and social control not only for criminals engaged in the daily enterprise of criminality but for everyone caught up in the larger social process of constructing and perceiving crime and control. (p. 298)

I find this conversation in criminology useful because visual resistance, as an artistic/political/cultural practice, uses symbolism and mediated meaning in a consistent, patterned style as a way to resist social control (Manning, 1999a). I agree with Ferrell (1997) when he argues that in the production of new cultural spaces, perception, meaning, and identity are constructed within relationships of power, inequality, and marginalization. Thus, I argue that those engaged in visual resistance tend to produce cultural spaces as they reclaim the city surface by disrupting the institutionalized avenues of political expression and by contesting formally prescribed understandings of the street.

Lyman Chaffee From Street Art and Political Protest

Understanding the fleeting visual communications on Barrone Street requires more than a redefinition of criminality. It also requires analysis of the visual media. Despite the varied approaches to resistance on the street surfaces and the construction of the activist as criminal, the visual in this public space does, indeed, function within several defining characteristics of public imagery. Lyman Chaffee (1993, p. 8) writes extensively on alternative communication and political propaganda and characterizes street art with five key features: collectivity, politicization, democratic competition, direct expressiveness, and adaptability. First, he suggests that street art is a primarily collective process, by which groups formulate political agendas and use the visual space to convey shared sentiments and confront social problems. The second characteristic of street art, according to Chaffee, is the nonneutral politicized medium. It serves as a forum for advocacy, usually from the marginalized, that discards any notions of objectivity. As the third feature, Chaffee recognizes the competitive, nonmonopolistic, democratic character of street art and defines the fourth characteristic of street art as direct expressive thought as seen in the powerfully simple words, symbols, and images. Extensive essays are not written on the walls. The messages are succinct, direct, and efficient, often condensed to a single word, slogan, symbol, or image. Finally, Chaffee suggests that street art is a highly adaptable medium, varying in relation to the changing political and social conditions. These five characteristics of street art, as defined by Chaffee, can be seen in the visual resistance that I have categorized under local issues, regional issues, and global issues.

Discussion of the Visual Data

Visual resistance carves out alternative spaces. I started this project by documenting the artist-activists' transformation of a public street space into a highly visible, yet socially contested site for visual resistance. Located between the historic French Quarter and the Central City neighborhood, the 300 to 600 block of Baronne Street in the Central Business District of New Orleans provided a site of rich visual data because the artist-activists marked the boarded windows of several vacant buildings with sophisticated political commentary, localized commentary, and critical dissent through ephemeral artwork. Together, symbols, slogans, posters, and written words confront numerous social issues, including some issues unique to the region and still others unique to New Orleans specifically. In this section, I present selections from the images collected on Baronne Street and organize the discussion under the categories of local, regional, and global issues presented in the images.

The visual resistance on Baronne Street employs several artistic communication techniques, including painting, written and sprayed graffiti, and mass-produced posters. At the immediately local position on Baronne Street, the artist/activists use satirical cartoons and visual symbols of affluence and

Photo 9.3   Questioning development on Baronne Street.

materialism to mock the potential commercialization of the urban space. The line-drawn figures, almost life size, are highly visible from the street. The markings on the wall—short and succinct slogans—convey the many possibilities for the vacant space's development: a gourmet grocery, bakery, coffee shop, or trendy European fashion store (see Photo 9.3).

Through a surface read of the images and texts, symbolic inferences can be drawn from the simple, yet powerful life-size cartoons. Even more, a closer inspection of the multiple layers may reveal the presence of an ongoing cultural conversation between those who have come in direct contact with the visual commentary. The artist-activist's depiction of the economic possibilities for the space's transformation confronts the complex issue of capitalist production and consumption, exhibited by the symbolic sparkling shoes, the array of baked goods, ingestion of coffee products, and the related transformation of this local urban neighborhood by a new professional class.

Another marking uses the words *homeless shelter* along with the unofficial symbol of the international squatter's movement. Efforts were made to cover up this addition, but the comments remained legible through the paint. These layers indicate that even though the artists promote a radical, progressive critique of the possible development of the space, there are some boundaries formed and maintained in satirical celebrations of the

Photo 9.4   Bad musician on Baronne Street.

detrimental effects of gentrification. Perhaps the idea of including a home-less shelter at this site did not support the satirical celebration associated with the invasion of young professionals and thus, warranted a cover-up to maintain a coherent visual message. If, indeed, the addition of the words *homeless shelter* is either too literal to fit within the satirical critique or too liberal in that it may not promote a radical overturning of the existing system, the cover-up indicates that artist-activists are also implicated in methods of social control, in efforts to close the conversation on the street. This also exhibits how power is multidimensional and dispersed in frag-mented ways, even in displays of oppositional politics. Again, visual resis-tance inhabits territories that are pluralistic, fragmentary, and in some ways contradictory.

In several places, the artist-activists invoke the term *yuppie* to describe the figures presented in the artwork (see Photo 9.4). One life-size, line-drawn figure depicts a musician playing a guitar for an imagined yuppie audience. In Photo 9.4, the figure speaks through a text-bubble written on the ply-wood, which reads, "I'm a shitty musician who wants to pimp my music to tone deaf yuppies."

The invocation of the term *yuppie*—juxtaposed with posters that warn of the gentrification of the neighborhood, stating, "their plans don't include you. TEAR IT DOWN + START OVER"—alludes to the class-based

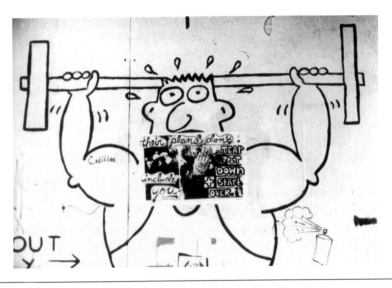

Photo 9.5   Workout Willy on Baronne Street.

politics and processes embedded in the transformation of urban centers, which may disproportionately affect marginalized groups (see Photo 9.5). Similarly, the detail of a Cadillac tattoo on the arms of a line-drawn body builder acknowledges the issues of materialism resulting in class struggles, meaning the conflict between residents who own status-symbol automobiles and those who do not.

Indeed, the body builder's figure represents the human body as a material commodity, not only the achieved status of an ideal masculine body but also the perception of a socially desirable good. The tattoo on the body parallels the marking of bodily space, like the visual markings on the wall.

Although much of the content of these images focuses on the material realities of class conflicts, the presentation draws heavily on the symbolic meanings. Mark Taylor (1997) associates the proliferation of media images with the human derma: "This explosion of images implodes on the surface of civilization and skin of our bodies. We are all tattooed by the media whose creation we have become" (p. 143). Taylor's critique focuses on the superficiality of surfaces and the disappearance of meaning beneath the surface in an examination of tattoos and dermagraphics. The ornamentation of the body and the wall, through tattoos and visual resistance, respectively, marks an association between the visual, media, and identity in a way that is skin/surface deep. The superficiality points to the importance of the symbolic dimensions of visual resistance strategies as discursive representations of social problems that are constructed through text and visual arguments. To some degree, the visual resisters are also implicated in the very processes that are critiqued in their messages, and this points to the paradox of their work. Following a postmodern politic, visual resistance is often contradictory. Drawing on existing symbols of material success—for example, the Cadillac—also reproduces the existing strength of the name within branding cultures. Unlike examples of culture jamming, which force corporate messages and advertising to work against themselves, the artists described here are caught in a circular system of strengthening corporate culture. It is no wonder some authors have argued about the "death of urban graffiti," as graffiti advertisements capitalize on the cultural practice of marking urban spaces for marketing purposes (Alvelos, 2004). Even more, the visual resisters may also be participating in an invasion of space themselves through the marking of visual territories, a process they critiqued as problematic for groups with more social mobility or cultural capital like the so-called yuppie class.

That said, these images of visual resistance confront issues both symbolically and materially and require an analysis that takes both into account. Manuel Castells (1977, p. 460), on the other hand, argues that *collective consumption* in advanced capitalism is the base of urban struggles, rather than a struggle over signs and signification. The artists confront the commodification of space by satirically questioning the prospective transformation of that specific abandoned space within the larger context of urban political/economic/spatial conflicts. The artists display the notion of the urban struggle base in a way that directly addresses the perceived and real disadvantages of a consumer society in late capitalism. Class conflict is embedded in this specific series of visual resistance examples. Even more, visual resistance is embedded in class conflict.

In addition to the drawn figures, the mass-produced posters also raise the issue of neighborhood fragmentation with the words, "Their plans don't include you. TEAR IT DOWN + START OVER," representing the larger conflict between those who benefit from urban renewal and those who are exploited and displaced by it. Another poster effectively gauges political sentiments with the title, "WARNING! *THIS* NEIGHBORHOOD IS BEING GENTRIFIED!". While this space was vacant and has still not been fully redeveloped,[1] the visual resistance symbolically marked the space as representative of the common spaces affected by urban renaissance projects and private investment, disinvestments, and profiteering when capital makes its return to older, redeveloping neighborhoods. Yet again, the art on Baronne Street confronts class struggles, this time in architectural and real estate consumption.

Unlike community murals, which are often legitimated through state sponsorship and planning, the techniques of visual resistance such as the mounting of mass-produced posters and of tagging written or sprayed graffiti have a temporary function in the public street space. This alternative form of communication also creates an open avenue for visual political thought outside of conventional, corporate-owned media. It is argued that conglomerating, for-profit media institutions, by pursuing their interests and agendas within closed commercial spaces, threaten democratic debate (Kellner, 1992). Thus, to challenge this media monopoly, "democracy demands an active participation and this can only be achieved today with renewed cultural activism" (Wallis, 1990, p. 10). Engagement and participation in political systems can take many forms—and visual resistance strategies are just a few—possibly to embrace the idea of cultural activism in the pursuit of democracy through creative cultural agitation. Using posters printed in large numbers, the artist-activist can paper community surfaces overnight, quickly and efficiently spreading a political opinion over a wide geographical area, thus participating in public debate and grassroots political activity. Although the corporate media promote government and military policies and contribute to the current "crisis of democracy" that disrupts the balance of power (Kellner, 1992, p. 45), it has be stated that "street art breaks the conspiracy of silence" (Chaffee, 1993, p. 4). Visual resistance, like independent and pirate media projects, becomes a source of agitation against centralized forms of power and sources of information, diffusing both power and resistance in microlevel transgressions.

Because artists use culturally available symbols to promote certain agendas and, in executing these symbols in different social/spatial contexts, manage to create new cultural spaces, it is also necessary to locate the significance of the sign in the urban environment. French theorist Jean Baudrillard (1976/1993) observes the power of symbols in the urban system in his study of the relationships between community murals, political art, and street graffiti in New York City during the 1970s. No longer the site of mass industrial production, the city has shifted from being the site of economic power to being a space of sign and code production, he argues. For Baudrillard, it is the "terrorist power of the media, signs, and dominant culture" (p. 76) that constitutes the new intervention in the city. Using the influx of graffiti in New York City for his arguments, he compares the symbolic meanings of politically significant community murals with the violent act of graffiti. He suggests that graffiti messages, in their claims to space with pseudonyms, are essentially *empty signifiers* because they reject any proper names and reference. In many ways, graffiti artists mark territory and make personal claims to space, including the vast transit systems, which put the appropriated spaces in motion.

I argue that the Baronne Street series falls somewhere between community murals, which focus on political issues, and graffiti, which functions only as an empty signifier. Visual resistance is more offensive and challenging than community murals; thus, this visual communication is not widely accepted as legitimate use/discourse/symbolism in the public domain. Consequently, visual resistance disrupts conservative and traditional spatial relations. The signs are unpredictable and radical, interrogating and challenging the common functions of the street surface. Yet, because there is a definite political message within the Baronne Street series, I suggest that it is not as empty as the graffiti in New York City that Baudrillard labeled *terrorist* in their complete dismissal of formal spatial relations. In any case, visual resistance continues to construct the spatial relationships by disrupting, challenging, and negotiating the meanings of the surface on the public street.

Like Baudrillard, W. J. T. Mitchell (1990, p. 37) also locates violence within the image and the sign in a discussion of the violent dimensions of public art. Mitchell distinguishes three forms of violence in public art: the image as *act, weapon,* and *representation.* First, the image is a violent occurrence in the act/event of vandalism or defacement. Next, the image is a weapon in that it can be used as an instrument to incite or coerce the public to react. Finally, the image is representation of violence in its reference to historical events or individual experiences.

The Baronne Street series exhibits all three forms of violence described by Mitchell. To begin with, the act of violence first occurred in the event of defacing the clean surface. Then, because of its political content, the series incited a reaction in the audience, in the form of yet another act of violence in the counterattack. This develops into an ongoing, violent street dialogue in which the original work was rejected by another street commentator.

Completing Mitchell's triad of violence, the representation of violence is one of self-infliction on behalf of the represented working-class figure (see Photo 9.6). The political cartoon depicts a figure with crossed-out eyes drinking from a bottle marked "XXX," inferring the ingestion of poison or at least alcohol. The 8.5 x 11-inch poster inside the figure's mouth reads, "They operate without you, but their decisions effect you *(sic).*" The visual representation of the alienated, suicidal worker is accompanied with the words, "The robos after 2 hours on day crew (damn its hot)." The combination of the exhausted worker with the satirical comment about the duration of the workday suggests that the figure, dehydrated from the heat, knowingly (and possibly in an act of suicide) turns to alcohol or a poison at the end of a long shift of mindless, alienating work in advanced capitalist societies.

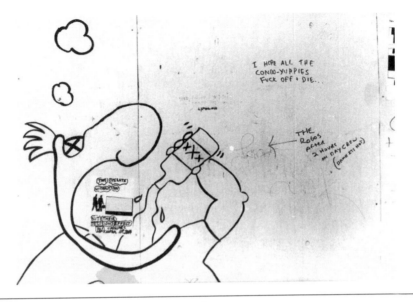

Photo 9.6   Self-medicating on Baronne Street.

Visual resistance cannot be discussed without making an attribution to the artist. In terms of authorship, the Baronne Street artwork is not attributed to an individual actor because it lacks any identifiable markings such as an initial or a signature. However, it appears that a local anarchist group sponsored this work (see Photo 9.7), illustrating Chaffee's idea that street art is a collective process; the linkage is indicated by a poster with the words, "Anarchist Art Attack: Long Live the Spirit to Fight Back," and by a URL to the website. The website makes no reference to the graffiti on Baronne Street, but for an observer curious about the artists' political stance, the site clearly gives reference to anti-establishment, anti-capitalist, anti-corporate sentiments. The URL posted in the vicinity of the Baronne Street graffiti series marks the connection between use of links in street space and community organizing within alternative art spaces.

Creating Borders and Crossing Boundaries: Colonialism and the Louisiana Purchase

While violent street dialogue/visual resistance is localized through development policies, the rhetoric claims additional authority by tapping into issues of a different scale that affect regional, national, and global issues. Next, I step out of the local block issues and see how the street surface is also used

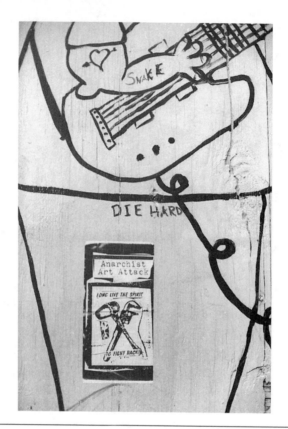

Photo 9.7   Anarchist art attack: Long live the spirit to fight back on Baronne Street.

to confront both regional and national issues. For instance, 2003 marked the 200-year anniversary of the signing of the Louisiana Purchase. Many individuals and organizations in the New Orleans area were promoting the Louisiana Purchase bicentennial celebration with items such as license plate holders, highway signs, U.S. currency, and postage stamps that commemorate the event. In addition to such novelty items, President Bush, President Jacques Chirac of France, and King Juan Carlos of Spain were invited to visit the reenactment of the signing of the largest real-estate purchase in history, which was scheduled in December 2003. The New Orleans Botanical Gardens hosted a show titled, "Plants of the Louisiana Purchase," and the zoo in Monroe, Louisiana, featured an exhibition called, "Animals of the Louisiana Purchase."

But against the institutionalized fervor of state celebrations, bicentennial conferences, and exhibitions at local museums, the Barrone Street space in

Photo 9.8   How will you expose Louisiana's purchased 200 years of sin and suffering? On Baronne Street.

New Orleans provided a public counteropinion outside of formal ideological systems in the form of a political poster stating, "How Will You Expose Louisiana's Purchased 200 Years of Sin and Suffering: forced migrations, mob violence, genocide, environmental shambles" (see Photo 9.8). The artist uses the street to vent political thoughts that might not enter the region's mainstream media, which remains increasingly inaccessible to the public thanks to efforts by both hegemonic corporate conglomerates and its corresponding political affiliations. In this way, visual resistance practitioners present oppositional views to political and social constructions of history and boundary formation. Through these methods, resistance groups attempt to inform the public about significant community issues.

The anonymous artist's local posting of the Louisiana Purchase poster in New Orleans is part of a larger international posting in Hungary, Italy, and France, which was documented photographically and then displayed more traditionally in an exhibition titled, "The Louisiana Purchase Dismantled: Re-visions of our History," at the Zeitgeist Multi-Disciplinary Art Center located in the Central City neighborhood of New Orleans in April and May 2003. Even in the gallery exhibition, the artist chose to remain anonymous. In this way, visual resistance in form and content presents critical views of boundary formation and the social constructions of geographic borders of the nation-state and allows these critical views on colonialism to reach the public as issues for conversation.

Photo 9.9   No more prisons on St. Charles Avenue.

About the same time, another slew of messages appeared on the streets of New Orleans that confronted issues related to the American South. In the week prior to the Critical Resistance South Regional Conference held April 4 through 6, 2003, "No More Prisons" slogans were written on surfaces on several major thoroughfares, including S. Claiborne Avenue and even the famous St. Charles Avenue (see Photo 9.9). Critical Resistance, a national grassroots movement trying to abolish the prison industrial complex, maintains that prisons do not make communities safer by putting people behind bars.[2] The local visual protest on public streets echoes the broader message of the regional conference.

Visualizing the Localized Global Anti-War Movement: War Keeps Kids off the Streets

The complicated struggles on the streets surrounding the "no more prisons" slogans centered around the idea of controlling the city's surplus population in capitalist economies. The relevance of the idea of surplus populations ranges from regional issues like the prison industrial complex to global issues such as war. The streets became testament to local anti-war sentiments. Another poster posted on Barrone Street reads, "War keeps kids off the

Photo 9.10   War keeps kids off the streets on Baronne Street.

streets." This mounted poster (see Photo 9.10) appeared on the streets of New Orleans during the first weeks of the second Gulf War in the spring of 2003; gravestones accompany the text. In keeping with the theme of localizing global sentiments, Photo 9.11 shows a gray square painted on the metal of an electrical box on Baronne Street. To the left of the Gray Ghost markings, a poster is mounted questioning Operation Iraqi Freedom through an image of a youth injured in the conflict.

Both ends of the (horizontal) political spectrum use the street as a propagandistic tool, especially when the subject is world affairs. The grassroots techniques developed historically by the opposition and the political left have been employed in return by the political right, embracing the tactics to show grassroots support for conservative sentiments. For example, a popular and timely slogan for the anti-war movement, "No War on Iraq," was stenciled in various locations around New Orleans, and supporters of the war responded by painting over the *No* to use the street space as a venue for advocating war. And so, the street dialogues continue.

While the local newspapers downplayed anti-war efforts in New Orleans, the streets became testament to the local sentiments of activists on both sides of the political spectrum. These efforts may not be covered in the commercial media, but the artist forced the political commentary into the realm of everyday life, not in the media or organized protest, but through navigational spaces through the city. Stop signs in high-traffic areas were stenciled

Photo 9.11   Operation Iraqi Freedom? And a Gray Ghost cover-up on Baronne Street.

with *WAR* or *Bush* under the word *STOP:* STOP WAR and STOP Bush. Even Do Not Enter signs were transformed into political street signs: Do Not Enter *Iraq.* Yet, within days, supporters of the war responded by covering the additions with paint or otherwise countering the original marking on the surface.

Unlike community murals, political graffiti emerges and disappears almost overnight. The cases on Baronne Street presented here illustrate an ongoing political conversation between resistance groups and authorities or individuals that seek to cover up these expressions. Thus, over time, the exchange of ideas in the street space exhibits the competitive and sometimes playful nature of street dialogue.

The above sample of images from urban visual resistance focuses on the three emergent themes: local issues, regional issues, and global issues. The local issues were gentrification and class conflict on Baronne Street in the Central Business District in New Orleans. At the regional level, the visual resistance looked at the construction of boundary formation in the Louisiana Purchase and was critical of celebrations that mask colonialism and genocide. Another regional concern was the growing prison industry in the southern United States. At the global level, the art focused on issues like capitalism and war. Even though all of these images appeared on Baronne Street as decipherable claims about local, regional, or global concerns, these themes unavoidably recur and overlap on each other. Corporations are both local and global, the Louisiana Purchase is a regional issue taken up globally in the exhibit, and war and lo-tech resistance make global policy local.

As I continued to collect these images of visual resistance in urban social movements, another theme emerged from the data in addition to the local, regional, and global issues. This fourth pattern was the inclusion of links to online resources in the form of posting a URL on the street along with the political graffiti. I have seen these URL links in three different forms: (1) alongside the political message, (2) incorporated into the mass-produced poster, and (3) posted by itself, a type of floating URL. The use of the URL posted as a form of resistance is significant because it uses the same resistance techniques as the other visual resistance, and more important, it changes the extent to which the sentiments are bound to that specific location. That is, the boundaries of local, regional, and global issues must now continuously be redefined as the messages make their way into electronic and hyper-communities. What first seems a local issue can become global, and what appears global can become local.

For those who are interested in the messages in the political graffiti, the URL serves as a link to more resources that may contain similar political sentiments. In this way, the political graffiti serves not only as social/political commentary but also as a possible recruitment tool to mobilize people with shared political leanings; visual resistance becomes a resource for community organization and group mobilization. It is no surprise that these efforts incorporate new technologies into methods of low-technology communication to draw support for grassroots movements. Jesse Drew (1995) proposes,

> A popular movement for social change must take advantage of the new technologies to further democratize the nation and to empower the disenfranchised. It is not the technology that will revolutionize society, but a movement of millions that must transform society. (p. 83)

Conclusion

Vito Acconci (1990) notes the advantageousness of public art in the city, especially for marginalized groups working against ideological hegemony. He writes,

> The built environment is built because it's been allowed to be built. It's been allowed to be built because it stands for and reflects an institution or dominant culture. Public art comes through the back door like a second-class citizen. Instead of bemoaning this, public art can use this marginal position to its

advantage: public art can present itself as the voice of the marginal cultures, as the minority report, as the opposition party. Public art exists to thicken the plot. (p. 179)

Visual resistance shows artist-activists engaging in an ongoing political dialogue with other activists and with state authorities. Visual resistance is a primarily collective process, as well as an interpretive process, involving the constant negotiation of style, meaning, and space in everyday criminality, authority, power, and resistance. In this competitive exchange for political visibility, the street becomes a battleground of words, signs, representations, and the effort to enforce the cover-up.

Consequently, it is easier for artist-activists to gain power by creating new symbolic images and new cultural spaces than it is to enter the restricted organizations, institutions, bureaucracies, and political structures (Dubin, 1992) that use authority to close or fix the meanings of symbolic representations (Hall, 1997). Hence, artist-activists compete for space and political visibility in a subversive fashion by using these visual resistance techniques. In doing so, visual resistance practitioners reject the closed media circuits, reclaim the public space for the marginalized, and discard the governmental rules of authority identified as state law.

Visual resistance interrogates and challenges the common functions of the street surface. Even more, it integrates technological tools, both high-technology mass communication and low-technology mass communication, into the visual resistance strategies as a possible method of mobilizing social movements. People pass artistic expressions on the street during the course of everyday life and pay no attention to the conflicts that give rise to the behaviors. But complicated relationships exist between the creation of alternative cultural spaces, the affirmation of group beliefs and values, and the conversation between resistance groups, social movements, and structures of authority.

In a moment of self-reflexivity in the picture/knowledge-making process, I see my actions replicate the actions of those engaged in the techniques and strategies of visual resistance (see Photo 9.12). In both cases, these expressions are made within structures of authority and the boundaries of legitimate knowledge production. Many of the cultural artifacts and sentiments that are made on the street go unnoticed. And in the same way that visual resisters contribute to the production of new cultural spaces, those scholars currently engaged in visual research methods, like the contributors to this volume and those who paved the way, are in a sense resisting the dominate modes of knowledge production that saturate Western rational thought. Here, the parallel between visual resistance and a subversive research politics has never appeared so clear.

Photo 9.12   Photograph of author photographing Gray Ghost cover-ups in the French Quarter.

SOURCE: By Jaclyn Reid; used with permission.

The work in visual sociology is visual resistance. Instead of making the discipline's boundaries clearer, visual research is a resistance to the milieu of social researchers who choose not to look at the world. While recognizing the marginalization of the visual relative to the verbal in mainstream social research, the literature in the field of visual sociology suggests that social scientists are paying attention to the role of the visual in social relations and to its potential contributions to the production of scientific knowledge (Becker, 1981, 1982, 1998; Chaplin, 1994; Collier & Collier, 1986; Emmison & Smith, 2000; Fyfe & Law, 1988; Holliday, 2000; Manning, 1999a, 1999b; Prosser, 1998).

Just as visual resistance on the streets forces us to continuously negotiate the meanings attached to street spaces, visual sociology blurs disciplinary boundaries and forces researchers to negotiate the lines around the discipline of sociology, which are constantly managed. Mainstream sociology is now opening its eyes, or at least, it passes this kind of work with increasing interest, like those passing the messages on the street who begin to register them. In this way, visual sociology is an act of resistance, much like visual resistance on the street, which attempts to carve out a space in relation to structures of academic authority and the gatekeepers that maintain the borders of the discipline. Visual resistance, on the street, in academia, and in everyday life, makes visible the conspiracies and pervasiveness of power: the power of those who choose not to look and the privileges created and maintained from a politics of invisibility. It is precisely at these (dis)junctures that scholars of visual cultures can begin to agitate. To paraphrase Acconci's comments on public art, visual resistance and visual sociology exist to thicken the plot.

Notes

1. Following interruptions related to Hurricane Katrina, construction resumed on high-end condo conversions in the Baronne Street building discussed in this chapter.

2. In a similar critique of the prison system in the context of crime and economics, radical criminologist Richard Quinney (1980) suggests that prison systems emerge in capitalist societies as a way of controlling unemployed surplus populations.

Acknowledgments

Earlier versions of the manuscript were presented at the 2004 American Sociological Association Annual Meeting, San Francisco, CA; the 2004 International Visual Sociology Association Annual Meeting, San Francisco, CA; and the 2004 Society for the Study of Symbolic Interaction Couch-Stone Symposium, Vancouver, British Columbia.

I would like to thank Edward J. McCaughan, Greg Stanczak, Anjie Rosga, and Janet Jacobs for their encouragement, challenging comments, and constructive feedback in developing the chapter. However, the positions and expressions in the chapter remain those of the author.

References

Acconci, V. (1990). Public space in private time. In W. J. T. Mitchell (Ed.), *Art and the public sphere*. Chicago: University of Chicago Press.

Alvelos, H. (2004). The desert of imagination in the city of signs: Cultural implications of sponsored transgression and branded graffiti. In J. Ferrell, K. Hayward, W. Morrison, & M. Presdee (Eds.), *Cultural criminology unleashed* (pp. 181–191). London: Glasshouse Press.

Baudrillard, J. (1993). *Symbolic exchange and death* (I. H. Grant, Trans.). Newbury Park, CA: Sage. (Original work published 1976)

Becker, H. (1981). *Exploring society photographically*. Evanston, IL: Northwestern University Press.

Becker, H. (1982). *Art worlds.* Berkeley: University of California Press.

Becker, H. (1998). Visual sociology, documentary photography, and photojournalism: It's (almost) all a matter of context. In J. Prosser (Ed.), *Image-based research.* London: Taylor and Francis.

Black, D. (1983). Crime as social control. *American Sociological Review, 48,* 34–45.

Castells, M. (1977). *The urban question: A Marxist approach* (A. Sheridan, Trans.). Cambridge, MA: MIT Press.

Chaffee, L. (1993). *Political protest and street art: Popular tools for democratization in Hispanic countries.* Westport, CT: Greenwood Press.

Chaplin, E. (1994). *Sociology and visual representation.* New York: Routledge.

Collier, J., Jr., &. Collier, M. (1986). *Visual anthropology: Photography as a research method.* Albuquerque: University of New Mexico Press.

Crusading graffiti-busters join Quarter cleanup team; $100 reward for tip leading to conviction. (2002, December 11). *Times-Picayune,* p. B3.

Drew, J. (1995). Media activism and radical democracy. In J. Brook &. I. Boal (Eds.), *Revisiting the virtual life: The culture and politics of information.* San Francisco: City Lights Books.

Dubin, S. (1992). *Arresting images: Impolitical art and uncivil actions.* London: Routledge.

Emmison, M., & Smith, P. (2000). *Researching the visual: Images, objects, contexts, and interactions in social and cultural inquiry.* Thousand Oaks, CA: Sage.

Erikson, K. (1966). *Wayward Puritans: A study in sociology.* New York: John Wiley.

Ferrell, J. (1995). Style matters: Criminal identity and social control. In J. Ferrell & C. R. Sanders (Eds.), *Cultural criminology* (pp. 169–189). Boston: Northeastern University Press.

Ferrell, J. (1996). *Crimes of style: Urban graffiti and the politics of criminality.* Boston: Northeastern University Press.

Ferrell, J. (1997). Youth, crime, and cultural space. *Social Justice, 24,* 21–38.

Ferrell, J. (1999). Freight train graffiti: Subculture, media, dislocation. In N. Websdale & J. Ferrell (Eds.), *Making trouble: Cultural constructions of crime, deviance, and control.* New York: Aldine de Gruyter.

Ferrell, J., & Sanders, C. R. (1995). *Cultural criminology.* Boston: Northeastern University Press.

Foucault, M. (1980). *Power/knowledge: Selected interviews and other writings 1972–1977* (C. Gordon, Ed.; C. Gordon, L. Marshall, J. Mepham, & K. Soper, Trans.). New York: Pantheon Books. Reprinted from Pouvoirs et strategies, in C. Gordon (Ed.), *Les revoltes logiques,* Volume 4, 1977).

Fyfe, G., & Law, J. (1988). *Picturing power: Visual depictions and social relations.* New York: Routledge.

Glaser, B., & Strauss, A. (1967). *The discovery of grounded theory: Strategies for qualitative research.* New York: Aldine.

Gray paint vs. graffiti. (2000, November 16). *Times-Picayune,* Metro section, p. 6.

Hall, S. (1997). *Representation and the media* (P. S. Jhally, Director). Northhampton, MA: Media Education Foundation.

Holliday, R. (2000). We've all been framed: Visualizing methodology. *The Sociological Review, 48*(4), 503–521.

Kellner, D. (1992). Television, the crisis of democracy, and the Persian Gulf War. In M. Raboy & B. Dagenais (Eds.), *Media, crisis, and democracy: Mass communication and the disruption of social order* (pp. 44–62). Newbury Park, CA: Sage.

Klein, N. (2000). *No logo.* New York: Picador.

Manning, P. (1999a). Reflections: The visual as a mode of social control. In N. Websdale & J. Ferrell (Eds.), *Making trouble: Cultural constructions of crime, deviance, and control.* Hawthorne, NY: Aldine de Gruyter.

Manning, P. (1999b). Semiotics and social justice. In B. A. Arrigo (Ed.), *Social justice/criminal justice* (pp. 131–149). Belmont, CA: West/Wadsworth.

Mitchell, W. J. T. (1990). The violence of public art: Do the right thing. In W. J. T. Mitchell (Ed.), *Art and the public sphere* (pp. 29–48). Chicago: University of Chicago Press.

N.O. man winning drawn-out graffiti war. (2002, August 26). *Times-Picayune,* p. B1.

Pride reflected in war on graffiti; Public's help needed in eradication efforts. (2002, June 23). *Times-Picayune, East New Orleans Picayune Section,* p. 01.

Prosser, J. (1998). The status of image-based research. In J. Prosser (Ed.), *Image-based research: A sourcebook for qualitative researchers* (pp. 1–7). London: Taylor & Francis.

Quinney, R. (1990). *Class, state, and crime.* New York: Longman.

Residents key to clean sweep. (1996, July 1). *Times-Picayune,* p. B4.

Strauss, A., & Corbin, J. (1998). *Basics of qualitative research: Techniques and procedures for developing grounded theory* (2nd ed.). Thousand Oaks, CA: Sage.

Taylor, M. C. (1997). *Hiding.* Chicago: University of Chicago Press.

Wallis, B. (1990). Democracy and cultural activism. In B. Wallis (Ed.), *Democracy: A project by group material* (pp. 5–11). Seattle, WA: Bay Press.

10

Performances, Confessions, and Identities

Using Video Diaries to Research Sexualities

Ruth Holliday

This chapter is based on research carried out between 1998 and 2000, through which I attempted to explore *queer performances* of identity and to investigate the use of video diaries as a research tool and method. In total, 15 video diaries were completed for the project, but this chapter discusses a smaller number. My focus in this chapter is on the ways in which participants constructed the diaries, the methodological problems and issues that were raised in the process, and the kinds of data made available through them. In particular, the project explored how identities are constructed (more or less deliberately) as texts on the surface of bodies, noting that the comfort or discomfort that diarists experienced in their identity work related to the extent to which they felt they were being read with or against authorial intention (see also Holliday, 1999). This issue is further complicated in a largely heterosexist culture structured by "the closet," in which misreading has been developed into a powerful normalizing mechanism. Video diaries have a strong resonance with an emerging *queer methodology*; here, this relates directly to the encoding and decoding of the visual and the body practices in which queer subjects are always actively engaged. Bearing these factors in mind, I will begin by describing the research process and some of the opportunities and drawbacks that video diaries afford.

My initial research problem was to investigate one postmodernist proposition—that individuals make and remake their identities according to the spaces they occupy. Some writers, in arguing against the essential self, have proposed that identities are simply a product of context and are taken up and thrown off *at will*. However, I feel this is a misreading of postmodernism because this approach re-centers the individual's will, positioning the individual as conscious author of his or her own identity. Furthermore, this certainly does not chime with my experiences of queer subcultures, in which there seems to be some attempt to communicate queer identification, however subtly, in whatever space is occupied. As a result, I decided to explore queer identities in three different spaces—*work, rest* (home), and *play* (the scene)—to chart the similarities and differences in identity performances between them. To capture identity performances, it seemed highly appropriate to employ a visual method.

As I began this study, I knew of no other similar research that had used video diaries. Photography had been central to much early sociology, in documenting slum conditions, for instance, but images were largely excluded from academic journals in the early 20th century as they became seen as emotive and subjective. More recently, however, a number of writers have renewed sociological interest in still photography, in looking at experiences of breast cancer, women's art, and homelessness, for example (see Chaplin, 1994; Knowles, 2000; and Spence, 1995; for examples). There has been a long tradition of filmmaking in anthropology as part of the objective recording of "other cultures." The tendency here has been to make the camera less and less visible to its subjects in the hope of capturing natural cultural performances such as tribal dances and village life. An invisible camera is not something that I could realistically employ in so many different spaces, and I also felt that such a method reduces participants' agency in creating their own self-representations. It is precisely this self-representation that some anthropologists have sought to evacuate from their own projects on the grounds that it would introduce bias (Schaeffer, 1995); instead, a distant view represents the only objective method, as far as these ethnographic filmmakers are concerned. There have, of course, been attempts to move away from this position, and some visual anthropologists have given their participants film cameras to produce an anthropology "from within." However, these films have been criticized for being more partial and subjective than anthropologists' own accounts. In my research, I wanted to use a method in which participants were active and reflexive in representing their own identities, so self-filming seemed an obvious choice.

At the time I was conducting the research, digital video was not freely available, so VHS video cameras were chosen as they were relatively cheap and easy to use. Furthermore, between 1990 and 1993, a series of short television programs called *Video Nation*, in which members of the public made video diaries, was broadcast nationwide in the United Kingdom on BBC2, documenting the extraordinary experiences of "ordinary" people. These gave the British public a familiarity with the concept of video diaries. Thus, many participants came to the research process with a clear idea of what a video diary might be, and consequently, none expressed concerns about either the practice of making one or the technology used. Indeed, since then, the straight-to-camera video diary has become a televisual mainstay, used in countless lifestyle, makeover, and reality TV shows, perhaps most famously in the United Kingdom in *Big Brother*'s diary room; the show's pervasive filming of housemates makes for a variety of more or less self-conscious performances, but the diary room is set aside as a private space to talk directly to "Big Brother." As I will discuss later, this framing of the video diary as a private space to discuss personal issues and feelings often gives such diaries a confessional feel; in televisual uses, this confessional quality is increasingly reflexively traded on as participants on shows learn the new skills of using confession on TV as a vote-winning tactic. Viewers, meanwhile, come to expect "truths" to be revealed in such diary confessions, even though they know these truths are performances for the camera and audience (Holmes & Jermyn, 2004).

The final format for the research process, then, was to give each participant, contacted through snowballing techniques (one contact passed the camera to a friend or associate and that contact on to another, and so on), a camera, microphone, and tripod plus a set of instructions. I conducted an initial interview to explain the process and the operation of the camera, and then I left the camera and blank tapes with the participant for up to two months. At the end of this time, I talked over the experience with the participant and reiterated the potential uses of the diaries in academic work. Each diarist was given a specific set of guidelines to follow. Key to this was the practice of dressing in clothes they normally wore for staying in, going out, or going to work. Diarists were then asked to film themselves in their typical choice of outfit for each setting and to comment on these settings and what the clothes, hairstyles, jewelry, and other bodily arrangements were designed to portray. Diarists were also asked to film themselves, where possible, in the different spaces, to capture differences between them in terms of comportment, demeanor, and behavior. No specific instructions were given on the involvement of others in the making of the diaries. Participants were also free to record and re-record their diaries at their own discretion. Once the diaries were completed, I viewed and coded them to identify points of similarity and difference as well as recurrent themes. In this sense, the analysis of the videos was similar to that of audiotaped research material, although the style in which the diaries were filmed as well as visual signifiers of sexuality were also noted. Finally, sections of different diaries were edited together around particular themes that emerged from them (see Photo 10.1).

Photo 10.1

Theory Matters

Besides the practicalities of the research methods they use, researchers need also consider their theoretical approach in relation to their methods. I would like to explore this in the context of a queer methodology, but to arrive at this, it is necessary to examine where this idea might originate. Debates in methodology have been moving quickly, largely mobilized around a critique of objectivism or what might be called the "view from nowhere" (the "God trick," according to Haraway, 1991). Feminists have been central to this critique and have argued convincingly that all views come from somewhere and that claims to objectivity most often mask the masculinist views that under-pin much of social science research. Furthermore, they argue that in this view, women's lives and experiences are overlooked or excluded or simply taken as natural rather than being seen as the product of networks of power. In attempting to redress the balance, then, early feminist research was designed to be "by women, for women, about women"—foregrounding the inclusion and emancipation of women both within and outside the academy. The academy reacted to this with charges of subjectivity and partiality: Objective research should be disinterested and verifiable by any objective researcher. Clearly research "for women" could not claim to be disinter-ested, and insisting on the importance of research "by women" meant that it was not verifiable by men. However, this formula soon came under scrutiny by feminists themselves, especially anti-essentialists and those who acknowledged that the category *woman* was not homogeneous but rather highly differentiated in terms of power.

Borrowing from Marx, Sandra Harding (1993) formulated a feminist standpoint. Marx said that only the proletariat could see the exploitative rela-tions of capitalism, as it was only the proletariat that experienced them: The bourgeoisie could not see this exploitation because they had an interest in maintaining it. Feminist standpoint used the same dynamic, proposing that only women could see the exploitative power of patriarchy—marginality from the patriarchal center afforded them epistemic privilege. Thus, the more one was oppressed, the clearer one's view. This "view from somewhere" or femi-nist standpoint Harding called *strong objectivity*—an implicit critique of the very notion of objective research (but also, perhaps, a lingering attachment to it). Feminist standpoint was not essentialist, according to Harding, because it was based not on the biological fact of womanhood but on women's marginal position within patriarchy—women's experience. However, in the assumption that all women are marginal and share the same experiences, she came in for criticism by feminists who wanted to recognize the relations of power *between* women. In the formulation "by women, for women, about women," *women* becomes the mask of sameness in what is actually a highly differentiated group. These arguments have been advanced most forcefully by Donna Haraway (1991), who has argued that all knowledges are situated in relation not only to gender, but also to class, race, disability, and so on. Furthermore, Elizabeth Grosz (1995), following Roland Barthes in her essay, "Feminism after the Death of the Author," has shown that no feminist text can guarantee a feminist reading (and no masculinist text can guarantee an anti-feminist one). Instead, meaning is made by *readers,* frequently against authorial intention. This idea has been used extensively by queer theorists, who have employed *queer reading*, reading queerness into heterosexual author(ity).

Where, then, does this leave us in terms of a queer methodology? To reinstate a formula such as "by queers, for queers, about queers" would be ridiculous, given that the de-essentializing of sex, gender, and sexuality is one of queer theory's central aims (Seidman, 1996). Queer theory is opposed to all normative regimes of sexuality, not only heterosexual but also homosexual ones. The category *gay*, for instance, also has its own internal power dynamic, producing gay subjects in disciplinary ways (especially in relation to conservative and liberal rights discourses of inclusion, or those based in theories of a "gay brain"). As a result, the term *queer* is always in transition, attempting to avoid reification as a normative category. Although some might want to insist on "insider" research to avoid the worst abuses of power, there is a question about what the "inside" might be, given the instability of the category. Furthermore, because conservative gay discourses come from within, being an insider is clearly no guarantee of political radicalism (Bell & Binnie, 2000). Can there be a queer standpoint, then, when *queer* is an umbrella term that catches many different and highly variegated identities, and when many of those identities are acknowledged as positions in flux? Rather than reinscribe such a formula, I would instead like to propose queer methodology as a *reading position*. Finally, the promiscuity of identity afforded to *queer* subjects might also apply to *academic* subjects. Shifting from being true to one's discipline toward using the best theory or method to get the job done might also be resonant with a queer methodology; as Judith Halberstam (1998) writes,

> A queer methodology, in a way, is a scavenger methodology that uses different methods to collect and produce information on subjects who have been deliberately or accidentally excluded from traditional studies of human behaviour. The queer methodology attempts to combine methods that are often cast as being at odds with each other, and it refuses the academic compulsion towards disciplinary coherence. (p. 13)

Perhaps the most distinct break between lesbian and gay studies and queer theory (aside from its greater inclusion) is the move from studying only the lives and experiences of lesbians and gay men to critical studies on heterosexuality, in particular a deconstruction of the binary of hetero/homo. Homosexuality is what (the later defined) heterosexuality has to exclude from itself to maintain its boundaries and definition. Queer theory reads the perversity back in and rediscovers the queer that has been sublimated from heterosexuality's consciousness or expelled into its "other"—the homosexual. As a profoundly subordinated identity, queers have been "invisible-ized" by heterosexual culture. There have always been those who could transcend this invisibility by virtue of class or collectivity, for example, but in day-to-day life, many queer subjects have faced the necessity of staying in the closet, communicating identity in surreptitious ways. To secure employment or maintain relationships with family members, for example, queer subjects have effectively walked a tightrope between being in or out of the closet and because of this have developed specialized reading skills concentrated around reading the identities of others, potentially alike. The pleasure of reading others, sometimes called *gaydar*, and the pleasure of reading queer into straight culture (TV shows like *The Golden Girls*, for example)—queer reading—is something in which many queer subjects have a particular expertise. That is not to say that *only* queer subjects have developed such skills: the derogatorily named "fag hag" is also a skilled reader, as is the homophobic extremist. However, whereas the homophobe reads queer as a negative threat to "normal family values," the queer reader reads queer as a way of dismantling normative and compulsory heterosexuality. Thus, perhaps video diaries could be said to have a particular affinity with queer methodologies in their visual representations of the encoding and decoding of queer (bodily) texts.

Dear Diary . . .

My intention in designing this project was to use video diaries to capture the *performativities* of identity in ways that are qualitatively different from other sociological research methods. Performativity is a concept developed by Judith Butler (1990); she proposes that rather than resting on an inner self that is stable and complete, identity is nothing more or less than a set of compulsory and repetitive performances. Butler demonstrates the ways in which men "dragging up" as women reveal the process by which women also drag up every day through the application of particular hairstyles, clothing, makeup, and even the ways in which women work on their bodies to reshape them as female. Part of being a normal[ized] woman is also to desire men and vice versa. Thus, Butler de-essentializes gender as simply a complex set of performances over which people have little or no control. Biological sex is not the foundation of gender but rather part of its discourse; the division into two genders and sexes only makes sense within a regime of compulsory heterosexuality. To de-essentialize gender and sex also makes a mockery of the binary division heterosexual/homosexual. However, this does not imply any slippage between (voluntary) performance and (compulsory) performativity. Moreover, performativities are just as central to the identities of lesbians and gay men as they are to heterosexuals because even realizing the discursive nature of sex and sexuality does little to help overthrow their powerful regimes.

Because I was interested in performativities manifest as bodily styles and behaviors, video seemed the obvious means of empirical investigation. The self-representation in a video diary is more complete than the audiotaped interview, which only provides aural data. The use of video as a *process* in the research is equally important (compared with, say, the use of still photography), not only in producing a visual representation of identities, but also in running alongside the narrativization of identity (through participants' commentaries) and in reflecting the selection, editing, and refining that constitute identity and performativity as *process* in everyone's lives (see Holliday, 2000).

Video diaries afford participants the potential for a greater degree of reflection than other methods, through the processes of watching, re-recording, and editing their diaries before submission. Against other methods that focus on accuracy or realism, then, this approach affords diarists greater potential to *represent* themselves; making a video diary can be an active, even empowering process because it offers the participant greater editorial control over the material disclosed. Accuracy or realism are not important to this project because (following Butler) there is no truth of the individual beyond performance. That said, in the material submitted by participants, two important but fundamentally different styles of diary emerged. One style was primarily associated with participants carrying out the guidelines of the project on their own. The other style was primarily associated with those participants who involved partners and friends in the filming process. These tended to be light-hearted pieces incorporating jokes and ironic statements. Although concessions were made to the overall aims of the project, these diaries appear to be specifically designed to be entertaining. So, for example, during the filming of one sequence, a friend of the diarist says, "Why are you being so witty and funny today? You're only trying to make out that you're a more interesting person than you actually are!"

These styles are not necessarily consistent throughout the diaries, and individual diaries include parts that are full of performances—dancing and singing, jokey telephone conversations, mock debates between soft toys, the baring of bottoms, and much giggling. This seems to suggest a high level of awareness of the camera. Of course, one would imagine that the diarists would be self-conscious in front of the camera; however, *alone* in front of the camera, these same diarists adopted a different style, as did those diarists who filmed themselves entirely without accomplices. The self-consciousness, thus, appears to be the result of performing in front of a *known* other person rather than the camera itself. Alone, the diarists appear to disclose more intimate details about themselves, so perhaps the relative candor is due not to a compulsion to confess but rather to the desire not to be overly self-examining among friends. Confession also becomes possible in the absence of potential contradiction by others (see Photos 10.2 and 10.3).

The style used by these diarists is, in fact, highly reminiscent of the confessional, a notion primarily associated with Michel Foucault (1979) in the *History of Sexuality*. The confession is certainly a structure of enormous importance, given its prevalence in the (post)modern media, manifesting itself in many areas from biographical documentaries to the most sensationalist popular shows such as *Rikki Lake* and most (in)famously *Jerry Springer*. As already noted, the televisual construction of the diary as a site of lone confession has become common to reality and lifestyle TV, perhaps making this mode of address seem especially appropriate to the context of the filming. Newer visual technologies such as webcams, videophones,

Photo 10.2

Photo 10.3

and moblogs have further expanded the possibilities for the production, circulation, and consumption of self-made representations, and these too seem to encourage a (knowingly) confessional tone.

Related to this, Michael Renov (1996) sees therapeutic discourse undergoing a transformation as it becomes media-tized. He argues that video is a particularly confessional medium:

> Confessional discourse of the diaristic sort addresses itself to an absent, imaginary other . . . In the case of video confessions, the virtual presence of a partner—the imagined other effectuated by the technology—turns out to be a more powerful facilitator of emotion than flesh-and-blood interlocutors. (pp. 88–89)

Renov sees confessional video as also empowering in the sense that it is beyond conventional media control. It is noncommercial and thus not susceptible to the whims of a viewing market. In some senses, it redresses the media imbalance, turning passive viewers into active producers: Video reclaims television as a two-way communication process. While Renov is perhaps a little overoptimistic, exaggerating the impact such video productions can make, two points in his argument warrant further discussion. The first is the concept of the confessional, which he employs in his analysis.

As Foucault and many others have pointed out, the confessional is itself far from a one-way process. Confessing in psychoanalysis, for example, although it is always conducted within a network of power, is not enforced through domination. The confessional is, rather, a power game. The analyst cannot force the patient to confess but instead must coax a disclosure. The patient may give a response willingly—with the aim of a catharsis or cure—but because these disclosures can be painful or embarrassing, there may be resistance to them. The confessional is, thus, a game played out *between* the analyst and the patient, and patients may choose to withhold or disclose information if they feel potential benefits may arise from this. Benefits may arise simply out of the fact of having a particular space in which to confess, an audience intent on listening. Patients may persuade the analyst that, after all, the disclosures are those of a normal subject. They might even dismiss the analyst if the latter cannot be persuaded of their point of view, as Dora famously did to Freud. Thus, the psychoanalytic encounter may also afford the patient the power and space to speak that normal circumstances preclude. What the patient risks, of course, is having that speech rendered into discourse. This paradox is one familiar to queer subjects, whose worlds historically have frequently collided with those of the analyst.

Diary Writers and Readers

In terms of the video diaries, the power to present one's identity may override the risk of having that speech appropriated by others (for example, the media, or indeed academics). Thus, the fullest confession opens up the greatest space for self-representation. If a distant authority subsequently appropriates that representation, then this is of little consequence to the diarists themselves. For example, in my study, Gill says,

> Why am I telling you all these things about myself? Well, I think that if you asked me I'd tell you, but you're going to tell other people; um, because I think that it's important and I think I've got things to say.

Although these confessions are by no means made externally to relations of power, the explicit nature of the material is facilitated by the unique space that participants are afforded to attempt to fix the meanings of what they say. In Photo 10.4, for example, Gill performs in the domestic space of the bedroom, a private space that she has "queered" through her sexual practices as a dominatrix; the bedroom has props and cues that signify these practices and its dual role as a playroom—she toys with a whip while talking to the camera and stands in front of a metal frame used for bondage scenes—but her framing of the diary entry in this space suggests that she has

Photo 10.4

chosen to let "us" (her assumed audience) into that space in the expectation
that we too can read these cues.

Although the diaries do appear confessional in style, it must be remembered that for this project, diarists were directed to talk around a number
of specific foci. These were in effect fairly mundane (in terms of how identity is expressed, rather than arrived at), and thus they cannot be compared
directly with, for instance, psychoanalytic encounters. In editing and
selecting extracts, moreover, I did not attempt to impose meaning on the
diaries, only to look for recurrent tropes or frames that helped illustrate
the ways that diarists constructed self-representations on camera: The
research brief, as already noted, was left open to diarists' own interpretations beyond the guidance about the focus on the places and performances
of identity. No prompt was given to participants encouraging a confessional style; rather, this emerged recurrently in the completed diaries.
Indeed, the frankness of the diarists' responses remains surprising. The cultural availability of the confessional it appears, may have made it seem
appropriate to the participants, who often demonstrated a clear media
consciousness in the construction of their diaries—in the framing of
shots, the use of dialogue, the editing, and so on. Yet, one should not be

overwhelmed into conceiving of this confessional frankness as the truth itself (traditional psychoanalysis has tended to assume that the more difficult the confession, the nearer it is to the truth): These accounts are representations. Nevertheless, the modes of self-storying used by the diarists does suggest that mediated confession is a mode of performance that subjects knowingly and self-consciously adopt when given the freedom to do so, highlighting a need to further explore the role of this kind of confession in contemporary media cultures.

A final point about the content of the diaries and their specifically visual nature is the possibility they afford for actions and props. Most people display their identities in visual ways through different arrangements of cultural products, such as clothes and interior décor, and the kinds of books, records, and CDs they display. In this respect, the diarists were no exception. The instructions to the project specified that diarists dress in the clothes they usually wore in specific situations, but many of them went beyond this, going through their wardrobes and identifying trends in clothing or specific items with special meanings. They often used panoramic shots to show music and book collections, posters, and prints, and they also pointed out items imbued with personally important meanings. For instance,

James pans the camera slowly around his bedroom, which is small and very tidy. It is decorated with blue striped wallpaper—the kind that parents might choose for their son. However, the walls are adorned with posters. The camera lingers first on a poster of River Phoenix, then on a postcard pinned to a board. Meanwhile James explains what we are seeing:

> This is the safe haven . . . that picture there is a Nicole Farhi model that I just thought was adorable, so he had to stay on the wall . . . um . . . My father never comes in to this room [*why not?*] so he wouldn't really take any notice [*James is not "out" to his father although he still lives at home with his parents*] . . . My bed is a mess, as you can see [*the bed looks remarkably tidy to me*] . . . lovely pictures of the goddess Madonna [*the camera lingers on one of two large posters of Madonna—this one part of the In Bed With Madonna promotion*]. (See Photos 10.5A and 10.5B)

The visual dimension of the diaries enabled a certain amount of acting out of particular situations or activities. There were shots of everyday work encounters or much more personal activities, such as the shaving of body hair or the taking of hormone tablets, accompanied by discussions about

Photo 10.5A

Photo 10.5B

these rituals. Such performances were frequently made central to the diarists' identities, but they were also sometimes discussed with a measure of ambivalence. Some of the diaries tended toward a more artistic structure and included, for instance, recitals of poetry and background music.

Video diaries capture the performance of identities and the ways in which they are mapped onto the surfaces of bodies, homes, and work spaces in fascinating ways. Put together, the intertextuality (as well as the limitations) of identifications becomes apparent in the ways in which similar props, or cultural products, occur across different diaries. In fact, identities may also be expressed in the very structure of the diaries themselves, which frequently borrow textual and visual codes from television programming and film. As James (1996) explains,

> While video provides the arena in which an autobiographical self can be talked into being, the talking is realised only via video; the verbal is always mediated through its specific electronic visualization. Investigating this mediation in successive tapes . . . the social relations that constitute [lives] are themselves similarly mediated through video as text and video as a social process, video as audiovisual electronic information and video as a network of social institutions and apparatuses in which this information comes into being. (p. 125)

However, to suggest that the diaries are *only* confessional would be misleading. For instance, Sue Dinsmore also looked at work on written diaries for her article concerning the BBC2 *Video Diaries* series. Simon Brett (1987) describes how the diary fulfills a variety of different roles:

> It can serve as a confessional or as apologia. It can be used to colour reality or to vent a spleen. It can be a bald record of facts or a Gothic monument of prose. It can chart the conquest of a libertine or the see-sawing emotions of a depressive, it can chronicle the aspirations of youth and the disillusionment of age. (quoted in Dinsmore, 1996, p. 44)

Certainly many of these elements appear in the video diaries I collected, and the styles employed varied considerably across different diarists and within diaries.

Closets and Comforts

I will now turn to a particular issue that emerged from the diaries as a way of elaborating their potential for queer methodology. Queer readings in literature or some parts of cultural studies have largely confined their analysis to written texts or film and TV, examining the heterosexist ideologies conveyed by them or deconstructing their omissions or silences. I would like to turn this instead toward bodily texts and the process of reading and *misreading* identities. In *Epistemology of the Closet,* Eve Kosofsky Sedgwick (1991) argues that sexuality is a primary structuring principle of modern society and culture and that the hetero/homo divide has remained fundamental to contemporary identities. Rewriting Foucault's analysis of the relationship between knowledge and power, in her discussion of the closet, Sedgwick focuses not on knowledge but on *ignorance:*

> The fact that silence is rendered as pointed and performative as speech, in relations around the closet, depends on and highlights more broadly the fact that ignorance is as potent and as multiple a thing there as knowledge. (p. 4)

The closet, Sedgwick (1991) says, is "the defining structure for gay oppression in this [twentieth] century" (p. 72); it is constituted through binaries such as public/private, in/out, majority/minority, knowledge/ignorance. The closet becomes secrecy itself and is the dividing line for hetero/homo. However, the heterosexual/homosexual binary is not manifest in distinct kinds of people but rather exists within each individual: It is the individual's homosexuality that must be confined to the secrecy of the closet. This dividing structure invokes a kind of institutionalized ignorance in which heteronormative culture claims a powerful ignorance of homosexuality with the intention of effecting its subordination through denying its existence. Diarists familiar with the politics of visibility, thus, used the research as a way to "queer" assumptions about heteronormativity; Photo 10.6, for example, shows a still from Shanice's diary, which features a lot of footage of familial domesticity, which it implicitly queers by asking such questions as: What does a lesbian wear to take her daughter to nursery?

This produces particular problems for queer subjects because mainstream culture systematically denies their existence, producing a closet through the presumption of heterosexuality. Thus, coming out (of the closet) is never a once-and-for-all event, but rather an unending process. Every new encounter erects new closets—the closet is a shaping presence for all gay people. Furthermore, coming out carries risks: "Even at an individual level, there are remarkably few of even the most openly gay people who are not deliberately in the closet with someone personally or economically or institutionally important to them" (Sedgwick, 1991, pp. 67–68).

In the context of my research, coming out was a process constantly being negotiated and renegotiated by the diarists. It was also shown to be extremely difficult and stressful, given heteronormative culture's reluctance to listen or to presume.

Photo 10.6

Sam lifts up her white medical uniform top to reveal men's low-waisted jeans of no particular label secured in place by a thick leather belt fronted by a bulky Calvin Klein buckle. She stands casually in front of her work space—a desk enclosed by screens and surrounded by medical equipment. Music plays quietly from a tinny radio beating out some of the latest club tunes. The camera, held by Sam's partner, pans slowly around the work space, lingering on two black and white postcards pinned to the screen at the side of her desk just below an official looking sign that reads SCANS 2–4 X-RAYS 2–3. The postcards both depict naked women in erotic poses—one lies on a blanket in what appears to be an empty warehouse, the other vertical and stretched out backward holds a sword in her hand. The phallic imagery of the second photo is not easily missed. Both of the postcards have an arty rather than pornographic feel. As the shot plays, Sam continues her commentary, although there is a marked difference in tone from her earlier clip. She has moved from standing, occasionally dancing along with the music from the radio, to sitting still and looking straight into the camera. Her expression is clearly troubled:

See, even with pictures like that on the wall, people still have no idea . . . You can be almost blatant and people still don't know. I never talk about men, I never talk about boyfriends . . . and that seems to be OK. Whatever I do seems to be OK. And yet I haven't told anyone here. There seems to be almost an understanding that I am . . . I think anyway . . . I think they know . . . but no one's actually ever said. But then again sometimes they say some really homophobic things, and I think, "well you couldn't possibly know then." But sometimes I say things to people here, and I think I'm surprised I get away with it, because sometimes it's really filthy! And I just keep doing it, and I think "surely they're going to get an idea sooner or later," but they just don't! (See Photos 10.7A and 10.7B)

In this case, Sam has tried to invoke a number of bodily and behavioral performances, work space adornments, and speech acts that have consistently failed to break her out of the closet. Her demeanor in front of the camera is uncomfortable. She is clearly torn between the idea that people should know and the anxiety that she should tell them. "Are you gay?" is the one question that will never be asked. Sam clearly wants to be read as lesbian and has made many moves to improve that possibility. Her discomfort derives from being consistently read against her authorial intention.

The lengths to which heteronormative culture will go to maintain ignorance of its other is clearly demonstrated in the following extract. James is a 20-year-old student living at home with his family:

James is sitting on the sofa in his partner's front room. The camera, operated by his partner, is focused close-up on his face, which is rather flushed. He talks quickly and urgently, looking rather flustered and bemused:

A guy I've started hanging around with, Greg, he's straight, I've met his girlfriend, or ex-girlfriend as it is now . . . he's very good-looking but takes an awful lot of pride in his appearance. Well, one day, the group that we were with, a group of girls, caught him looking at a lad that he thought he knew and started taking the piss out of him to say he was gay . . . um . . . I wasn't there at the time, and I came back after my lecture and they were all saying, "Greg's gay, Greg's gay," and anyway . . . I haven't told them I was gay . . . If any of them had asked, I would have told them, but they haven't and . . . um . . . Greg turned round and said, "For all you lot know, James and I could be having an affair." . . . One of the girls turned round and said, "Don't be stupid, you can tell James isn't gay just by the way he acts [*James starts to scratch uncomfortably at the back of his neck and laughs nervously*]. You're too prissy, Greg, you're always playing with your hair and everything," and as she said this, I turned

Photo 10.7A

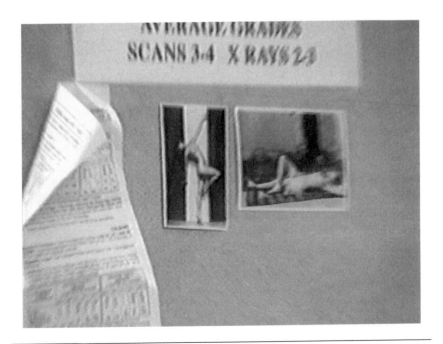

Photo 10.7B

round and said *[He throws his head back in an exaggerated gesture]* "Au Contraire!" and I launched into an "I am Gay" speech . . . because I've worked hard for this reputation, and I'm not about to let it die now *[he giggles and his voice turns up in pitch]*. But they just burst out laughing at me! And one of them said, "Oh you're so funny! I've told my parents all about you, you're such a wit and a wag" and *[incredulously]* they didn't believe me!

In this extract, some of the particular motivations for ignorance of James's declared homosexuality seem more obvious. It seems likely that the girl he refers to has a special interest in James being heterosexual—perhaps she carries a torch for him. However, more interesting, James insists that Greg is straight, evidenced by his ex-girlfriend. Because Greg openly proposes the possibility that he and James could be lovers (for all the girls know), then Greg's undisputed heterosexuality seems at the very least open to contestation. Even if this were said in a jokey, "homosocial" way, the slippage between homosocial and homosexual would simply suggest that Greg is excluding his own homosexuality into the closet (as all heterosexuals do). However, as I suggested earlier, and as is borne out in James's denial of Greg's potential homosexuality, it is not only heterosexuals who police the boundaries of the closet. That a sign as arbitrary as an ex-girlfriend could be used by a gay man as proof of someone's heterosexuality makes visible the ways in which heterosexuality is the normalized category of the majority.

Finally, I would like to refer back to an earlier clip by James. He mentions that his bedroom in the family home is a "safe haven" where he can put up pictures that he feels are clear markers of his (homo)sexuality. He also tells us that his father never enters his room. Why would a father *never* enter his son's room, were it not for avoidance of discovering some secret that in reality he already knows? By avoiding the room, James's father can remain ignorant of his son's sexuality, while in the practice of avoiding it, he displays that he already has this knowledge. This is what Sedgwick refers to as the "open secret," a powerful structuring mechanism of the closet. The denial of knowledge of sexuality confines it to the bedroom, the most private space, preventing it from entering public space and thereby disrupting the heteronormativity of the public.

The following extract is taken from a diary by Stevi, a transsexual woman who is in the process of gender reassignment. In this sense, she currently (at the time of the video diary) occupies a liminal position, passing convincingly neither as male nor female.

Stevi reclines along the sofa dressed largely in black, her long legs bent at the knee, alternately holding a cigarette, then a cocktail, then a cigarette in her hand. The camera is motionless, set on its tripod to focus on the orator. A large yucca plant forms a backdrop, along with a large window through which only the tops of distant buildings are visible. The shot is backlit by a lamp, which casts an orange-red glow up toward the yucca and over the collection of ethnic ornaments that fill the rest of the frame. The mood is somber; only the faint clanging of wind chimes is audible in the background. She talks calmly and slowly and movingly about her background, family, love, intimacy, therapy, Bowie, Bolan, gender dysphoria . . .

> So anyway, here I am, 18 months down the line, 9 months on hormones which really did kick in and help . . . and the sense of freedom was just overwhelming . . . after all the years of just maintaining this façade . . . not really subscribing 100% to the masculine club . . .

Police sirens pierce the calm of the room but Stevi does not react to them—a common occurrence? Somehow they seem to enhance the melancholic mood of the piece rather than intrude upon it. She reaches with a leisurely gesture for another cigarette and lights it. She continues:

> I suppose it's more mind games than war games . . . I find that now that I'm managing to blur the boundaries of gender more than I've ever done before *[inhales and exhales slowly]* I have more power and control over my situation, and therefore I have more ability to actually live it. *[laughs slightly bitterly]* . . . the negative reactions and um . . . influence people's thinking a bit more.

It might be expected that a position of gender liminality would produce the greatest degree of discomfort, then, because although wanting to move toward being a woman (her authorial text), she is constantly read as not being one. However, it seems that it is not being read *as a woman* that is important, but rather *not being read as a man*. In this sense, it is not an appeal to heteronormative society that is being made, but rather to the transgender community. Being read as male (in the normative gender closet) is a position (coded by her as apolitical) of extreme discomfort. Embodying gender queerness is what brings satisfaction.

In all of these extracts, then, embodying one's identity is central to feelings of empowerment and comfort (for a more detailed discussion of comfort, see Holliday, 1999). In one sense, this is clearly a reaction to heteronormativity and the constant threat of being pushed back into the closet. In another sense, however, identity politics produces a powerful discourse of its own, in which being visible is a mark of political commitment, of being principled. Queer subjects clearly occupy an extremely tenuous position—pushed toward invisibility on the one hand and visibility on the other. In the diaries, this was clearly observable in the constant negotiation of signifiers manifest in choices of clothing, hairstyles, and speech and bodily performances. Psychic comfort could be attained only when bodily texts were read as their authors intended. Given the arbitrary nature of signs, as well as the powerful forces structuring their misreading, comfort is something that queer subjects seem destined rarely to achieve.

Conclusion: Re-Presenting Visual Diaries

There are a number of issues raised by the video diary method that I would now like to address. First, and perhaps most significant, is the issue of the presentation and re-presentation of material. In spite of the visual nature of the data that inform this chapter, I am left to present it using only text and a few still images. To capture the flavor of the diaries in text is extremely difficult and takes up an enormous amount of writing space. Still images don't always speak clearly if they have been constructed as part of a live-action video. Having to explain in text still images that are used to stand in for moving images inevitably leaves little space in the average book chapter or journal article for analyzing the findings, and this impoverishes the reader in relation to the writer. Conducting research presentations where clips from the diaries can be shown allows a quite different dynamic between diarist/researcher/audience to come into play. Diarists make self-representations (although clips are, of course, edited by me) directly to the audience, and this has, on occasion, led to members of the audience challenging my analysis or adding to it. The nuances available in an audiovisual text are such that many simultaneous interpretations are possible. For instance, I have been challenged over my use of the term *queer* in referring to subjects who described themselves in clips as gay or lesbian. Thus, the audience refers directly to the diarist in a way that I have rarely witnessed while using written transcripts. The diarists and their views are foregrounded in presentations, and the audience is similarly skilled at reading video diaries due to their near-constant use in lifestyle and reality TV (and indeed beyond).

Another issue specifically related to video diaries is that they are essentially a one-way conversation. This has sometimes been frustrating when

I have wanted to explore some of the points made by the diarists, to enter into dialogue. One way to address this is through follow-up interviews, although these might fruitfully be conducted after research presentations to incorporate some of the observations made by the presentation audience. Also, the spaces in which my participants were free to film were sometimes limited. Given the constraints of the closet, using a camera at work or in a gay club, for instance, was often impossible. Diaries were filmed largely, if not exclusively, in the home. When filming did take place at work, it was frequently done after hours or in individual offices, so that the spaces seem strangely devoid of other people and social interactions.

Developments in digital video, electronic journals, computerized data storage, and the Internet have now made it possible to envisage electronic papers in new ways. For instance, a Web space could be used to store a paper that is part text (and hypertext for notes and additional explanations), part video. Clips could be easily incorporated into theoretical or conceptual elaboration and argument. The reader could simply click on the relevant icon to run the clip. Given the large number of journals now online and books with linked Web spaces on their publishers' sites, it should be possible to incorporate this technology more easily into existing content, publishers permitting (and not forgetting access issues, of course). Academics are increasingly using their own institutional home pages to host visual and moving images, Web logs, and e-archives, suggesting further possibilities for circulating visual material, subject to available server space and institutional regulation. E-books or publication on CD-ROM could provide another solution for relatively low-cost distribution of audiovisual materials. All these developments would, of course, bring with them new questions of access, permissions, copyright, and ethics.

My central aim in this chapter has been to offer an account of my own experiences of using the video diary method, an account that has some valuable lessons for others seeking to use and understand this approach. At the heart of my discussion is the idea of the confession. As noted, confession is now commonplace across the (post)modern media, with the televisual construction of the diary as a site of lone confession being a staple of reality and lifestyle TV, and increasingly bleeding into other TV genres. This ubiquity shaped the ways that participants in my study made their diaries and thought about both how to "write" them and how they might be "read." New media technologies (webcams, videophones, moblogs and so on) are increasingly being used for the production, circulation, and consumption of self-made multimedia representations, and these are likewise routinely marked by a (knowingly) confessional tone.

Participants were clearly media savvy in making their diaries, drawing on available cultural codes for how to do this kind of reflexive, mediated self-storying. But readers must not forget that these accounts are representations, self-consciously filmed and edited by participants clear about the aim of my project and also about how they could engage with the process; as Gill said, one reason for making her diary was "because I think that it's important, and I think I've got things to say." Ultimately, therefore, the modes of self-storying in the video diaries suggest that mediated confession is a performance in which participants knowingly, reflexively, and willingly engage; in a media-saturated and confession-saturated culture, this confirms the value of this method and suggests the need to more fully understand the cultural work of the confession as a site of local mediated meaning making.

In this chapter, then, I have attempted to show the value of video diaries and their potential for representing identity performances and performativities. I have also tried to elaborate a link between them and what might be called a queer methodology through the excerpts presented here. I hope that I have demonstrated (as far as is possible in a text-based medium) the extremely rich data that can be provided by video diaries, as well as some of the problems and issues that are raised around their presentation and representation.

References

Bell, D., & Binnie, J. (2000). *The sexual citizen: Queer politics and beyond.* Cambridge, UK: Polity.

Brett, S. (Ed.). (1987). *The Faber book of diaries.* London: Faber & Faber.

Butler, J. (1990). *Gender trouble: Feminism and the subversion of identity.* London: Routledge.

Chaplin, E. (1994). *Sociology and visual representation.* London: Routledge.

Dinsmore, S. (1996). Strategies for self-scrutiny: *Video Diaries 1990–1993.* In C. McCabe & D. Petrie (Eds.), *New scholarship from BFI research* (pp. 41–57). London: BFI.

Foucault, M. (1979). *The history of sexuality* (Vol. 1). Harmondsworth, UK: Penguin.

Grosz, E. (1995). *Space, time, and perversion: Essays on the politics of bodies.* London: Routledge.

Halberstam, J. (1998). *Female masculinity.* Durham, NC: Duke University Press.

Haraway, D. (1991). *Simians, cyborgs, and women: The reinvention of nature.* New York: Routledge.

Harding, S. (1993). Rethinking standpoint epistemology: What is "strong objectivity." In L. Alcoff & E. Potter (Eds.), *Feminist epistemologies* (pp. 49–82). London: Routledge.

Holliday, R. (1999). The comfort of identity. *Sexualities, 2*(4), 475–491.

Holliday, R. (2000). We've been framed: Visualising methodology. *Sociological Review, 48*(4), 503–521.

Holmes, S., & Jermyn, D. (Eds.). (2004). *Understanding reality television*. London: Routledge.

James, D. E. (1996). Lynn Hershman: The subject of autobiography. In M. Renov & E. Suderburg (Eds.), *Resolutions: Contemporary video practices* (pp. 124–133). Minneapolis: University of Minnesota Press.

Knowles, C. (with photographs by Ludovic Dabert). (2000). *Bedlam on the streets*. London: Routledge.

Renov, M. (1996) Video confessions. In M. Renov & E. Suderburg (Eds.), *Resolutions: Contemporary video practices* (pp. 78–101). Minneapolis: University of Minnesota Press.

Schaeffer, J. H. (1995). Videotape: New techniques of observation and analysis in anthropology. In P. Hockings (Ed.), *Principles of visual anthropology* (pp. 245–258). Rotterdam: Mouton de Greuyer.

Sedgwick, E. K. (1991). *Epistemology of the closet*. Harmondsworth, UK: Penguin.

Seidman, S. (Ed.). (1996). *Queer theory/sociology*, Oxford, UK: Blackwell.

Spence, J. (1995). *Cultural sniping: The art of transgression*. London: Routledge.

11

The Symbolism of Video

Exploring Migrant Mothers' Experiences

Yolanda Hernandez-Albujar

In the summer of 2003, I began fieldwork for a qualitative project on migrant mothers in Italy. Working from a postmodern feminist approach, I wanted to highlight the peculiarity and uniqueness of the migratory experience of Latin American mothers in Italy through in-depth participatory interviews and narrative analysis. I realized that including visual methodologies in my research would allow me to further a holistic, critical, and reflective understanding of the participants' experiences. My original goal was to produce a short video ethnography of the everyday lives and experiences of these women. However, I soon concluded that conventional ethnographic videotaping would not be plausible because it would disclose the identities of these immigrant women, many of whom are undocumented and have tenuous legal status in Italy. In this chapter, I detail the evolution of this project as I reconfigure video representation and push the boundaries between social scientific methodology and symbolic filmmaking.

Migrant Mothers in Italy

Throughout human history, people and populations have migrated to other regions or countries in search or in need of better life conditions. The last two decades have seen an overall increase in the number of migrants around the world: Today's migratory movements involve an unprecedented number of people (Berry, 1997). The major destinations are wealthier Western countries, including Italy, which in the last decades has become a site of immigration rather than emigration. For the last 10 years, Italy has been the country of choice for a number of Latin American migrants. Rome is the city with the highest concentration of Latin American migrants and is therefore the location of this study.

Historically, women have migrated as much as men, but they have been considered nonactive participants of the migration process (Barsotti & Lacchini, 1995). Classical migration theories have considered this subject from an ungendered point of view, focusing on the analysis of different factors such as economic issues or the labor market. Just few decades ago, sociologists started including new important reflections on gender, race, and class. Thanks to that, the recognition of migrant women developed, and researchers started considering them as active participants who experience migration in ways that frequently differ from those of migrant men (Fouron & Glick Schiller, 2001; Kelson & DeLaet, 1999). In fact, the migratory experience of women is greatly influenced by gender.

Women are vulnerable and exposed targets who face discrimination at multiple levels of their public and private lives (Buijs, 1993). Some specific factors negatively affect migrant women. First, Italy historically is a primarily white society that started confronting modern issues of racial prejudices most acutely with the arrival of migrants. Latinas with interracial or nonwhite features evoke social prejudices and are challenged by sexual myths attached to their race. For example, black Latinas or *mulatas* tend to be stereotyped as *calientes* and sexually promiscuous. Because of this assumption, black Latina women are more likely than Italian women to be the object of disrespectful sexual approaches.

Second, although working women represent an important thrust for the economic development of both home and host country (Barsotti & Lacchini, 1995), they are discounted or degraded as unskilled and dispensable workers. This public perception contributes to the low wages that immigrant workers are afforded as well as the types of jobs that they are allowed to perform. As with other cases worldwide, migrant workers in Italy accept hard, unhealthy, or demanding jobs that Italians usually reject. Many Italian employers prefer migrant workers and migrant women for these very reasons. Migrant women in Italy work mainly in domestic services, an occupation that has slipped further into the realm of low-level work with the influx of migrant women. For instance, Italian women performing domestic duties were usually paid by the hour, whereas female migrants are typically employed as round-the-clock live-in help (Andall, 2000). Domestic service and the pejorative view of immigrant labor and wages position migrant women within a class hierarchy and patterns of male domination while at the same time reproducing those patterns.

The main purpose of my study is to highlight an important yet frequently neglected experience of migrant women: motherhood. In the midst of the challenging milieu that migrants find in Italy, they also need to cope with new roles and identities for themselves, including the readjustment of their family relationships (Handlin, 1973; Zlotnik, 1995). Because of the deep-rooted social constructions of women as the main family caretaker, mothers struggle to balance their cultural values and traditions as nurturers, wives, and women with the customs and rules of the host society. Women who join the labor market are still responsible for child care and domestic labor at home; therefore, they simultaneously experience a double adaptive stress: as individuals and as mothers (Liamputtong, 2001; Schecter, 1998).

In the host country, mothers who migrated with their children often need to face the stress that accompanies the frequent changes in power relationships between mothers and children. Such changes transcend the common developmental process and challenges of childhood and adolescence because the processes of identity formation for both children and parents are now embedded in the new society and culture. For instance, children often learn Italian more easily and more fluently than their parents, and they are more easily involved in new social contexts, such as schools and peer networks, which often are very different from the realities or experiences of migrants' home countries. Some of these migrant children help their mothers with language translation and assume positions of power and responsibility that mothers often perceive as disrespectful. Such role changes may challenge the mothers' idea of adequate parenting. Mothers struggle to find alternative ways of parenting to develop or regain satisfactory relationships with their children. More complex is the situation of those mothers who moved without their children, facing the issue of separation from and rejoining with children who grew up far from them (Hondagneu-Sotelo & Avila, 1997).

For my study, I was particularly interested in exploring the experiences of migrant mothers. I wanted to develop the concept of motherhood into the feminist discourse of migration to address one of the most universal roles that many women of all statuses acquire and face around the world. The main goal of my research was to understand and expose the ways in which women migrants reconstruct their identities as mothers in the host society under multiple stressors such as family separation, racism, gender-role expectations of mothers, and international differences in mothering styles.

Developing a Videographic Eye

Before this research, I was passionate about black and white photography but had only a little experience working with video. Through an inspiring course at the University of Florida, I learned the basic techniques of shooting and editing video, but most important, I received an introduction to visual theory and to a way of critically thinking about communication and interpretation in the contemporary world. I became familiar with video as an engaging methodology and started experimenting with it as a technique in my projects. Learning how to shoot and edit a video revealed the power of narrative image and the numerous possibilities of applying alternative visual methods to social research.

Impressed by the potential of visual methodologies, I considered including the visual aspect in my study. This intention grew stronger when I started reading about the topic of gender and migration and the frequent affirmation in social literature of the invisible and voiceless role of women on the migration process (Andall, 2000; Morokvasic 1983, 1984; Pessar, 1995). At that point, rather than pursuing conventional academic venues of publication, I decided that I wanted to expose these women's stories in a place and in a way that they could not be ignored. Including visual information could allow me to present a more holistic and personal perspective on the experiences of migrant mothers by increasing the complexity of research through diversifying my methods, my data sources, and my forms of articulating findings (Becker, 1974). My choice of video over photography was related to the importance I gave to watching and listening to my participants. My assumption is that video does more than just tell a story: It more closely reproduces the feelings, lived experiences, and sensations of the participants. Video methodology allowed me to narrate the experiences of migrant mothers in a new dimension that included texture, sound, color, and movement.

The choice of adding visual devices to an inquiry implied a reformulation of the general theoretical framework of the project, including methodological, technical, and ethical concerns that appeared during the course of the shooting, editing, and presentation of the study. An additional rationale was that visual communication is nowadays an emblem of Western societies. Because of this, I believed that compared to conventional text-based analysis, my video could be more effective in reaching broader audiences and spreading interest in the topic of migration and motherhood.

Mediating Social Knowledge

In the same way that industrial development and its social and cultural consequences were among the main starting points of the modern era in the 18th century, broad access to and use of communication systems are among the precursors of the postmodern age (Vattimo, 1997). Western societies live in cultures based on mass communication, in which "to be in contact" with the rest of the world is a priority, even though this exchange is frequently unidirectional. In the postmodern time, the range of interactions in our lives has spread and is not as limited as it used to be by rigid physical, geographical, and temporal dimensions. Our immediate, daily world has expanded toward cultures and societies that are not familiar through conventional lived experiences. Everyday, we see on television images of people and places from around the world, mainly related to political events or natural catastrophes. Such a way of relating to these cultures is typical of consumerist sides of globalization in our postmodern era (United Nations Development Program [UNDP], 2004).

The images and information that accompany the narratives on this "exotic otherness" (UNDP, 2004, p. 103) are frequently presented in an objective way, as if that were the only truth. Such supposed neutrality tends to create in the audience an illusion of absolute knowledge. Television, radio, and the Internet enable people to become a voyeuristic audience in an unequal power game, in which one individual or group of people watches a counterpart that is passively watched (Frosh, 2001). One of the consequences of this dynamic is that the group of watchers gains knowledge about the other, whereas the watched group gets no new information from this interaction. This can be seen as a postmodern form of colonization. In fact, knowledge is not neutral: It goes hand in hand with power and, in its turn, with the circular creation of knowledge by allowing specific selections of truths (Foucault, 1980).

My critical interpretations of visual information in the mass media should not be interpreted as negative. In fact, in the globalized context of mass communication, the audience acquires a new reflective and constructive role in the assimilation and interpretation of events. Communication and its visual aspect are interpretations that are inevitably specific to the social, personal, cultural, and political contexts in which the information is recognized as important enough to be narrated. When people endorse this perspective on knowledge and on the information they receive, they create the conditions for the development of critical awareness on dominant discourses, ideologies, and games of power and knowledge. Such awareness entails the potential liberation from rigid conceptions and final judgments about what is shown in the media. The realization that we see through the eyes of others allows us to position ourselves as conscious, skeptical, yet participant individuals looking for something once called reality. We construct our reality by comparing different sources, by seeking more information, and by creating our own and unique interpretations and narratives. Besides any manipulation of images and information, visual information provides richer and more complex data than its merely verbal counterpart, therefore allowing more occasions for the process of critical deconstruction and reconstruction of information. In this sense, visual information is an important tool for people to use for their advantage. The camera may facilitate a switch from the detached, positivist study of an object to a localized, critical, and collaborative interpretation of subjects' experiences.

By embracing the above considerations, I arrived at the conclusion that migrant experiences in their entirety are too complex to be deconstructed and constructed in a 10-minute short or in any video, no matter how long it is. As with conventional approaches to ethnographic analysis, I did not develop my video with the intention of producing absolute or exhaustive knowledge of gendered immigration and labor in Italy. Instead, I intend to call attention to certain aspects of what it may mean or feel like to be a migrant mother and, in doing so, to generate interest in the public around the topic, creating discussion and facilitating reflexivity. Indeed, I expect the audiences to be engaged in an active exercise of introspection and reflexivity. The video that I titled *voices* gave me the opportunity to implement my theoretical and ethical considerations and to reach readers/audiences that would require and generate a more participative involvement in the narration.

Video-Aesthetics, Reflexivity, and Social Inquiry

My project was grounded in a specific research question: In your personal experience, how does your identity as a mother in your home country transfer to your new life in Italy? Working from a feminist-postmodern framework, I emphasized the importance of being sensitive to the construction of gender and personal experiences, while acknowledging cultural differences. Feminist researchers implement and combine a variety of dynamic and changing methodologies, depending on the research question and project design (Whaley, 2001). Qualitative methods are the most common framework for feminist research. Nevertheless, consistent with postmodern philosophies, no qualitative methodology can be considered *the one* for the feminist paradigm, which in fact has no "single qualitative idiom" (Holstein & Gubrium, 1997, p. 215; Pink, 2001).

My theoretical positions led me to explore new alternatives to gathering and analyzing interviews. However, in spite of the importance I attached to the video portion of my research, my aim was to organize my study in ways that would equally build and embrace both theoretical and filming aspects. An important concern of this endeavor was to ensure my study's validity as social research. In other words, I wanted to keep in mind that theory is the one aspect that guides my research (Becker, 1974). I wanted the video to be an integrative part of an analytic project instead of an extra or an end in itself. Visual data that social researchers produce are typically part of a project that starts from theoretical questions, which shape the research framework and inform the way findings are articulated (Banks, 2001). However, it is interesting to point out that the data in my visual project do not correspond with traditional ethnographic parameters. The women who appear in the video are not the interviewees, and the surroundings have not been filmed just in Rome. My video is a montage of metaphorical images recalling feelings; these images are neither facts nor linear narratives. However, the video's value as data comes from its ability as a whole to generate information as well as introspection on the topic of migrant mothers.

In this context, the validity of nonconventional visual projects requires a different approach. For example, when talking about validity on documents of life, the sociologist Ken Plummer (2001) affirms that this kind of account produces a "continuum of constructions," which makes it improbable to achieve the positivistic conception of validity (p. 166). From a positivistic perspective, validity refers to the neutral and universal "truth claims" of inquiry (Gatenby & Humphries, 2000, p. 90). Alternatively, qualitative researchers consider that the validity of a project relies on the consensus about the findings among participants, researchers, society, and academics (Gee, 2005). In the latter case, researchers do not deal with absolute, observable realities or targets. Instead, they work with, or even better, collaborate with, the participants, implementing Patty Lather's (1997) reflection that "the effacement of the referent in postmodern culture has made [knowing about] 'the real' contested territory and created anxieties about narrative will and interpretive weight" (p. 295). The goodness of the research is, therefore, defined by the specific context of scientific discourse (Foucault, 1969/1972). Nevertheless, it is important to seek dialogue among interpreters, and it is in this sense that feminist scholars argue that often "validity focuses on how to create a dialogue that emphasizes partiality as a condition of being heard and activism as a means to make a change" (Koro-Ljungberg, 2004, p. 611).

The researchers' interactions with the participants and their personal interpretations of the outcomes influence the findings of the research. Again, social research goes beyond the mere collection of data to become a collaboration between researcher and participants; a co-construction of meaning (Banks, 2001) that eliminates the possibility of impartial objectification in research involving human beings. Sarah Pink (2001) also notes, "Reality is subjective and is known only as it is experienced by individuals. . . . It is not solely the subjectivity of the researcher that may 'shade' his or her understanding of 'reality,' but their relationship between the subjectivities of researchers and informants that produces a negotiated version of reality" (p. 20).

In sum, while the understanding of validity of positivistic studies does not apply to qualitative social research, qualitative sociologists using visual methodologies still have points of reference that guide their inquiry. Two provide the main lines for my reflection. First, I wanted to support my visual data with a coherent and philosophical framework, especially regarding epistemology and philosophy of knowledge. Second, I wanted to reflexively identify myself as an active participant, to reflect on my position in the performance of science and creation of knowledge, and to know how the realities I pursued were changing personal, local, and sociocultural narratives and collaborative constructions of meaning.

To conclude, my project was informed by a feminist framework that allowed for the combination of critical epistemologies (knowledge formation and validity) with the distinctive feminist awareness on power and gender differentials. Such combination resulted in the active cooperation of participants and researcher in the construction of meaning. In fact, this project posed ethical and methodological challenges that required a greater degree of collaboration and explicit participation in the processes of interpreting, retelling, and mediating the narratives of these women.

The Process of Filming:
Issues and Ethical Considerations

During the summer of 2003, I spent one month in Rome conducting in-depth interviews for my study on motherhood and migration. Quite naively, I expected to spend just a few days interviewing and filming the participants, who were introduced through social and humanitarian organizations that worked with local migrant women. These groups were also providing me with an office where I could conduct the inquiry. However, due to the slow mechanisms that regulate the internal functioning of those organizations, I could not get enough support in a reasonable time. Thus, I found myself alone in such a beautiful city carrying with me a handy camcorder that

I bought for the occasion, but with nobody to film. Soon, I realized I had to actively search for potential participants at their meeting points, and the street was one of them.

A priest told me that many Latin American migrants used to meet near a central, 15th-century church called Santa Maria degli Angeli, right behind Termini train station. That location became my starting point, and my study acquired an unplanned ethnographic dimension. I frequented Santa Maria degli Angeli every Thursday afternoon and late Sunday morning, when the backyard of the church transformed itself into the surprising setting for a gathering of hundreds of Latin American immigrants. There I started to talk with some of the women. Because Spanish is my mother language, idiom was not a barrier in my communication with the participants. During my conversations with these migrants, I came to know that the gathering days at Santa Maria degli Angeli were the times when people working as housekeepers, nannies, or elderly caretakers had part of their day off. In that short time together, migrants exchanged news from home, made new friends, and gave to those who were leaving packages for their relatives back at home.

The get-togethers around Santa Maria degli Angeli were also an opportunity to create and develop social networks among immigrants. The casual encounters were occasions to find new jobs or accommodations by word of mouth. At the same time, immigrants exchanged information about how to obtain visas and the permanent *permesso di soggiorno* (equivalent to the U.S. working permit), how to travel for less money, where to find special or ethnic foods, or what doctors or hospitals provided better care to their patients without asking for papers. The Thursday and Sunday meetings fulfilled the function of a social service by creating an unofficial but efficient information center where immigrants could speak their own language and where many of them did not need to expose themselves to the consequences of disclosing their legal status as unauthorized aliens. People from different cultural backgrounds, countries, ethnicities, races, and gender did not have to deal with their otherwise pervasive feeling of being foreigners. Finally, but not less important, they interacted with each other without the sense of powerlessness and marginalization that characterized many of their everyday relationships.

My first conversations were with a group of very kind, older women from Peru. These women, who appeared to be in their early 70s, knew the family situation of everybody in the meeting place. They not only were valuable sources of information about the community but also were able to introduce me to mothers who could be potential participants for my research. Moreover, because the group of older ladies were regulars at the church and very respected by the migrant community that met there, they facilitated the openness of many women who otherwise may not have participated in the interviews.

At that time, a more important problem emerged. The women I was interviewing were ambivalent about whether or not they should be videorecorded. Some of them did not have the legal papers to reside in Italy and did not want to expose themselves and their families. Others told me they were very shy and that they were afraid of the camera. Even though it was important for me to be able to present the protagonists of the story in the video, I had to consider important issues of ethical professionalism, respect for privacy, and the risks and benefits for the participants. Because of the relative newness of video ethnography, nothing has been written in stone about ethics and moral codes regarding visual methodology (Harper, 2005), and I had to rely on my personal judgment. All participants preferred that I tape-record the interviews, and of course, I respected and acknowledged their position. With that decision made, I confronted a methodological dilemma: How could I offer a visual representation of a subject who was not visible on the tape? Could I expose relevant information about migrant mothers' experiences using the power of imagery to narrate their stories? I could not use their faces, but still, I had their words. I decided to use a different system from the "talking heads" film (Martineau, 1984, p. 257) I had in mind at first.

In the same way in which postmodern and feminist thought have liberated qualitative methods from rigid interpretations of validity and truth, postmodernism has also opened the door to innovative and experimental construction of representation in films (Folkerth, 1993). The issue of not being able to include the research participants in my video (at least in the way I wanted to include them originally) made me rethink the possibilities that visual methodologies offer to researchers. I was and still am convinced that for me to expose those migrants' experiences, I had to insert some visual aspect into the project. Therefore, I reinvented my personal approach of imagining these women in the film. I was particularly influenced by an Australian short made by Tracey Moffatt, *Night Cries: A Rural Tragedy,* in which the filmmaker beautifully narrates a story without words, using non-figurative suggestive images that translate the viewers into that woman's personal history. The viewers do not get to know the relationship between the actors or their personal histories. Nevertheless, the bitterness of the actors' gestures and the intense background colors create a dark atmosphere that is able to suggest the internal conflicts and unhappiness of the protagonist. Moffatt's movie illustrated to me the power of evocative images, which can speak for themselves and are able to communicate emotions that may transcend traditional narratives. Finding Moffatt's example an inspiring and thought-provoking elaboration of data, I decided to create my movie from a more phenomenological perspective, even if the theoretical background and framework are informed by feminist and critical postmodern theories.

Capturing Stories

My research was based on in-depth, participative interviews of 10 mothers. The participants' ages were between 28 and 50 years, with children between 2 and 19 years old. Their countries of origin were Argentina, Colombia, Nicaragua, and Peru. Four were working as housekeepers and nannies, one worked as a caretaker for elderly people, two were housewives, and the last one worked in an information center. Three of these women lived in the suburbs of Rome, while the other five lived in the city. Three of the participants were white, four were of mixed indigenous race, and one was mulatto. This classification was from my direct observations of the participants, and as I did not specifically ask about their racial identity, it could have been different from the participant's own perspective.

I analyzed the interviews using narrative analysis, which allowed me to remain open to different cultural perspectives and interpretations and therefore to fulfill the exploratory nature of the study. However, to capture the issue of motherhood and migration, it was not enough to just analyze the interviews and present a paper-based theory or research alone. These women's stories went beyond a simple sequence of events: The emotional aspect of their adventures had a bodily component that could not be avoided and that reinforced my initial belief that something important would have been missed if I had not included a visual dimension to my inquiry.

The final video, *voices*, emerged as a practical solution to the participants' refusal to be video-recorded. The short developed toward a narration of feelings and sensations through symbolic representations. I substituted the participants' faces and their gestures and actions in front of the camera by symbols that engaged metaphors of the verbal and visual narrative. This translation of embodied life experiences to visual metaphors required several stages. After transcribing and analyzing the interviews, I selected some paragraphs considering two main features. First, probably still influenced by Moffatt's film, I preferred to emphasize suggestive images rather than speaking narratives. Consequently, the paragraphs had to be concise yet adequate representations of migrant women's experiences.

I looked for parts that could represent the mothers' views of how the migration process affected their relationships with their children. In this respect, all participants pointed to one or more of the following issues relating migration: personal tensions due to economical crisis back in their home countries, the difficulties of taking the decision to migrate, and the drama of separation. During my conversations with the participants, their recall of those personal issues created the most emotive moments: Some of the interviewees cried; others had long moments of silence. In the short film, I wanted to share with the audience the emotions I experienced from hearing those stories and accounts because, from my perspective, this is an effective method to create understanding, respect, and interest on the topic of migration and motherhood. Emotions, therefore, became a central axis of the analysis, elaboration, and presentation of the data, adding a phenomenological and human character to the research, which can be so powerfully expressed through videos and which frequently remains hidden behind the detached wording of scientific journals.

Second, I selected parts from the interviews that had a high-visual dimension and that were strong enough to suggest metaphors able to trigger the reader's imagination. My intention was not to reproduce in the video those particular images in the traditionally literal way (an articulation that is bound up in our taken-for-granted expectations of visual grammar), but to represent the evoked emotions using symbolic images through video narration. I selected the following passages:

> We were very bad out there. It is sad to lose everything. It is very sad, and to explain it to your children is impossible. With the economic crisis everything just falls from your hands: It is like sifting water, you are working for nothing, you are going nowhere, and everything seems sad, heavy. (Victoria)

> I left him when he was one year old; I just started seeing him grow up. He was taking his first steps, saying his first words, but I have to leave him because I had to work. The first time we met was very touching for me and strange for him. He knew me through my voice and pictures. He realized I was his mother. He knew my voice. It was the first time he met me in person. Little by little, I got to know him. It was a great joy, after five years without seeing him. (Alicia)

> I thought a lot about it . . . We can hurt our children a lot because they have to leave behind their friends, their security, their space, their "everything" . . . because a house does not fit in bags, a life does not fit in luggage. (Cristina)

> [referring to mothers] What would one not do for her children, even this, migrate, in order to try to give them a better future? (Isabel)

The first account was narrated by Victoria, a woman in her late twenties, mother of three children who at the time of the interview were 6 months, 3 years, and 5 years old. Victoria migrated with her husband, who worked long hours in a factory every day while she worked at home taking care of the children. In the above paragraph, Victoria explains how the unstable economic situation back in her home country influenced her decision to migrate. She also relates feelings of sorrow and sadness and makes an interesting analogy between her situation and the action of "sifting waters," pointing out the difficulties her family faced.

The second paragraph was extracted from Alicia, a middle-age woman working as housekeeper, who arrived alone in Italy leaving her one-year-old son back home with her mother. Alicia did not see her son for the first 4 years. Ultimately, when she legalized her status and saved enough money, she brought her son to Italy. I chose Alicia's narration because it depicts the emotive experience of the first encounter with her son after years of separation. Alicia's story also grabbed my attention because of the way in which this woman explains how her voice and some pictures helped her son to reconnect with her.

The third paragraph I selected was from Cristina, a woman in her late forties who migrated to Italy with her husband and her five children. In Italy, she worked taking care of an elderly man. The decision to move to Italy was very difficult for her because not all the children wanted to migrate. Migrating to Italy provoked many tensions in the family who, up to that point as Cristina recalled, had always maintained excellent communication with each other. Cristina's story reveals her worries about the difficulties of having to separate her children from their friends and their original culture. She included a profound and suggestive sentence relating life and luggage.

Finally, the fourth paragraph, which I used to close my video, was from Isabel. She was in her late thirties and was working in domestic service. She moved to Italy alone, leaving behind her two children. Three years after Isabel migrated to Italy, she was reunited with her children and her mother in Rome. During those initial 3 years, she was able to visit her family just once. Isabel concluded the interview with a smile, while commenting that all the sacrifices and efforts she had to make as an immigrant were worth it because of the better opportunities she created for her children. I decided to conclude *voices* with that same sentence because those few words exposed the main rationale behind the migration of the 10 women I interviewed: to improve their children's life conditions. In my opinion, that affirmation characterized the interviewees' experiences and gave to their narratives a distinctive character.

From the four personal accounts described above and the imageries they suggested to me, I edited some of the shots I took in Italy during the interview period. I captured most of the scenes representing movement in Rome. I selected specific locations like the center for Latin American Culture, street scenes near Santa Maria degli Angeli, or areas in front of some Latin American embassies. I also included some shots I took that same summer in Belgrade, Serbia, like the old woman walking on the park. I was shooting on the streets, in different locations, and for many hours. I used to put my camera on a tripod and wait for women to pass by. I was video recording mostly women who in my opinion, because of their physical appearance, could stand as a visual proxy for the women from Latin America. I took images of women alone, women walking with their partners, groups of women talking among themselves, women with children in parks, and so on. From all the scenes I shot, I selected the few that in my opinion had a poetic background that evoked the analytic metaphors and emotional prompts of my research, such as the old woman, or children playing in a fountain. (See Photos 11.1 and 11.2.)

Photo 11.1

Although evocative of time and place, the abstract street scenes themselves could not fully capture the sentiments of the women whom I spent hours interviewing and whom I hoped to represent; I turned to other constructions, as well. When I returned to the United States, I produced more abstract images, such as a box from a video editing program that had an eye painted on it and where I projected different lights (see Photo 11.3). I asked some girlfriends of mine to pose for a picture of their faces. Then, I attached those pictures to a wind chime made of boxes.

Photo 11.2

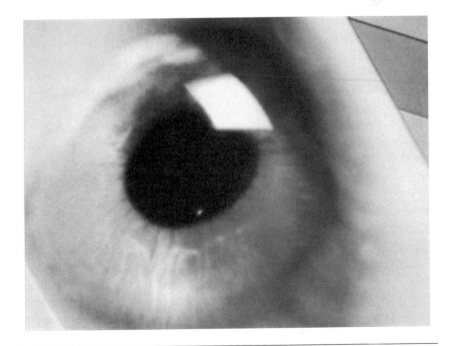

Photo 11.3

voices

At this point, I would like to describe briefly the video, focusing particularly on the main symbols I used. I would like to reiterate that what was meaningful to me might be less relevant for another reader/viewer. I was particularly interested in producing a video that allowed for and facilitated the creation of personal interpretations by the audience. In this way, viewers could reflect on and develop a dialogue between their own experiences and the issues of gender, migration, and motherhood. In the research design, I anticipated that the viewers' plural interpretations would promote the desired dimension of multiple voices in the video.

The fact that a video can be fully understood only by watching it represents one of the main limitations of visual sociological research that articulates its findings through video production. At this point, the readers of this chapter are familiar with the context of the work, which puts them in a privileged position. If the video were screened for people who have this familiarity with the project as a whole, the watchers could identify the metaphors more easily, making *voices* less abstract. On the other hand, people who watch *voices* without the theoretical background and framework described here may still gain critical access to the topic of migrant mothers' experiences. In this sense, the video gains sociological value because it has the power to reach audiences and provoke critical discussion among viewers.

The short film *voices* opens with a brief introduction of the topic of motherhood and migration. Initially, I point to the approximate number of migrants worldwide and the percentage of them who are mothers who left their families behind through a text-based overlay that states: "There are currently more than 120 million migrants worldwide. Fifteen percent of them are women who migrate alone, leaving their families behind." This is the only empirical information in the video and functions to situate the context of action. The very first image on the video is the ocean seen through the window of a ship in movement (see Photo 11.4); there is no sound. That scene includes the two main symbols I use, with diverse meanings, in many of the sequences: water and movement.

Many cultures consider water a symbol of life. We need water to survive. Water is the main component of the Earth as well as our bodies, and it is also a literal and symbolic feature of motherhood and fertility. Once we are conceived, we grow in our mother's belly, where we are surrounded by liquid. One of the first signs that a woman is ready to give birth is when her water breaks. However, water may also have another sense, the one of separation. The physical separation between Latin America and Italy is the ocean. In this

Photo 11.4

case, water represents the thousands of miles that separate those migrant mothers from their countries and, more significantly, from their children.

Water appears on two other important occasions. The first is in a scene in which two children are playing with the water of a fountain. In this case, the happy children take us to the heart of the video, that is, to narrate one of the most difficult events that many migrant mothers experienced: separation from their children. That scene asks what a migrant mother who was separated from her family would feel when seeing those children; what emotions would emerge in a mother while considering issues of family adaptation and hopes for a better future. I tried to put myself in those different situations, and the result was a mix of sadness and tenderness, emotional tiredness for the efforts made, and a reflective internal peace. Of course, that was my personal interpretation, and viewers will develop their own particular meanings from those images.

The image of a woman's hands playing with a small waterfall is the third instance in which water symbolically appears. (See Photo 11.5.) In that scene, I recall Victoria's comment about "sifting water." Many of the mothers I interviewed told me about how difficult it was for them to make the decision to leave their families to migrate to Italy. Recalling that episode was very emotional for many of the participants, who described feelings of sadness and guilt, as well as the sensation that their worlds were just falling apart. The water is falling through the woman's hands in the same way in which these mothers' daily lives fell once, back in their home countries.

Photo 11.5

Movement is another constant in *voices*. I present images of a landscape from a train in movement, of the ocean from a ship, of the city from a bus. I understand the movement of migration not only as the physical change from one place to another but also as the introspective, personal change that an experience like migration (with all the negative and positive consequences) may have for people. To include movement was important because all the experiences of the participants were related to before and after the migration experience. Migration is not a static experience; it is not a picture we can take and observe; it changes and evolves with the protagonists and the personal, sociological, and political circumstances of the migrating process.

The old woman who appears in the video represents the historical and ancient aspect of migratory movements. Migration is not a new process: Women on the move were, are, and will be present as long as migration continues. We cannot think of the issues of migrant mothers' as an extraordinary event of our times. On the contrary, as a female researcher, it is important for me to present this as an atemporal issue, to remark how little information we have about this particular group of migrants. Because of my first-person experience with migration, I was able to identify with the participants. My parents migrated to Barcelona when they were very young. I migrated to the United States 6 years ago; and who knows where my son will choose to live in his adulthood? The suggestive image of the old woman in slow motion is repeated twice in the movie, once at the beginning and once at the very end, to give a circular and interrelated narration of the events.

In the movie, I opted to draw attention to women's voices and silences as well as their words. The words of Victoria, Alicia, and Cristina, which are quoted earlier in the chapter, appear as subtitles in *voices*. Their narratives can be read but not heard. Instead, Isabel's voice concludes the video, in Spanish and with no subtitles. I wanted to create in the audience, which I assumed to be mainly English speaking, the sensation that something was still missing from these women's stories, that their picture is still unfinished for the viewer. This strategy has the effect of provoking personal reflection on the participants' motherhood experience, as opposed to the feeling of having fully understood the situation. In other words, I tried to avoid creating the illusion of absolute knowledge that characterizes dominant forms of analysis of exotic otherness, such as Latin American mothers in Italy.

In the moments of silence, viewers can read the texts. When, instead, voices can be heard, the subtitles disappear so that viewers can focus on the suggestive images. Another critical dichotomy I chose to present in the film is in relation to words versus bodies: When we see women talking, we do not hear them; there is no voice attached to the body. When we hear them, there are no women on the screen talking: Quite literally, no body is listening or involved in the conversation. There is no possible reply to those women's words because they are voiceless and alone in the room (the women who appear in this scene are friends of mine, and they are not the research participants). With this metaphor, I wanted to symbolize the underrepresentation of migrant women in traditional migratory studies as well as in the political and public arena.

The analytic choice of presenting the voices versus bodies dichotomy may appear as reinforcing the idea of voiceless women. To this potential criticism, I would like to explain that I do not agree with the presumption of "giving voice," which I consider a paternalistic and disempowering expression. In fact, women are entitled to their own voices. They do not need any researcher to give them a voice. What I intended to do instead was to situate their existing voices within political interactions and cultural constructions, so that they could be heard, understood, and acknowledged, with a consequent improvement in mothers' life conditions. As the video departed from a traditional, linear presentation of images toward an abstract and symbolic film, readers need to consider that what I did (to show women without voice and to hear women without bodies) was precisely to underscore that in our society and, specifically, in the realms of politics and family, those voices are not represented.

In some scenes, we can hear many women talking at the same time but using different languages (Spanish, Catalan, and English). I intentionally overlapped voices and languages to make it difficult to understand what the women are saying. I did not try to represent the universality of migratory flows by using different idioms. Instead, I tried to leave in the viewers' ears the echo of many women who simultaneously narrate their stories to legitimize, by the very process of storytelling, their own narrations (Lather & Smithies, 1997). At the same time, such overlapping, unintelligible voices and narratives function as a critique of a text-based or narrative approach to research, which assumes the domination of verbal communication and its linear, structural narration.

These are just a few examples of the dialectic among symbols, images, and personal narratives I used in the film, but they are not the only ones. My intention in this section was to show how symbolism may work on the dialectics between social research and visual methodologies in the context of migrant motherhood. However, I do not think it is possible to translate the video into words or accurate descriptions without changing it and without falling into clichés. We have to consider that *voices* was born as a continuum of interrelated images that, if explained one by one, would risk losing the holistic and phenomenological conception of the video. Perception and appreciation of *voices* are inevitably co-constructions between the viewer and the researcher, within a specific medium. After all, the pictures on the boxes, the sounds and the silences, the slow motion, and many other features are each watcher's interpretations and constructions of the dynamic between signifier and signified. Translations and interpretations are performed at the level of sociocultural discourses as well as personal narratives, and such hermeneutic processes are crucial for any sociological endeavor that wants to analyze complex relational phenomena as motherhood and migration.

Limitations

voices is an experimental idiom of negotiation and consensus among participants, audiences, and me. By pursuing this emotive and reflexive line of representation, I was able to resolve some of the potential limitations that I perceive within the conventional analytic ethnographic study of migrant mothers. In particular, I see the video as a contemporary expression that transcends text-based analysis alone by collaborating with the research protagonists as well as the potential audience. Nevertheless, such co-production added frequent methodological and ethical concerns, such as the unwillingness of the participants to be videotaped, which I described above. The turn of the video toward symbolic representation based on the reluctance of the participants definitely influenced the project. This was the major obstacle that I had to face for the realization of the video and probably a common limitation for many visual researchers. The challenge of finding and involving participants in any sociological study becomes even more difficult when visual devices and methodologies are introduced. Participants are concerned with the use of their images, the sociological representation of their persona, and the audiences to whom the video will be shown. Video-recording exposes people's faces and voices and as a consequence eliminates the guarantee of the anonymity that many text-based researchers extend to their participants. This is an important issue, especially when the participants involved in the project are in a delicate legal situation.

While I view *voices* as a strong film in its own right, screening the video may have limitations for generating sociological knowledge. Admittedly, *voices* is an integrative part of the broader ethnographic research that I conducted and therefore should be presented alongside conventional text-based analysis of the project to achieve the most comprehensive sociological implications of the study as a whole. However, access to visual data is a common limitation of video methodology in the social sciences. It is in general more difficult to integrate the movement of images into the final format of the research. For instance, visual studies based on photography may easily incorporate the photographs in books or articles, whereas this is not the case for video. E-books or Web articles have interesting potential, but those communication systems are still not used with the same regularity as text-based literature. Usually, the journals that are on the Web are online reproductions of their paper version, so the inclusion of videos is again limited to the constraints of having just one standard format. This combination of media (text and video) is not yet fully embraced by the discipline.

These limitations affect video-based researchers. For example, most faculty members at my university did not acknowledge the two formats (text and video) with the same emphasis. Conventional outlets of the discipline, outlets that impart legitimacy and reproduce the parameters of valid social analysis, could not review or publish these two formats equally. Yet my inquiry was about motherhood and migration; it was not a presentation of the use of video methodologies. As a consequence, the lack of familiarity with and outlets for visual formats of production hinders the recognition of the video as a generator of social information. If compared with text-based research, the film *voices* was almost neglected by academics, with the exception of those who were specifically interested in visual methodologies.

Although certain forms of visual data are making headway into the mainstream of the social sciences, it remains difficult to integrate alternative visual data with formal research and to generate interest in such projects as a whole. In my opinion and in this particular case, the discounting of video is reinforced by two main elements. First, *voices* remains an abstract construction of images that differs from traditional visual representations. The people looking for data in the mode of classic anthropologic documentary may have difficulty relating with the video and therefore struggle to engage its reflective intentions. Second, although the research focuses on migrants' constructions of identities related to motherhood and on some of the issues that migrant mothers may face, the video ultimately developed toward a symbolic representation of emotions and feelings, a field that is less explored and often difficult to convey in social research.

Conclusion

Video methodologies allow us to explore new forms of social language. Video is already part of our daily lives. When we go to an ATM, when we enter a supermarket, or when we park our car in a parking lot, we are video-taped. Our friends video-record every single smile of their newborn babies, and many of us take a mini camera on every trip. In addition, cell phones have incorporated small devices that can capture 1 or even 2 minutes of action. Video is definitely around us; it is accessible, cheap, fun, and easy to operate, so why not use it? The answer to this question is complex and involves many factors. Talking from my own experience combining sociology and visual methodologies, I want to underscore the inevitable relation between the researcher's personal curiosity and passion for a specific visual device and his or her sociological interest. In other words, I do not think there is a sociologist using photography who does not love photography. In the same way, it would be very difficult to find a researcher using video who does not enjoy the process of shooting and editing. The appreciation of aesthetics, form, movement, color, and light does not have to be (perhaps should not be) coolly denied in pursuit of social knowledge and the methodological and analytic benefits of media alone. For the sociologist who uses visual methods (and perhaps the sociological audience who views the final products), the love of visual art and the love of social research converge into a unique whole. Qualitative methodologies courses that do not include visual research are rapidly changing with the introduction of postmodern and feminist theories that push the boundaries of traditional ways of understanding sociological experiences and events.

Including visual methods in social inquiry is another way to see and understand our world. Similarly, the use of video in social research also responds to specific agendas that seek to interpret the way in which people relate to their personal histories and to the cultural and political social constructions of a particular period. Visual sociology implies social constructions as well as active dialectics between researcher, society, and technology (Becker, 1998). It has the advantage of being malleable and able to adapt to different idioms, from empirical documentary to artistic translations and phenomenological interpretations (see Wagner, Chapter 2, this volume). Video stories depend on the personal ways the social researchers choose to capture, interpret, and share the parts of the world they are observing. The critical use of video allows researchers to find and develop their own personal social vocabulary. In the postmodern era, nothing is considered fixed (Lather, 1997). On the contrary, the world is in constant change, metanarratives are challenged, and multiple social constructions make impossible the description of one reality using just one scientific methodology or approach (Lyotard, 1984). While talking about human and social sciences, postmodern researchers accept that the focus is not on objects but on subjects and subjectivities: persons, groups, or populations that deconstruct and construct themselves, their memories, and experiences. Such experiences can and should be represented in a number of different ways.

Besides photography and video, social researchers can apply many other visual methodologies still unexplored. The boundaries of including numerous video possibilities into research are set by the limits researchers place on themselves. There are alternative solutions to any methodological problems. As Ken Plummer (2001) said about video and sociologists,

> It is everywhere—a volatile expansive, proliferating media with a seemingly inexhaustible array of functions: to prove, document, persuade, analyze, archive, and play with events. Once again, I can only express my surprise at how few sociologists have made much use of it; and indeed a whole new generation of "video" experts seems to have emerged outside of sociology to do sociology's work! There are now several generations of "video workers" who have used video as radical means of transforming the orthodox visual image and of providing a whole library of "alternative video forms." (p. 71)

To conclude, in this chapter, I introduced the topic of gender, migration, and motherhood by describing some of the social stigmas and personal challenges that migrant mothers face. I talked about the importance of having a theory behind a visual representation and about the need to realize that visual data are a valuable alternative method to interpret reality and co-construct meanings without claiming to add objective truths to the sociological record. I also discussed how postmodern and feminist positions replace scientific conceptions of validity with subjective perspectives of interpreting the world. The result invites researchers to find new languages to conduct their inquiries and increase the complexity of their research. I explained the circumstances that drove me to include video in my project and how and why I rebuilt the original idea of an empirical video into phenomenological images.

I cannot finish this chapter without talking about the personal implications that the creation of *voices* had for me. Symbolic representations of constructed realities represent an alternative to missing actors while still presenting them as the core of the story. I created a short movie that, instead of narrating stories, tried to evoke some of the feelings of many migrant mothers with whom I spoke. The video was also a pretext to explore and interpret my own personal experiences as a migrant woman. I did not realize at that time how much I needed to express that side of my life. Even now, just writing about the video in front of a computer represents for me an introspective work. *voices* embodies my perspective on the world, which of course is inseparable from my own history of life. There are many things I would like to change in the film, images I would like to add or scenes I would have preferred to delete from it or to edit in a different order. However, I think the video works for its main principle: to get to know migrant mothers, a crucial part of the migrant community that has been neglected in the social sciences. When I see the movie, it reminds me of the women I interviewed, their accounts, their gestures, their smiles, and their voices.

The use of video in qualitative research actively responds to the social needs of an era in which technology, communication, images, and identities cannot be unlinked. It is not my intention to sustain that visual methodologies are the only approach to explore human experiences, but in my experience, visual work is decisively one of the best for conveying the lived experiential components of social life. This chapter is an invitation to all researchers in general to keep seeking the numerous possibilities of integrating visual art into the sociological discourse, establishing a sensitive dialogue between the two of them.

References

Andall, J. (2000). Organizing domestic workers in Italy: The challenge of gender, class, and ethnicity. In F. Anthias & G. Lazardis (Eds.), *Gender and migration in southern Europe: Women on the move* (pp. 145–172). New York: Berg.

Banks, M. (2001). *Visual methods in social research*. Thousand Oaks, CA: Sage.

Barsotti, O., & Lacchini, L. (1995). The experience of Filipino female migrants in Italy. In *Proceedings of the United Nations Expert Group Meeting on International Migration Policies and the Status of Female Migrants*. New York: United Nations, Department for Economic and Social Information and Policy Analysis, Population Division.

Becker, H. S. (1974). Photography and sociology. *Studies in the Anthropology of Visual Communication, 1*, 3–26.

Becker, H. S. (1998). Visual sociology, documentary photography, and photo-journalism: It's (almost) all a matter of context. In J. Prosser (Ed.), *Image-based research: A sourcebook for qualitative researchers*. Bristol, PA: Falmer Press.

Berry, J. W. (1997). Immigration, acculturation, and adaptation. *Applied Psychology: An International Review, 46*, 5–34.

Buijs, G. (Ed.). (1993). *Migrant women: Crossing boundaries and changing identities*. Oxford,UK: Berg.

Folkerth, J. A. (1993). Postmodernism, feminism, and ethnographic film. In R. M. Boozan Flaes & D. Harper (Eds.), *Eyes across the water two: Essays on visual anthropology and sociology*. Amsterdam: Het Spinhuis.

Foucault, M. (1972). *The archaeology of knowledge and the discourse on language*. New York: Pantheon. (Original work published 1969)

Foucault, M. (1980). *Power/knowledge: Selected interviews and other writings, 1972–1977*. New York: Pantheon Books.

Fouron, G., & Glick Schiller, N. (2001). All in the family: Gender, transnational migration, and the nation state. *Identities, 7*, 539–544.

Frosh, P. (2001). The public eye of the citizen-voyeur: Photography as a performance of power. *Social Semiotics, 11*, 44–59.

Gatenby, B., & Humphries, M. (2000). Feminist participatory action research: Methodological and ethical issues. *Women's Studies International Forum, 23*, 89–105.

Gee, J. P. (2005). *An introduction to discourse analysis: Theory and method*. New York: Routledge.

Handlin, O. (1973). *The uprooted* (2nd ed.). Boston: Atlantic Monthly Press Book.

Harper, D. (2005). What's new visually? In N. K. Denzin & Y. S. Lincoln (Eds.), *The Sage handbook of qualitative research* (3rd ed., pp. 747–762). Thousand Oaks, CA: Sage.

Holstein, J. A., & Gubrium, J. F. (1997). *The new language of qualitative method*. New York: Oxford University Press.

Hondagneu-Sotelo, P., & Avila, E. (1997). I'm here but I'm there: The meanings of Latina transnational motherhood. *Gender and Society, 11*, 548–571.

Kelson, G. A., & DeLaet, D. L. (Eds.). (1999). *Gender and migration*. London: Macmillan.

Koro-Ljungberg, M. (2004). Impossibilities of reconciliation: Validity in mixed theory projects. *Qualitative Inquiry, 10*, 601–621.

Lather, P. (1997). Drawing the line at angels: Working the ruins of a feminist ethnography. *Qualitative Studies in Education, 10,* 285–304.

Lather, P., & Smithies, C. (1997). *Troubling the angels: Women living with HIV/AIDS.* Boulder, CO: Westview.

Liamputtong, P. (2001). Motherhood and the challenge of immigrant mothers: A personal reflection. *Families in Society, 82*(2), 195–201.

Lyotard, J. F. (1984). *The postmodern condition: A report on knowledge.* Minneapolis: University of Minnesota Press.

Martineau, B. H. (1984). Talking about our lives and experiences: Some thoughts about feminism, documentary and "talking heads." In T. Waugh, (Ed.), *Show us life.* New Jersey: Scarecrow Press.

Moffatt, T. (Producer). (1990). *Night cries: A rural tragedy* [Motion picture]. Australia.

Morokvasic, M. (1983). Women in migration: Beyond the reductionist outlook. In A. Phizaclea (Ed.), *One way ticket: Migration and female labour* (pp. 13–32). London: Routledge,.

Morokvasic, M. (1984). Birds of passage are also women. *International Migration Review, 18,* 886–907.

Pessar, P. R. (1995). On the home front and in the workplace: Integrating immigrant women into feminist discourse. *Anthropological Quarterly, 68,* 37–60.

Pink, S. (2001). *Doing visual ethnography: Images, media, and representation in research.* Thousand Oaks, CA: Sage.

Plummer, K. (2001). *Documents of life 2. An invitation to a critical humanism.* London: Sage.

Schecter, T. (1998). *Race, class, women, and the state: The case of domestic labor.* New York: Black Rose Book.

United Nations Development Program (UNDP). (2004). *Human development report 2004: Cultural liberty in today's diverse world.* New York: Author.

Vattimo, G. (1997). Postmodernidad. In P. L. Osés & A. Ortiz (Eds.), *Diccionario interdisciplinar de hermenéutica.* Bilbao, Spain: Universidad de Deusto.

Whaley, D. E. (2001). Feminist methods and methodologies in sport and exercise psychology: Issues of identity and difference. *The Sport Psychologist, 15,* 419–430.

Zlotnik, H. (1995). Migration and the family: The female perspective. *Asian and Pacific Migration Journal, 4,* 253–271.

12

Website Design

The Precarious Blend of Narrative, Aesthetics, and Social Theory

Stephen Papson, Robert Goldman, and Noah Kersey

Our original essay about website design was published in *American Behavioral Science* a year ago. In it, we discussed our venture as sociologists: building a website to present our data rather than following the traditional route of publishing a manuscript. In this chapter, we leave the original essay intact. We feel that it captures the struggles with building a website and also the aesthetic and communicative nature of the medium in relation to our project. We rejoin this essay in our conclusion where we muse that unlike publishing a book, website work went on and on and on ad infinitum. Now we have entered Phase 2. Our musings were an accurate prediction of our present state. In the addendum to the original essay, we discuss three new moves we are making. The first step is backward: We now are turning the website into a book. The second move is sideways: We published a chapter as an article in an electronic journal in a PDF file with embedded video. Our third move is forward: We have begun to restructure the website from an ensemble of static pages produced through an HTML authoring program to a dynamic database-driven site. In each of these cases, we have had to explore the shifting relationship between producing a written text and new digital possibilities that allow for not only the presentation and discussion of moving images but also the production of new relationships between user and hypertexts. The original article begins here; if you have read it, you should jump to the addendum.

For some years now, our approach to sociology has been straining to become more visual because our empirical field of inquiry—advertising—is so heavily visual. But publishing our work has been frustrating because of the limits set by our discipline's journals and book publishers in how, and to what extent, we might include visual materials in our work. With our study of television advertising, the dilemma has intensified because our textual data are not just visual, they take the form of video. The book form is obviously antagonistic to the presentation of video, as are print journals. We fantasized about creating a CD of Nike commercials to go with our last book, *Nike Culture,* but our publisher resisted. At the start of our current research project, we were determined that this study must include the objects of our inquiry—the TV ads that we analyze. We decided to write an "Internet book" as opposed to another conventional book. To answer the question "Why?" at this point was fairly easy. The medium of the WWW allowed for the presentation of video within the text. That quality of the medium was the basis of the decision to step into the unknown, into "Web design," a whole new field of HTML editors, digital video editing, image manipulation, navigation, FTP clients, database design, and other unforeseen challenges, unknown software programs, and unfamiliar terms. With such an investment of effort the "why is this better?" question immediately surfaces. It is better because it allows us to more closely relate the process of our translation from lived experience to sociological analyses through a medium where we attempt to show rather than tell; where we can present the visual, the textual/lingual, and the audible together, to more closely convey what we envision in our minds to the receiver, be it student or stranger.

What would be different about an Internet book from the print book? In print, the page is undifferentiated—pages are pages are pages. The basic unit is the chapter or sections within the chapter. But on the Internet, the page is the fundamental unit. The technology of print sequences the pages; on the Internet, the relationship between pages may be nonsequential. Whereas the print medium is often characterized by a spare, ascetic aesthetic, the Internet amplifies the importance of layout and design and aesthetics.

We quickly sensed that the look of our pages was going to be key in trying to get people to read rather lengthy analyses on the Internet. Most literature on Web use suggests students surf and graze across the Internet—reading sideways across the Internet. The very strength of the Internet—its capacity for hyperlinks—seemed also to be its pedagogical weakness. The Internet had become the new, and hippest, medium for superficiality.

How could we write in chapter form under such circumstances and hope to have it read from beginning to end? "Nobody will read that much on the Web," was the usual warning we heard. Yet measuring the Internet page by the standard of the print page blinds us to the dynamic multimedia possibilities the Internet might provide. For sociologists to overcome the poverty of the Internet, we must begin to challenge the hegemony of the numerical symbol and the written word. This emphatically must not mean that we abandon the written word, but that we find new ways to incorporate visual meaning systems. It means we must learn to tell our stories in new ways. As Berger and Mohr (1982) put it, images offer us "another way of telling."

For the most part, sociologists' use of the Internet has been unimaginative, minimalist, and mechanical. Initially, sociologists—like all other academics—created pages that organize lists of categories that connect with hyperlinked websites. One of the best of its kind is UC Santa Barbara's *Voice of the Shuttle* (Liu, 2003), which offers a virtual compendium of academic writings. Such sites are difficult to maintain—links go dead and must be constantly monitored—and they continue to be almost exclusively logocentric. In fact, most academics think so little about the form of their presentation that they simply import their Microsoft Word documents into an HTML editor. Now, in defense of all this, for most of us, the slow baud rates on modems greatly limited the willingness of users to deal with the large file sizes of photos, much less video. Broadband bandwidths are changing, but sociologists (in fact, most academics) seem terribly unprepared to take the next step. We came to this project as sociologists trying to think about how we could leverage the possibilities of the Internet to more fully convey our work.

Although novices, we nonetheless made several important decisions at the start. First, although we wanted to engage the power of hyperlinking to make connections, we decided not to have external links to other sites outside ours. Our effort to create a "sticky" text aimed at countering the usual slip and slide of surfing readers going from site to site. We knew we could not fully constrain or steer readers in this new domain, but we wanted to hold their attention as long as possible. Second, we have been mindful that we could not simply write this as a conventional Microsoft Word manuscript that could then be converted into HTML pages. Instead we tried to craft our writing according to the structural pluses and minuses of the Internet—this meant writing in HTML programs and forcing ourselves to think about the page as a set of visual relationships. Conceptualizing "pages" as canvases made incorporation of visual materials not an afterthought but part of the page design itself. Third, we decided to experiment with new tools for visually presenting and displaying information. So we began to experiment with rollovers, floating boxes, QuickTime movies, Flash presentations, and databases.

We have structured this article to highlight a dialogue between the practices we have adopted along the way and the issues raised by theories of hypertext. The issue is not simply one of how our narratives change when we rearrange the relationships between written texts into hypertext, but also what new ways of telling sociological narratives emerge when we are willing to engage a language of images. Having said this, we should caution that we have hardly been willing to give up our love affair with the written word, sentence, paragraph, or chapter. Rather we have engaged the struggle of how to find a new balance between image and text in narrating our research.

Our reflections here focus on the relationship between the formal elements of our site: hypermedia, written textual analyses, aesthetic and stylistic choices, and navigational devices. Taken together, these constitute an epistemology of hypertext. We interrogate the theories of hypertext from a position of grounded theory, from the ground of website construction.

Four sets of questions weave through this discussion. First, hypertext theory stresses that the navigational structure of hypertext shifts the power from author to reader because of its nonlinear parameters. Readers/users have multiple choices in how they select the order of pages that they read, or which pages. Hence, readers/users can read in an unintended order and make links/connections that result in new "ways of seeing." Questions of navigational design become paramount. How do we design a navigational structure that increases users' agency while also serving the authors' rhetorical stance and agenda? Does the hypertext context also require a different kind of writing than academics normally use in publishing our work?

Second, hypertext mimics the process of mapping. It is spatial in design. It lays out, rather than argues. In our case, how might we use hypertext to both map the corporate representations in our study, while also theorizing a relationship of those representations to changing economic formations?

Third, the production of hypertext is a form of bricolage. It enables us to gather images, audio-video clips, print text, graphs, and so forth and then reassemble and "remediate" these elements to create intended associations. These practices lie at the margin of traditional scholarship. How might we construct a hypertext that is scholarly and yet visually engaging?

Finally, we have constructed a particular type of hypertext: a website. Cognitive theory concerning user practices stresses the tendency to surf rather than to read deeply. Web design theory stresses the use of *lexias,* short pieces. How do we build a website that orients users to do critical readings of representations?

The Project

Over the past 3 years, we have been constructing a website entitled *Landscapes of Capital: Representing Time, Space, and Globalization in Corporate Advertising* (http//it.stlawu.edu/~global/). We have built a database of 900 corporate commercials that aired between 1995 and the present. The TV commercials are drawn primarily from the telecommunications, information technology, and financial sectors. The site addresses how Capital depicts and defines itself in advertising discourse. Our project consisted of taping commercials, digitizing them into a Web-friendly format, keywording the commercials, analyzing commercials, and inducting broad theoretical categories to organize our analyses. The site contains 200 pages of written text with embedded images and commercials. The site also contains a searchable database of the commercials, along with an extensive illustrated glossary that defines analytical concepts that we use. Multiple navigational devices are used to engage different reading styles and to structure the site.

Our project intent is to frame and analyze the relationship between a system of advertising signs and the emerging global system of production and investment, also known as post-Fordism, flexible accumulation, and transnationalism. We see advertising as a discursive landscape that reflects social and cultural change, while recasting those changes to fit the interests of corporate sponsors. As a genre, corporate TV advertising frames emergent economic formations as landscapes that legitimize the corporate policies and practices that bring them about. As such, this cultural form is a powerful tool that "enables people to construct new cosmologies that aid in making sense of such intense and rapid changes" (before proceeding, the reader should visit the website at http://it.stlawu.edu/~global/).

The Site—The Content

In substance, the site is divided into six categories: Mapping Global Capital, Global Capital, the Semiotics of Advertising, Grand Narratives Revisited, Landscapes: the Geography of Capital, and Speed: Conquering Time and Space.

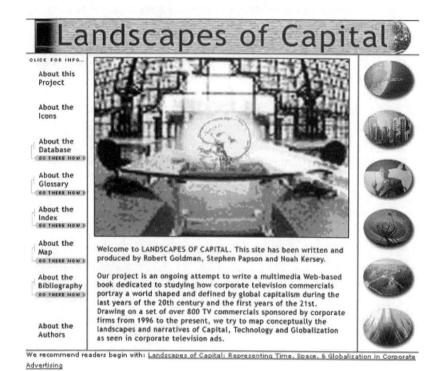

Welcome to LANDSCAPES OF CAPITAL. This site has been written and produced by Robert Goldman, Stephen Papson and Noah Kersey.

Our project is an ongoing attempt to write a multimedia Web-based book dedicated to studying how corporate television commercials portray a world shaped and defined by global capitalism during the last years of the 20th century and the first years of the 21st. Drawing on a set of over 800 TV commercials sponsored by corporate firms from 1996 to the present, we try to map conceptually the landscapes and narratives of Capital, Technology and Globalization as seen in corporate television ads.

We recommend readers begin with: Landscapes of Capital: Representing Time, Space, & Globalization in Corporate Advertising

Photo 12.1 Our opening page. It contains links to navigation devices, the database, the glossary, the bibliography, and linked icons to the six section introductions.

Mapping Global Capital serves as an introductory section that discusses the process of mapping in relationship to advertising. Here we suggest that corporations construct a cultural landscape composed of motifs, recurring visuals, and narratives that when taken together, create a hegemonic worldview, a way of seeing the process of globalization and the role of corporations and their practices, such as capital investment, and scientific and technological development.

In Global Capital, we use advertising as a catalyst to describe the morphology and processes of post-Fordism. Corporate advertising displays how Capital "works." It offers visual representations of the social relations of production in a "global information economy" (see Castells, 1996). However, we note that here "morphology becomes mythology." New economic and technological formations are generally represented as beneficial, exciting, secure, and just. The aura of a just civil society appears to be one and the same with that of the sponsoring corporation. And, when representations of failure or disruption are used to show the underside of these economic formations, corporate advertising has a remedy available.

The Semiotics of Advertising section foregrounds advertising as a discourse composed of signifiers, formula, and codes. This section also functions as the methodology center on the site where we break down the semiotic mechanics of advertising and the methodologies of brand construction. Here we look at the agenda of commercials (the branding process), at the shorthand of visual signification (recurring signifying clusters), and at the underlying grammar of ads (narrative structures) used in this genre of corporate advertising. It is in this section that we have thus far made the most use of Flash—a program that permits the construction of animated presentations through the writing of scripts.[1]

Despite postmodernist declarations regarding the demise of modernist grand narratives, corporate advertising clearly connects the matter of individual well-being and social and economic progress to corporate practices. Questionable as these narratives may be, advertising gives the discourse an ideological coherency that alternative visions lack. The Grand Narratives Revisited section explores recurring narratives, or what Roland Marchand (1985) identified as modernist parables. These are organized around three themes: the contradictions of development, the stories of science and technology, and reason and progress.

Reading landscapes is a way of visualizing the relations of power that underlie and constitute them (Zukin, 1991). In Landscapes: the Geography of Capital, we use the physical metaphor of "scape" to look at the way social and cultural spaces are fabricated by Capital. The architecture of Capital is symbolically represented by urban, technological, and organizational formations. Moreover, the cultural landscapes of "nonmodernized" peoples are also highly represented in this genre of advertising. In this section, we look at the way in which corporate ads ideologically blend images of place and nonplace to connote that Capital simultaneously protects place as it modernizes through technological development and financial investment.

Advertising equates gains in speed not only with general notions of progress, but also with disruption, anxiety, and uncertainty. Sometimes referred to as time-space compression, sometimes as deterritorialization, this process threatens/promises to transform not only the ways in which we work and do business, but also the ways in which we live. In Speed: Conquering Time and Space, we look at how corporations use speed to depict organizational adaptability, the flexibility of Capital, and technological integration.

The site also contains a glossary, a bibliography, and a searchable database. The glossary provides extensive discussions on 25 theoretical concepts (e.g., abstraction, commodity sign, reification, simulacra, social tableaux) that we use in our analyses of advertising. The glossary is essentially a self-contained website that could be used in courses that deconstruct advertisements. Users have access to the glossary via the toolbar on the header without leaving the page they are on.

Likewise, the database is accessible from any page without taking readers away from their page. The database contains approximately 900 keyworded commercials from which we've drawn commercials for analysis and illustration. The database also contains the narrative text for each commercial as well as a field that identifies the business/industrial sector and key metrics of the corporation's size and profitability.

The database provides users with an opportunity to explore their own interest on particular areas and search via keywords and corporate names. Most important, it offers the reader immediate access to a miniaturized QuickTime video of the commercial itself. We hope this combination of features might be attractive to faculty who wish to use these materials with their students. For example, students could do their own analyses of selected commercials, engaging them more deeply in the methodological and theoretical issues of studying advertising.

The Production of the Site

The tasks of conceptualization and execution were intertwined. We had to learn how to use new tool sets. First we had to learn an authoring program that would allow us to proceed. We selected Adobe GoLive. We learned enough to take ourselves through several incarnations of the website. Later, we were joined by Noah Kersey, a skilled designer who made fuller use of GoLive and Photoshop tool sets. At that time, the site acquired a new level of design consistency across all our pages. Moving to cascading style sheets also permitted more effective management of what has grown into an extraordinarily complex site composed of thousands of files. The current page design is a product of extensive experimentation with various ways of organizing pages (each page an analysis and an argument) and their relationships with one another.

To build an electronic database, we needed to learn a database program—FileMaker Pro was our choice. As we began to tape and accumulate enough commercials to initiate an analytical process, we also began cataloging, extracting, digitalizing, keywording, and then converting the ads into

QuickTime fast start files. Although recording commercials is often a hit or miss approach, over time the database fills in. In the early days of this project, storage, server space, and bandwidth issues were concerns. But we worked with the expectation that these issues would solve themselves as computer technology developed. The database continues to grow in terms of the number of records, while it evolves in terms of the searchable fields and the questions that interest us. For example, version 2 has become more user friendly, now permitting the user to search by year of the commercial.

Third, rather than approach the project with the goal of extending or applying a particular theoretical perspective, we conceptualized the project as a dynamic mapping process. We inducted categories to serve as the foundations for organizing our map. However, a central characteristic of hypertext is temporal continuance. It can be changed, re-edited, and added to continuously. Add to this both the historically accelerating pace of advertising production and the accelerated appearance and disappearance of major corporations. An issue that we continuously face is: How does one map a landscape in continuous flux?

Constructing Hypertext/Hypermedia

Writing about advertising for many years has compelled us to confront the problem of trying to convey the meaning of audiovisual texts in the absence of the text itself. Many who write about advertising focus on magazine ads because these can be easily scanned and inserted into the text. Even when writing about audiovisual texts, we tend to lift and freeze key frames and juxtapose them with our descriptions of the commercial. Another approach is to make videos that overlay commercials with a critical narration (e.g., Sut Jhally's *Advertising and the End of the World*). We found these practices limiting. The former fails to provide the viewer with the complete text; the latter imposes a didactic tone, compelling the viewer to absorb the analysis or critique at a prescribed pace. The hypermedia/hypertext nature of the website not only provides a means of integrating a myriad of visual elements, but also enables a dynamic means of presenting the semiotic and narrative structures used in this genre of advertising.

Although the distinction between hypertext and hypermedia is often blurred in the form of the website, it is useful to separate the terms for analytical purposes. *Hypertext* refers to links between pages or sections within a page (anchors) and is "designed to be entered at any point and read non-sequentially" (Felker, 2002, p. 326). Navigational choices determine the hypertextuality of a piece. Theoretically, once external links are made possible, hypertextuality extends over the entire Web. *Hypermedia* is defined as "a collection of text, sound, video, and/or images, linked electronically to one another (and possibly to other hypermedia)" (Felker, 2002, p. 326). Hypermedia is by its nature hypertextual. Links between text and image, video, flash animations, and so forth, even though hidden, always create possibility and choice. Bolter and Grusin (2000) observed that "the ultimate ambition of web designers seems to be to integrate and absorb all other media" (p. 208).

Website production integrates three elements: an aesthetic (the use of repetition alignment, proximity, and contrast), the use of images and audio-visual texts, and a system of navigation. These three factors frame the substance of the site and serve as the visual markers that guide the viewer through both the page and the site. Moreover, these markers privilege some elements of the website over others. Essentially, a hierarchy of information is constructed.

The Aesthetic

Hypertext (hypermedia) is, before anything else, a visual form. Hypertext embodies information and communications, artistic and affective constructs, and conceptual abstractions alike into symbolic structures made visible on a computer-controlled display. (Joyce, 1995, p. 19)

The aesthetic is the overall look of the site. Although semiotic analysis tends to reduce text to signifiers and signifieds, it is essential that analysis recognize the gestalt of an advertising text. The site blends and arranges signifiers to convey both affect and meaning. The aesthetic must not only capture the eye but must also separate elements on the page from the clutter of other elements. The use of repetition, alignment, proximity, and contrast creates the visual boundaries for the site. The user must be able to recognize that they are within the site. The aesthetic is the grammar of the site. It not only guides the reader around the page but also directs the reader to make associations. In this sense, the aesthetic serves as a rhetorical device.

The aesthetic of our site serves two often-contradictory demands: design and academic literary culture. Design refers to maximizing the visual elements of the page to engage a user. Hypermedia is a closer kin to the advertiser's photomontage than the printed manuscript of the scholar. Visual culture operates on the principle of recognition, fascination, and search, often privileging graphics over words. As a visual medium, our website blends style with substance, making aesthetics substantive.

The aesthetic is read socially. For example, commercials that mix gold tones, classical music, and soft intonation of the narrator's voice will connote upper-class taste. Likewise, website aesthetics create an affective relationship with the site. The aesthetic adds sign value and salience. To be trusted, the site must look professional. Although the site design guides the viewer's affective relationship to the subject, we argue that substance—the multimediated analyses—remains the essence of this project. Although the images and other visual constructs are the first elements to engage the eye, academic culture privileges the printed text. Therefore, we must walk a fine line between a visual style that is inviting to the reader, while still encouraging a perception of the site as intellectual and serious in content and not frivolous.

> Like other forms of change, the expansion of writing from a system of verbal language to one that centrally involves nonverbal information—visual information in the form of symbols and representational elements as well as other forms of information, including sound—has encountered stiff resistance, often from those from whom one is least likely to expect it, namely, from those who already employ computers for writing. Even those who advocate a change frequently find the experience of advocacy and of change so tiring that they resist the next stage, even if it appears implicit in changes they themselves advocate. (Landow, 1992, p. 49)

Just as our database continually changes, so has our aesthetic. We have gone through several site designs and navigational systems. Much of our time has been spent revamping the site. Presently, we are considering two new strategies. First, we are discussing the production of a written manuscript. This would allow us to reduce the amount of text in the site and create more dynamic pages. Second, we are considering layering each page in which the dynamic pages would sit above text-heavy analysis. The user could then link to a printable analysis. Creating new designs that make the site pedagogically more useful has become a central concern. Our conversations about the representation of Capital include a discussion about how we might design a page to visually represent that relationship. Website construction necessitates a reflexive stance on media (see Photo 12.2).

Integration of Images and Audiovisual Texts

Bolter and Grusin (2000) noted that digital media lend themselves to remediation—appropriation, borrowing, commenting on, and reforming mediation:

Landscapes of Global Capital

The Death of Marxism

|Bibliography| |Database| |Glossary| |Index| |Map|

Francois Lyotard argued that in postmodernity, knowledge forms express an incredulity towards metanarratives, a rejection of metaphysics, philosophies of history, and any totalizing theory (Lyotard, 1984).But master narratives of development have not disappeared; instead, they have taken on new appearances in response to the material infrastructure now dictated by communications technologies and dominated by the interests of a highly concentrated few corporations. New capital formations associated with flexible accumulation, digitalization, and cultural commodification generate new legitimation myths (narratives) to sustain it.

New Economic Formations

Commodification

- Global currency
- Tracking commodification
- ...the most elusive commodity of all: an idea
- Hypercommodification
- **The death of Marxism**

Social Relations of Production

Information Economy

Neo-liberal ideology may now be the reigning myth. We have seen in the **Traveler's** and **Merrill Lynch** commercials how this ideology proclaims the social good of investment while glossing over any moment, or even hint, of exploitation. The Marxist narrative could not withstand the power of capital as it now freely flows across all territories. One dimension of neo-liberal ideology constructs the death of Marxism as a consequence of the power of free market capital. No longer a viable threat, the angst disappears from capitalist discourses about communism. The comic wins out -- not only has state capitalism been vanquished, its ideology of socialist man can be taunted.

The comedian, Denis Leary did a series of **Lotus** commercials drawing on his fast talking, abrasively cynical persona. One **Lotus** ad takes place in a small store run by the 'Palm Beach People's Party.' The store is filled with Soviet paraphernalia and iconography. Hammer & sickle posters hang on the back wall. Their computer monitor featuring their own e-commerce site reads "Our Beach Collection." Beneath are catalogue-style pictures of t-shirts and sunglasses from the collection. On another monitor it states, "Welcome to the PBCCCP." Beneath the copy is an image of Lenin in sunglasses. Leary enters the store and begins an interview with the store manager.

Photo 12.2   Death of Marxism.

Remediation is reform in the sense that media reform reality itself. It is not that media merely reform the appearance of reality. Media hybrids (the affiliations of technical artifacts, rhetorical justifications, and social relationships) are as real as the objects of science. Media make reality over in the same way that all Western technologies have sought to reform reality. Thus, virtual reality reforms reality by giving us an alternative visual world and insisting on that world as the locus of presence and meaning for us. Recent proposals for "ubiquitous" or "distributed" computing world do just the opposite, but in the service of the same desire for reform. (p. 61)

Because this site is about advertising, its primary data are audiovisual texts. How does one present visual analysis? What images does one draw from a commercial? By gathering, selecting, extracting, juxtaposing, framing, and reformulating, we use texts created by corporate Capital in an unintended way. By reframing elements, such as narratives, themes, signifiers, and so forth, remediation creates a critical dimension that allows for alternative readings. Culture jammers, such as Adbusters, add a didactic tract in the form of new visuals and copy. Our approach is to use advertising texts in relation to one another to explore the cosmology of Capital itself. We both lift texts out of their context (e.g., playing on CNBC) and reformulate these texts creating space for reflexivity on the structure of the text and also on its role in constructing a mythology of Capital. To that end, we use stills and video clips in multiple ways. (See Photos 12.3 through 12.6.)

Another device that we commonly use is the extraction of key frames or clips from of a commercial. (See Photos 12.7 and 12.8.)

Designs that make use of these orientations might attract viewers but move the site away from the longer analyses associated with print culture. Academic sites must always negotiate the contested terrain of the perceptual styles associated with these media. Presently, we are reformulating pages to be more visually dynamic and interactive. At what point does the problem of clutter occur? Like good advertising, should each page contain a single unified concept? Or does that simplify the complexity of the arguments linking representation to Capital?

A System of Navigation

One of a website's most important elements is its system of navigation. How do we make it easy for users to recognize where they are, particularly in a site that contains a large number of pages? There are two theories on the use of hierarchical maps for websites. First, cognitive load theory suggests that maps lessen the user's cognitive load and therefore allow him or her to more easily learn the structure of the website. The second theory stresses cognitive learning processes in which the user constructs a map as the user explores and navigates a site. The lack of a map necessitates an active deeper learning process (Nilsson & Mayer, 2002). We started using icons but found that visual markers often cluttered the page and didn't lock into memory as much as linguistic markers. We minimized our icons to the six section headings. The icons are composed of frames from commercials. Each image is selected because it pictorially represents the section heading. When a user scrolls over

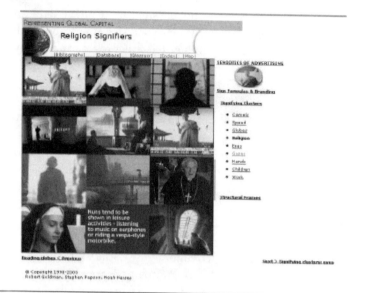

Photo 12.3   In Photos 12.3, 12.4, and 12.5, Live Motion was used to demonstrate the use of reoccurring signifiers in this genre of advertising. Religious signifiers such as nun, monks, and priests are used to signify the harmonious blend of technology with traditional belief systems.

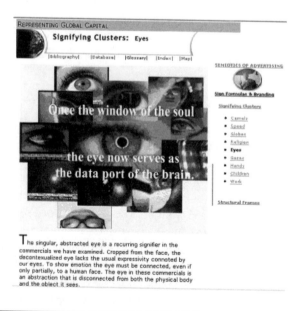

Photo 12.4   Images of eyes are associated with the speed of data transmission that often enters the eye as a beam of light.

Photo 12.5   The upward gaze is less about space than time—Capital's vision of the future.

these images, the title of the heading appears. However, images are too visually rich to serve as directional signs. Most directional icons, whether found in an airport or on a toolbar, are simple line abstractions. Nevertheless, these images support an aesthetic that locates the viewer in a section of the site.

McGann (2001) argued that hypertext decenters, that one can get to other parts of the text by passing others. (See Photo 12.9.)

> Unlike a traditional edition, a hypertext is not organized to focus attention on one particular text or set of texts. It is ordered to disperse attention as broadly as possible. Of course it is true that every *particular* hypertext at any particular point in time will have established preferred sets of arrangements and orderings, and these could be less, or more, decentralized. The point is that the hypertext, unlike the book, encourages greater decentralization of design. Hypertext provides the means for establishing an indefinite number of "centers" and for expanding their number as well as altering their relationships. One is encouraged not so much to find as to make order—and then to make it again and again, as established orderings expose their limits. (p. 71)

True hypertext extends beyond the boundaries that the author imposes. We found that a hypertext that features text links to pages outside the site tends to create navigational havoc. Likewise, creating links within the textual analysis to other pages in the site resulted in losing one's sense of direction. Because the body of the site has approximately 200 linked pages, we

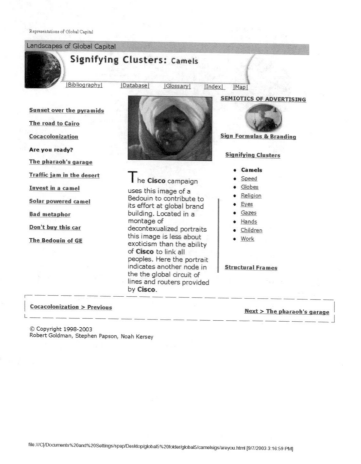

Photo 12.6   Images of camels, Bedouin, pyramids, and desert are used to signify the global reach of corporate Capital.

felt it was essential to have a navigational system that would allow users to spatially locate themselves. Moreover, it is our position that the hierarchical structure also contains a rhetorical dimension. Unlike McGann's (2001) position, we created a hierarchical order. The user, however, can move around the site using multiple navigation systems that are linear, sequential, and Web-like.

We have four systems of navigation:

- An index. The index is a printable page and looks like a table of contents for a book. Users can get to the index from the toolbar.

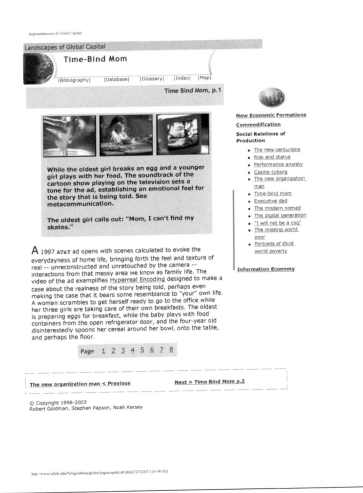

Photo 12.7   Time-Bind Mom is divided into eight pages. Each page builds around key frames from an AT&T commercial. The analysis relies heavily on Arlie Hochschild's (1997) work.

- A visual site map that allows the viewer to mouse over to see what is in every section. This map is a spatial representation of the site. By mousing over section icons, subsections appear. This is also accessible from the toolbar.
- A list of pages in a frame located on the right side of each page. This list locates the viewer in the subsection. It also provides a sense of how topics are related to one another.
- A previous/forward link at the bottom of each page. The user could read each page in a preconceived order.

Holly in Kosovo! Hi, I'm Holly from Philip Morris.

At first Holly is all smiles, naïve and innocent. She just wants to help. Her face lit from the side expresses hope in a drab and dull world. She identifies herself as a representative of Philip Morris.

Less we forget that Philip Morris is aiding these people the company's name is mentioned 8 times in this commercial.

Voice-over, Holly of Philip Morris: And I went along to see that it got there.

Returning to a voice-over Holly explains that her role is overseeing that the food is delivered. This statement is juxtaposed with a truck driving over snow covered roads. Perhaps we could imagine Holly helping to push out the truck if it got stuck. Her primary function is to star in this commercial.

Photo 12.8   This image is a fragment of a page that deconstructs a Philip Morris legitimation commercial. Here we juxtapose frames and narration with analysis.

The user has a choice to work through a section linearly or to use the document as a hypertext. Linking pages only serially or as a Web without a guide (map) lacks the rhetorical power that we as authors wanted. The intent of the project is to map representations of Capital. We imposed the structure that hermeneutically emerged on the analysis in the form of a navigational system. It serves not only to allow the user to locate himself or herself easily, but also acts as our map of these representations. Navigational devices serve to imprint our construction of the representational landscape of Capital in the user's mind. Because the project is about mapping representations, the navigational system (the authors' map) functions as a tree on which specific analyses are hung. We present it in numerous ways to reinforce our constructed version on the user.

Hypertext—A Discussion

Discussions of the epistemological implications of hypertext emerged from the convergence of three theoretical perspectives via literary theory.

Postmodern theorists, such as Harvey, Hassan, Lyotard, and Baudrillard, stressed the indeterminate and fragmented nature of knowledge generated by the rise of electronic communications. Cultural fragmentation was linked to the accelerated production and circulation of signs created by electronic technology motivated by Capital's ongoing quest for profit. Generally, postmodern theorists focus analysis on macro-level social formations and their reading of texts is used to represent these formations. Hypertext theory draws heavily on this emphasis on fragmentation and indeterminacy found in postmodern theory. Websites such as *ctheory* (http://www.ctheory.net/) blend postmodern sensibilities, theory, and aesthetics collapsing discursive boundaries in reflexive hypertext/hypermedia. Poststructuralists are concerned with the nature of discourse itself. Barthes, Foucault, Derrida, and Kristeva struggled to undermine the essentialist assumptions associated with concepts such as author, text, sign, and structure. They extended the concept of text beyond its traditional boundaries, often reversing the roles of readers and writers. They repositioned the reader in relation to texts and unveiled the implicit assumptions in discourse. Computer theorists, such as Vannevar Bush and Theodor Nelson, positioned as the forerunners for hypertext, are interested in developing information retrieval systems (i.e., Memex) that mimic human thought. As new computer programming devised ways of storing and retrieving data (i.e., Apple's Hypercard), new models for intelligence and memory were constructed.

These three strands were brought together by literary theorists George Landow and Michael Joyce and writing historian Jay Bolter. Landow (1997) stated that

> hypertext has much in common with some major points of contemporary literary and semiological theory, particularly with Derrida's emphasis on decentering and with Barthes' conception of the readerly versus the writerly text. In fact, hypertext creates an almost embarrassingly literal embodiment of both concepts, one that in turn raises questions about them and their interesting combination of pre-science and historical relations (or embeddedness). (p. 32)

Landow (1992) celebrated the hypertext as a new form of writing that promises empowerment: "I contend that the history of information technology from writing to hypertext reveals an increasing democratization or dissemination of power" (p. 277). The fragmented indeterminate nature of hypertext is positioned as a revolutionary form. Joyce (1995), author of the seminal literary hypertext *afternoon, a story* (Joyce, 1993), drew heavily from Derrida's (1991) essay *Living On* to argue that texts overflow endlessly into other "differential traces." Here the reader becomes the writer by choosing the direction of the flow. In this regard, "digital technology is turning out to be one of the more traumatic remediations in the history of Western writing. One reason is that digital technology changes the 'look and feel' of writing and reading" (Bolter, 2001, p. 24). Bolter emphasized the electronic nature of hypertext and its ability to include visual and aural representations: "The electronic writing space is inclusive, open to multiple systems of representation" (p. 36). He further noted that the visual "threatens to overwhelm the text on the Web page" (p. 73). Computer technology and Internet applications privilege digitalization and hyperlinking. This relationship opposes the privileging of text in the Western academic tradition. Hypertext theorists emphasize a relational shift between author and reader, a textual shift from written to visual, and a directional shift from linear to nonlinear.

The posited equivalence between poststructural theory and hypertext theory has, however, been questioned. Ganascia (2002) argued that there are some crucial differences between hypertextual theorists and neostructuralists such as Derrida and Barthes. He distinguished between underreading and overreading. Ganascia argued that, on the one hand, "hypertext encourages 'under-reading' by giving easy access to pieces of information" (p. 16). Readers surf leisurely and often superficially across lexias, garnering fragments of information. Writers, such as Barthes, on the other hand, used lexias as a way to dismantle a text and facilitate new readings. "'Over-reading,' adding sense, bringing fresh material to ancient concepts, is contrary to 'browsing' and picking up bits and pieces here and there in a text, unreadable through its sheer immensity" (Ganascia, 2002, p. 16). Ganascia argued that poststructuralism fails to legitimize hypertextuality. Likewise, Aarseth (1997) questioned the equivalence between poststructural concepts such as network, writerly, and lexia and their use in hypertext theory. He concluded that

> the politics of the author-reader relationship, ultimately, is not a choice between paper and electronic text, or linear and non-linear text, or interactive or noninteractive text, or open and closed text but instead is whether the user has the ability to transform the text into something that the instigator of the text could not foresee or plan for. This, of course, depends much more on the user's own motivation than on whatever political structure the text appears to impose. (p. 164)

Although the metatheoretical discussions of hypertext target the infinite nature of linking, it is its visual character that radically turns readers into users. As noted, hypertext privileges the visual in three ways: its aesthetic serves a visual rendering of the analysis; it incorporates audiovisual media

Photo 12.9   Navigational icons: Mapping Global Capital; Global Capital; Semiotics of Advertising; Grand Narratives; Landscapes of Capital; Speed.

and operates as hypermedia; and its navigation system functions as cognitive map. It is the integration of these elements that underlies and stimulates user decisions to hesitate or travel onward. If a page is too cluttered, we mouse click away to a user-friendly aesthetic. If the visuals lack salience, we surf on. If the navigation system is incoherent and we cannot construct a cognitive map, we experience disorientation and frustration. As hypertext theory matures, discussions of its visual nature and the centrality of design take on increasing importance.

Empowerment—Reader Versus Writer

How do we position our site against this discussion? Does hypertext theory, drawn from a literary tradition, neatly apply to a scholarly site? Do these theories take into account the practice of a work in progress? In the process of making this site, we have been mindful of the tension between competing ideals and competing perils (e.g., writing in shorter blocks can help us avoid the overly linear text, but it also risks fragmentation). Can one hold on to modernist ideals of intellectual coherence in a medium that could easily be labeled as postmodern? Does our site liberate the user from a linear rhetorical reading designed by the authors? Although it is true that users can enter the site wherever they want, change direction, and read in an unintended order, aesthetics, integration of visuals, and navigation still imprint an authorial hierarchy on the site.

We also need to rethink the concept of empowerment. Postmodern schizophrenia traversing a world of white noise composed of fragments and factoids is not necessarily empowerment. Empowerment is based on reflexivity and both access to and understanding of relevant discourses. Hypertext creates an open often-unbounded system of information creating new and unexpected associations. "In a hypertext environment, nothing stops the user from entering your argument at the conclusion, the problem statement, or anything in between. In this way, a hypertext resembles associative thinking more than reading or writing" (Felker, 2002, p. 329).[2] Associative thinking is not necessarily conducive to critical thinking. Keep in mind that advertising discourse is built on associative thinking. Signifier/signified/commodity are linked simply because they share the same space, the advert. Advertising creates strange bedfellows (i.e., happy active people smoking cigarettes). Association does not necessarily enhance critical thought, deep readings, and reflexivity. Agency is not located in form but in the relationship of a subject to a text. The formal structure of the text certainly orients that relationship but in no way liberates nor determines it. We hope that our reading of advertising texts will encourage alternative readings. By providing a searchable database and by placing commercials on pages, the site empowers the user to move beyond our analyses. (See Photos 12.10 through 12.12.) Nevertheless, the power of the user lies in the experience and knowledge that the user brings to the site.

Mapping Versus Theoretical Coherence

What we have tried to do is to assemble the map, to find the pieces and link them together with the intention of providing a rough guide for navigating the symbolic world of Capital. We are not just discussing the maps produced by Capital, we are ourselves mapping (even if critically) a discourse constituted by cultural criticism. By bringing these ads together, categorizing them, and connecting them to an outline, we are creating a map that was previously unspoken. (Landscapes of Capital website at http://it.stlawu.edu/~global/)

We associate maps with the physical landscape. Mapping cultural texts, particularly the flow of advertising texts, appears to be much more unruly. The physical referent for our map has both leaky amorphous boundaries and is a scape in constant flux. Moreover, a map built upon cultural deconstruction and interpretation rather than on physical measurement appears much more subjective.[3] Nevertheless, mapping serves as a methodological strategy that allows us to impose order and sense on what otherwise appears as disjointed, competitive, and unconnected texts.

The process of mapping is hermeneutic; each individual commercial is part of a fluid mosaic. The categories used to spatially organize the commercials are derived both from the literature on globalization and post-Fordism and from the analyses of the commercials. These categories act back on the commercials to make sense of them both individually and collectively. As authors, we mediate this process with our theoretical understandings of advertising and Capital.

Mapping is a form of power. The history of mapping correlates with the rise of nation states. The map asserted control over politically claimed territory. Corporate advertising selectively maps the effects of its practices across the globe.[4] Because advertising materializes as an ever-present flow across mediascapes, its relationship to its referent becomes taken for granted. And so, there is a hierarchy of signification here. There are the actual corporate practices, corporate representations of those practices, and our map and analyses of those representations.

What is the relationship of hypertext, mapping, and social theory? The spatial character of hypertext mimics the map. Joyce (1995) notes that in hypertext, "the writing process, as we have come to understand it, becomes geographic" (p. 161). Because the primary element of hypertext is the link, this format privileges the relationship between writing spaces. It forefronts the getting from here to there. Links and navigational structures visually (spatially) spell out our version of the relationship between representation and Capital.

The principal epistemological concern, however, is the relationship between mapping and theory construction. On the one hand, hypertext focuses on the relationship of representations to one another. On the other hand, it lacks the linear certainty, a form of argumentation that we associate with theory. Landow (1997) argued that

hypertext linking, reader control, and variation not only militate against the modes of argumentation to which we have become accustomed but have other,

LANDSCAPES OF GLOBAL CAPITAL

City of the Future I

[Bibliography]   [Database]   [Glossary]   [Index]   [Map]

LANDSCAPES

Abstraction and
Deterritorialization

Cultural Geography

The Architecture of Capital

* The skyscapes of
  capital
  * Global Cities
  * Towers
  * City of Future
  * City of Future
    2
  * Virtual Cities
  * City of capital
  * Nodes & Flows
  * World Trade
    Center
* Capital's skyline

Boeing's artful imagery of the city of the near future. The mixing of elements is suggestive of a postmodern motif. The landscape itself captures the movement of data at blurring speeds. The metaphor of the highway transit flows defined by light beams is used repeatedly in these ads to signify the electronic movement of information. Here is the landscape for the information Age – postmodern citadels of corporate culture presiding over a smoothly functioning society — so smooth, it actually whizzes along without any apparent need for external intervention. The flow of reddish color can also conjure up the imagery of blood coursing through the body system, keeping it alive, healthy and functioning.

Towers of capital < Previous   Next > City of the Future II

LANDSCAPES OF GLOBAL CAPITAL

Virtual Cities

[Bibliography]   [Database]   [Glossary]   [Index]   [Map]

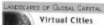

LANDSCAPES

Abstraction and
Deterritorialization

Cultural Geography

The Architecture of Capital

* The skyscapes of
  capital
  * Global Cities
  * Towers
  * City of Future
  * City of Future
    2
  * Virtual Cities
  * City of capital
  * Nodes & Flows
  * World Trade
    Center
* Capital's skyline

One vision of the coming electronic city is provided by BAP's "city of a" which seems to float over the edge of the planet as a hologram or an apparition (depending on one's theoretical point of view). Upon entering the "city of a," we may perceive that it internally replicates the vertical lines and shapes of the modern city, this time as a self-contained cyber-fortress. This is a city conjured up by computer technologies and clean, ultra-national, market-like exchanges of goods and commodities. In this way, society is made apparently a better place, driven by the apparatus of efficiency and rationality.

NASDAQ offers another version of the cybercity in which the cybercity is depicted as a product of the computerized world of business and science. This freeze frame captures the overlay of scenes that combines the 'Enter' key on a computer keyboard with an aerial shot of skyscrapers comprising a global, centercity business district.

City of the future II < Previous   Next > City of capital

Representations of Global Capital

Landscapes of Global Capital

Microchip Landscapes

|Bibliography| |Database| |Glossary| |Index| |Map|

The micro-technology revolution that underlies advances in semiconductor chips, fiber optics, biotechnology, and telecommunications has its own landscapes. A **Computer Associates** commercial touts a product called Neugents (derived from Neural Agent) that it claims can think for itself! Part way through the commercial, in a long string of "high-tech" signifiers intended to bolster the astonishing assertion of a technology that "thinks," the following scene of a complex circuitboard appears. But it's how it appears that interests us -- it resembles a "panoptic" overview of a modern city. It looks like a map -- like a geographical map that seems to map a landscape. This must be the high tech landscape of miniaturization.

Abstraction & Deterritorialization

* Representing space
* Ad cartography
* Global panorama
* Decontextualized sunsets
* Virtual place
* Placeless places
* **The landscape of microtechnology**
* Cyberspace

Cultural Geography

The Architecture of Capital

This scene appears but for a brief second, vanishing as it abruptly as it appeared, flushed away in the stream of images that follow. The image barely has time to register, but much less permit reflection upon its meaning. And yet, a similar shot of this signifier, framed comparably, recurs in ads from other large technology providers. **Siemens** uses the same device here to frame circuitboard "components" as evocative of an urban landscape. Perhaps a tacit meaning in this panopticism is that computer circuitboards are the 'ground' of a global unification of digital telecommunications. The grids and networks that appear in these landscapes, speak to the rationalized delivery of services and goods. Even more precisely rationalized grids are evident in the imaging system at right. But if Virilio is right that territory becomes outmoded by the micro-electronics revolution, why construct a visual analogy between the technology and the territorial landscape?

One available meaning in these circuitboard landscapes is that they represent landscapes of speed and rationality. Such a reading is, however, immediately contradicted by the inverse relation between speed and territorialization. But perhaps it is precisely the latter tension that accounts for this type of symbolization. Turning the material of microelectronics into landscapes may offer a modest reassurance about the stability of social forms. Mapping offers a way of ordering our world. And electronic forms of mapping offer the imagery of precision in ordering the world.

Photos 12.10, 12.11, and 12.12   The hypertext allows users to follow their interest by assembling the order of pages. For example, the user could go from "The City of the Future" to "Virtual Cities" to "Microchip Landscapes" using a hypertext map. Likewise, once in, the user can proceed directly to individual pages or through different thematic portals (i.e., Landscapes: The Geography of Capital). The visual elements on the page serve as icons of salience. Easily scanned, the visual elements function to valorize a decision to invest time in the page by reading the text.

far more general effects, one of which is to add what may be seen as a kind of randomness to the reader's text. Another is that the writer, as we shall see, loses certain basic controls over his text, particularly over its edges and borders. Yet a third is that the text appears to fragment, to atomize, into constituent elements (into lexias or blocks of text), and these reading units take on a life of their own as they become more self-contained, because they become less dependent on what comes before or after in a linear succession. (p. 64)

In *The End of Ideology,* Daniel Bell (1966) distinguished between the scholar and the intellectual. He noted,

The scholar has a bounded field of knowledge, a tradition, and seeks to find his place in it, adding to the accumulated, tested knowledge of the past as to a mosaic. . . . The intellectual begins with his experience, his individual perceptions of the world, his privileges and deprivations, and judges the world by these sensibilities. (p. 402)

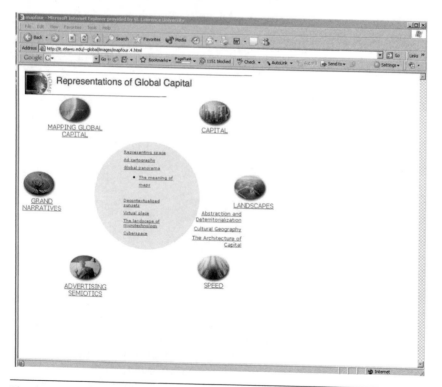

Photo 12.13   Visual site map.

Bell went on to note that in the postindustrial society, the role of the intellectual had greatly weakened, replaced by an ideology of accommodation and accumulation. We might add a third character to this dichotomy: the bricoleur. For Lévi-Strauss (1966), the term *bricoleur* refers to someone who works with his hands and uses "devious means" in the act of production. Although there is no equivalent in English, the term refers to a man who does odd jobs, a jack-of-all-trades. Lévi-Strauss compared the bricoleur to the engineer. He noted that although the bricoleur can carry out a variety of tasks, the engineer subordinates tasks to the availability of specific tools or the proper raw materials. The engineer conceptualizes, whereas the bricoleur improves:

> And the decision as to what to put in each place also depends on the possibility of putting a different element there instead, so that each choice which is made will involve a complete reorganization of the structure, which will never be the same as one vaguely imagined nor as some other which might have been preferred to it. . . . It might be said that the engineer questions the universe, while the "bricoleur" addresses himself to a collection of oddments left over from human endeavors, that is, only a sub-set of the culture . . . the engineer is always trying to make his way out of and go beyond the constraints imposed by a particular state of civilization while the "bricoleur" by inclination or necessity always remains within them. This is another way of saying that the engineer works by means of concepts and the "bricoleur" by means of signs. (Lévi-Strauss, 1966, pp. 19–20)

Although scholars and intellectuals are idealized, even mythologized, production practices within academia increasingly resemble bricolage. This is a consequence of the explosive production and the accelerated distribution of cultural texts. Keeping up with the flow of information even in fairly specialized fields is often daunting. The strategy of bricolage recognizes the impossibility of placing scholarly boundaries around knowledge fields. Moreover, images and audio/video texts dominate the flow of this electronic montage. They are much more unruly than the printed word. Hypertext, and the electronic information technology that supports it, lends itself to bricolage. Ironically, although hypertext adds to the chaos of the electronic flow, it can function as a flexible and dynamic tool that can impose at least a momentary semblance of order on segments of cultural texts. By blending mapping and analysis, the hypertext can "rope off" and boost media reflexivity.

> Any perceived fragmentation or chaos instigated by hypertextual links is only problematic when viewed from a print-centric vantage point. While the print medium holds up stability and order as ideals, in the electronic age masses of

reticulated, even self-contradicting texts are connected via the unity that hyperlinks provide. (Feldman, 2001, p. 154)

In our site, adverts are collected and assembled in relation to other adverts. The categories in which we place the analysis give cognitive order to this relation. Yet many of our analyses of specific adverts could easily be placed in other categories. Building this site draws heavily on the production practices of gathering, cutting and pasting, and reassembling. Moreover, the user also can move in whatever direction he or she desires. We might think of bricolage as a consumption practice in which the user assembles a cognitive map of the data and analyses. Does this style of production suggest that the fragmented cut-up nature of hypertext/hypermedia makes theoretical coherence an impossibility?

We are not convinced that this is so. First, throughout the site, we have attempted to engage in conversation with relevant theories. This conversation is woven into the fabric of analysis. Second, theoretical generalization emerges later in the process and is generated out of the process of bricolage. As authors, we are constantly rewriting and reorganizing. Although this is also part of the process for writing a manuscript, the lack of closure associated with building a hypertext not only extends but also privileges this task. Consequently, theory is inductive and grounded. For example, we are now discussing a seventh section with the preliminary heading of Crisis and Contradiction (no icon yet). Here we plan to explore the relationship of representation and the emergent economic formations through the relationship of contradiction to visual abstraction. Essentially, we see the process of constructing hypertext closely akin to bricolage. But unlike the bricoleur, our goal is to move beyond signification to conceptualization.

Conclusion: Print Versus the World Wide Web

Calise and Lowi (2000) authored *Hyperpolitics*, a hypertext of interconnected matrices composed of concepts ands axes that allow the user to see relationships between political concepts that were extracted from dictionaries and encyclopedias of political science. They argued that "hypertext brings an interactive and dynamic quality to theory-making" (p. 285). They also noted,

> However, a caveat is in order here. The recent spread of the World Wide Web on the Internet has greatly enhanced the possibility of surfing from one term— or site—to another through a hypertext-like interface. Yet, the philosophy of the Net is a bottom-up approach: making available for the user as many sources as possible, but *with no closure*. Unlimited—and unguided—access to

a massive number of sources is equivalent to hardly any access at all; an excess of freedom can be a one-way ticket to chaos. (p. 285)

Hypertext can be distributed as CD-ROM or website. We didn't have the resources to publish and distribute the project as a CD-ROM. As long as our institutions provide server space, distribution is instant and global. Because we use both institutional servers, we often have two different versions of the site: a clean functioning one and messy innovative one. Now we must consider publishing in the context of the Web. "The Internet generally privileges speed of connecting authors and readers, serendipity, and novelty over epistemological reliability (as mediated by peer review, publishing houses, and curated libraries)" (Kling, 1997, pp. 434–444). Two new concerns emerge at this point in the process: publicizing the site and establishing credibility in a virtual world in the absence of gatekeepers. We have presented papers on the site at academic conferences. We have recently e-mailed a description and address of the site to a number of journal editors with the hope of getting it reviewed. We have encouraged colleagues to use and link to the site. We have also sent the address to other websites that serve as clearinghouses for critical sites on advertising. Unlike book publishing, in which the distribution network is more or less fixed by the publisher, WWW distribution is variable and uneven. It also is cumulative and grows geometrically. It is not constrained by geography, temporality, or economics.

Will this project ever end? When does one stop adding data to the site? When do its authors become intellectually disengaged from the site? As we move toward completion, we must now engage with these questions. McGann (2001) aptly noted,

Unlike a traditional book or set of books, the hypertext need never be "complete"—though of course one could choose to shut the structure down if one wanted, close its covers as it were. But the hypertextual order contains an inertia that moves against such a shutdown. (p. 71)

Think of sending that final draft of a manuscript, proofread and ready for the printer, back to the publisher, to receiving authors' copies in the mail, running across your book in a bookstore, a colleague's note telling you that he or she is using the book for a class, initiating a new project. There is pleasure to closure. Think of the tons of website detritus reflected by nonfunctioning links. Perhaps at some point, despite our best intentions, our site will join the electronic rubbish heap. It is hoped that until then, it serves as a useful research and pedagogical tool.

Addendum

In the time since we wrote the preceding article, this project has spawned three unique avenues of exploration. Wrestling with these diverging yet intertwined initiatives illustrates the important lessons we learned from this project, and these lessons point to where we see it heading in the future. We previously argued in favor of hypertext as a medium because it provided flexibility and a particular suitability for presenting multimedia materials so obviously lacking in a traditional manuscript.

In comparison to a manuscript, however, hypertext is a fragmented format in which the voice of authorial narrative is weakened. Much of the literature on hypertext celebrates this weakness, arguing that this characteristic empowers the reader. Hypertext appears to be the uber-writerly text of Barthes (1977). As he noted, "the birth of the reader must be at the cost of the death of the Author" (p. 148).

Because our website was necessarily a hybrid of traditional academic writing and experimental multimedia artifact, we attempted to create an alternative narrative structure by using navigational devices. We employed a comprehensive site index; each page contains links to other pages in each section to provide a sense of location to the reader. We felt that theoretical narrative demands that readers are able to locate themselves in the narrative. A recognizable structure not only allows readers to traverse the site in an informed way but also allows authors to produce a narrative flow while recognizing that users have the agency to move easily outside the structure to follow their own interests. And yet we had a sense that the narrative was not necessarily being pursued. The website is a collection of small pieces loosely joined, and both the benefits and drawbacks have become more apparent to us.

One Step Back

The first of our three divergences is that we now find ourselves producing a manuscript from the website. Moving in this direction generates a number of questions. Why go backward? At this stage, why write a manuscript? How does one go from a hypertext to a linear text? What are the problems that we are encountering along the way?

We are going back to a manuscript format for a number of reasons, not the least of which is the cultural mores of academia. Books make work legitimate in a way that the Web cannot yet—and may never—do. A book goes through a gatekeeping apparatus. When we had a stable version of the site, we sent an abstract to the editors of relevant journals, requesting that our website be reviewed. Despite the numerous e-mails that we received commenting on the site, no journal editor deemed it worthy of review. Academia continues to hold a strong bias toward the hard copy that travels through gatekeepers of the publishing industry. There is an interesting contradiction here. The publishing industry, including university presses, is increasingly driven by cost-efficiency protocols that can restrict subject matter, limit the size of documents, and determine the style. Website production bypasses not only gatekeeping but also all the economic pressures to produce a profit-making commodity. Despite this, the benefits of independent screening, professional editing, and the extended temporal space for refinement, akin to the waiting period necessary to purchase a gun, all come into play here and are good reasons for pursuing the traditional form.

The site is so large that no one can sit in front of a computer screen and read through it. The printed page, the book on one's lap, is much more amenable to a complete reading and more pleasurable for longer engagement spans. In this first generation of Internet users, we recognize that the Web is most often explored quickly; decisions are made in nanoseconds. We are continually told readers do not bother to scroll down a page. Simply, the book, in all its physicality, is superior for engaging a reader in an extended theoretical narrative, and it was frustrating to try and shoehorn that element of the project into a webpage-based structure. As authors, we want to allow the unfolding of an argument across many chapters, and we predict that because of this need, the book will continue to be an important part of the experience.

As an example of the kind of narrative sabotage we observed, we have heard anecdotally that some readers, on entering the site, went to the section entitled *camels* or other similarly nominated subsections of the semiotics-focused portion of the site. Readers tend to bypass narrative to pursue what is salient, but salience is often more about spectacle, a particular task (i.e., fact hunt), or just a passing fancy—a critique leveled at the nature of information within postmodernity.

This process of transformation from hypertextual to linear has been both challenging and illuminating. Putting a theoretical narrative to each chapter has demanded that we rethink our analysis. As we revisit the site, our focus now is not just on the content of Capital scapes but on the structures that are used to frame adverts. We are interested in how corporations reproduce grand narratives out of decontextualized signifiers. We see the thematic montage as a dominant structure in which signifiers are assembled and given affect through music and given salience through narration. Now we struggle to develop this discussion as our own narrative and weave it through the manuscript. Consequently, we had to rethink style. On our website, analyses of ads were equivalent to one another. Each analysis could be read as a closed completed text. Users could then jump to anywhere in the site to read another analysis if they so chose. In this sense, the website flattened the information. The manuscript has made a different demand on us. We have decided to choose specific ads to highlight as representative analytical pieces while other ad analyses are shortened and integrated into the narrative. Here, information is hierarchal and a function of authorial decision.

The website sprawls, and despite our efforts to cut, chapters seem to grow. Moreover, even though readers will be able to access commercials on the website, we feel the need to include more frames to exemplify our analysis. Length has become a major problem. We even have discussed producing a two-volume piece. Website length is a function of the amount of memory allocated on a server. As server size has grown and cost has dropped, this is no longer a topic of conversation. The printed text demands that we focus and refine our argument.

Finally, the work of manuscript writing demands continual engagement. All academics struggle with finding time for continuous writing amid the demands of teaching or academic committee work. Although hypertext design demands continual engagement, hypertext writing is much more fragmented and is more easily integrated into our fragmented lives.

The issues here are voluminous and being continually redefined with each passing year as traditions change, curricula change, teaching methods evolve, and the economics of academia exerts its gravity.

One Step Sideways

Our second divergence is the development of electronic multimedia documents that blur the line between traditional print pieces and the Web pages we were creating. Through the use of electronic publishing software such as Adobe InDesign and the emerging video capabilities of the Portable Document Format (PDF), we are able to embed video and sound clips into a consistent and recognizable document structure that is easily distributed.

One of the main issues that we encountered was getting attention to the site. One method was to present papers at conferences, often in a section on advertising or globalization. Drawing from different sections of the site, we also wrote articles for journals. Here we were able to go through a peer review process, advertise the site, and focus our theoretical narrative. One such article, "Speed: Through, Across, and In—The Landscapes of Capital," was published in an electronic journal (http://www.fastcapitalism.com). Here, we produced a narrative that both focused on the depiction of Capital and on the processes of decontextualization, fragmentation, and abstraction in relation to the representation of speed. We also explored the use of speed in highly accelerated flows of signifiers across our screens. The journal provided two versions to readers: text only and video embedded. Using Acrobat Reader (6.0 and above), readers could play the commercials on the metaphorical page.

Although we gave up some of the virtues of hypertext, we were able to include commercials for readers to view. For our specific needs, the learning curve for InDesign was a fraction of the time spent on learning Web-authoring software. Publishing video-embedded PDF files offers scholars an easy solution for providing visual texts to readers. And electronic publishing offers speed of publication, ease of access, the inclusion of image and video texts, and virtually no page length restraints. As all of these technologies continue to merge, it seems that this will be a fruitful arena for bridging the gap of traditional publishing and full-blown multimedia Web productions.

One Leap Forward

The third divergence we are pursuing is that of reconfiguring the website so it is contained within the framework of a database. This journey looks like it will be a complete reexamination and reimagining of the work we have done so far. This excerpt from a discussion on the SIGIA-L listserv for Information Architecture lays out in stark terms the paradigmatic shift that such a move entails.

> What also helps here, as Jonathan mentioned, is the withering notion of a "page." Once you go from website -> online application, page is an anachronism. Data drives the interaction and the architecture reflects this compression of the distance between data and interface, rendering paper/printing as road kill.

What do we write if not pages? Our site relied on static pages managed through our HTML editing program, Adobe GoLive. To make changes to a page, we had to edit several pages and add new links to our navigation systems. This was cumbersome and frustrating. Moreover, we located the site on two different servers at academic institutions at opposite ends of the country. We first did this to use one site as experimental space. When we were satisfied with the changes, we would post them on the other site. As we wrote articles and presented papers, multiple versions proliferated. Some of these changes found their way into the site; others did not, partly because of the complexity of our editing process. Our Web publishing system presented a real impediment. In the interim, many different software packages have emerged in the area of content management systems; one of these may help remove some of the burden of this process. Content management is still a developing field, and there is no clear path. Rather, interested parties are left to adopt or develop whatever seems to suit their needs best. In contrast, once a manuscript is printed, unless another edition is to be published, continuous revision is not a concern. For a website, revision is unending. This is even more true for a website about advertising. The flow of new commercials is unending. Our database now includes more than 2,000 commercials and continues to grow. Being novices, where we failed initially was to develop a clean efficient system to allow us to make macro-level changes.

The database component began as a simple tool for organizing the ads we digitized. Having worked with that for a few years, we can now see the possibility of using it for much more. The system we are now working toward will be driven by the database itself. As we envision going forward, the essential form of the project will shift from hundreds of individual html files to a database containing thousands of records. The look and feel of pages will be separated from the content, allowing things to be rearranged much more easily, depending on the needs of the authors or users. With the inherent search capabilities, there are opportunities for more user-created pathways through the material. The appearance and usage of this type of site could be similar to a site based on static pages; however, its behavior will be easier to control on a large scale. Edits are reflected immediately. The possibilities for conceptual reorganization are numerous. Navigation could become more a result of the search function. Linearity could exist for those who want it or be abolished for those who don't.

Dynamic sites have become much more common. From January 2000 to November 2005, usage of the scripting language PHP (commonly used as a go-between for a database and Web browser) has gone from virtually several to more than 2 million sites, leading to more development of tools that may be useful in an academic context (*PHP*, 2006). *Voice of the Shuttle* has gone through this transformation. Its introductory page states,

> Welcome to the new VoS. Started in 1994 as a suite of static Web pages, VoS has now been rebuilt as a database that serves content dynamically on the Web. Users gain greater flexibility in viewing and searching, while editors are able to work more efficiently and flexibly. We've tried to maintain most of the original structure of the site, which models the way the humanities are organized for research and teaching as well as the way they are adapting to social, cultural, and technological changes. But some shifts in organization and navigation are necessary for technical reasons. *Voice of the Shuttle* (April 17, 2006)

As we move into this new terrain, four new sets of concerns arise.

The Question of Metadata

One of the initial tasks when constructing a database is defining the fields, and this has led us to look very closely at how we describe the digitized commercials and in the future the analytical essays. We use the term *metadata* here in referring to the data *about* the data, any input we attach to a particular object to describe it. Obvious choices—company, title, length, size, and format—are givens, but what about trying to code for theoretical concepts through keywords? By engaging in semiotic analysis, we already approach these artifacts with the premise that there is a multiplicity of signifieds for each signifier, and yet it is analytically disconcerting that there is no visible end to that road. From our current vantage point, we hope to provide a coherent structure so that we can allow for the continual evolution of our description of the artifacts. Our understanding will always be only partial. This challenge is compounded by having multiple researchers working on the same dataset, but with their own unique subjectivities. Whereas one person may code attentively to one facet, the other may not notice it at all. A controlled vocabulary for keywording is tempting for its consistency, yet uncomfortably limiting when something new and unexpected is encountered. This process serves as a potent reminder about the power of the language we use to describe the things we perceive and how that shapes our experience of them.

The World Outside

After all of that navel gazing, we are also concerned about how the database that we create operates with other structures on the Web. The data we do end up creating need to make sense to other researchers and other automated electronic systems that are growing around the world. One goal we have for the site is that it can become a gathering place for those interested in studying advertisements, whatever the context may be. Our vision is to open up the site to include external authorship by providing space for user responses and analyses. At this point, the site authors will become less creators and more moderators and community leaders.

Usability

The way in which we tie all of the elements of our site together and present them to our visitors is something we want to have in mind at all times. How do we make the site transparent, allowing for meaningful interaction, searches, and responses? Our ability to relate the different data we create will largely determine our ability to tease out new patterns and construct new narratives that had been previously obscured. The degree of internal relatedness will broaden the pedagogical possibilities for the project, allowing users to examine an analysis from many different angles.

Storage and Growth

With hundreds on hundreds of analog videotapes lying around, we are not yet completely satisfied with our ability to choose archival "best practices." Digital video is still expensive to store because of its size, although storage is coming down in price all the time, and we must assume that soon that point will be moot. With some VHS tapes more than two decades old and degrading noticeably, we like very much the prospect of storing digital copies in their full resolution in two or more places. From those master copies, we would be able to derive versions appropriate for whatever means of distribution we require, be it small and compact streaming video for the Web or mid-size copies for projection in the classroom. So what is the most appropriate system for producing master copies? How can we ensure storage safekeeping and the funding and institutional support to keep the project ongoing? How do we go about automating the process to improve efficiency? At present, we are struggling with the complexity of new technologies in a rapidly changing technological landscape. What we hope is that the work will endure, so that it can serve others and be a foundation for future scholarship.

Our goal for the newly emerging site is tighter integration in which textual analysis becomes a component of the database structure. By linking the analysis with the video records, we hope

- A deeper view of the analytic process will emerge.
- New correlations that have gone unnoticed will appear.
- New cognitive linkages will generate pedagogical utility of user connections within the material.
- New patterns that we disguised by the use of individual files will be generated by users themselves.
- New usages will be driven by users' needs rather than authors' intuitions.
- Glossaries, course modules, PowerPoints, and other organizational devices will be interactively developed by teachers and scholars using the database.
- Community involvement will increase as the site serves users not only as a resource but as an interactive space.

The database is a construct fast becoming one of the predominant forms in our society. In a constantly changing landscape, be it within the scope of one research area or the larger sphere of a digital life, the ability to add to, search, manipulate, and visualize the steady stream of incoming information is absolutely crucial. It will be essential for new sociologists to be critically trained in the use of databases both as a research tool and as a space in which they organize their data and from which they distribute their findings, insights, and observations.

Notes

1. Here, we began with Adobe's Live Motion program—their version of Macromedia's Flash—and are moving to Flash in our next generation—upgrade—of the site.

2. Most users tell us they go from index to signifying clusters: camels first. The unexpected and unique draws attention. What is the relationship of nonlinear reading to scholarly reading?

3. Critical geographers question the myth of objectivity that hovers above the map. "Because [an interested party] selects from the vast storehouse of knowledge about the earth what the map will represent, these interests are embodied in the map as presences and absences. Every map shows this but not that, and every map shows what it shows this way but not the other. Not only is this inescapable but it is precisely because of this interested selectivity—this choice of word or sign or aspect of the world to make a point—that the map is enabled to work" (Wood, 1992, p. 1).

4. In contemporary society, "mapping has become an activity primarily reserved for those in power, used to delineate the 'property' of nation states and multinational companies" (Aberley, 1993, p. 1).

References

Aarseth E. (1997). *Cybertext: Perspectives on ergodic literature*. Baltimore, MD: John Hopkins University Press.

Aberley, D. (1993). *Boundaries of home: Mapping for local empowerment*. Gabriola Island, BC: New Society.

Barthes, R. (1977). The death of the author. In *Image, music, text*. New York: Noonday Press.

Bell, D. (1966). *The end of ideology*. New York: Free Press.

Berger, J., & Mohr, J. (1982). *Another way of telling*. New York: Pantheon.

Bolter, J. D. (2001). *Writing spaces: Computers, hypertext, and the remediation of print*. Mahwah, NJ: Lawrence Erlbaum.

Bolter, J. D., & Grusin, R. (2000). *Remediation: Understanding new media.* Cambridge, MA: MIT Press.

Calise, M., & Lowi, T. J. (2000). Hyperpolitics: Hypertext, concepts and theory-making. *International Political Science Review, 21*(3), 283–310.

Castells, M. (1996). *Rise of the network society, the information age* (Vol. 1). Oxford, UK: Basil Blackwell.

Derrida, J. (1991). Living on. In P. Kamuf (Ed.), *A Derrida reader* (pp. 254–268). New York: Columbia University Press.

Feldman, S. (2001). The link, and how we think: Using hypertext as a teaching & learning tool. *International Journal of Instructional Media, 28*(2), 153–158.

Felker, K. (2002). Ariadne's thread: Hypertext, writing, and the World Wide Web. *Library Hi Tech, 20*(3), 325–339.

Ganascia, J.-G. (2002). On the supposed neo-structuralism of hypertext. *Diogenes, 49/4*(196), 8–19.

Hochschild, C. R. (1997). *The time bind: When work becomes home and home becomes work.* New York: Metropolitan Books.

Joyce, M. (1993). *Afternoon: a story* [CD-ROM]. Cambridge, MA: Eastgate Press.

Joyce, M. (1995). *Of two minds: Hypertext pedagogy and poetics.* Ann Arbor: University of Michigan Press.

Kling, R. (1997, July). The Internet for sociologists. *Contemporary Sociology, 26*(4), 434–444.

Landow, G. P. (1992). *Hypertext: The convergence of contemporary critical theory and technology.* Baltimore, MD: Johns Hopkins University Press.

Landow, G. P. (1997). *Hypertext 2.0: The convergence of contemporary critical theory and technology.* Baltimore, MD: Johns Hopkins University Press.

Lévi-Strauss, C. (1966). *The savage mind.* Chicago: University of Chicago.

Liu, A. (2003). *Voice of the shuttle.* Santa Barbara: University of California. Retrieved from http://vos.ucsb.edu

Marchand, R. (1985). *Advertising and the American dream.* Berkeley: University of California Press.

McGann, J. (2001). *Radiant textuality: Literature after the World Wide Web.* New York: Palgrave.

Nilsson, R. M., & Mayer, R. E. (2002). The effects of graphic organizers giving cues to the structure of a hypertext document on users' navigation strategies and performance. *International Journal of Human-Computer Studies, 57,* 1–26.

Wood, D. (1992). *The power of maps.* New York: Guilford Press.

Zukin, S. (1991). *Landscapes of power: From Detroit to Disneyworld.* Berkeley: University of California Press.

Index

Note: In page references, *p* indicates photos, and *f* indicates figures.

Aarseth, E., 326
Aberley, D., 343nn 4
Acconci, V., 249, 251
Adams, A., 31, 68, 121
Adler, P., 170, 173
Adobe Photoshop, 44, 147, 314
Advertising, 308
  capital and, 319
  constructing hypertext/hypermedia
    and, 315–316
  empirical inquiry and, 31
  hypermedia and, 316
  mapping and, 328–329
  narratives and, 338
  revision and, 340
  thinking and, 328
  visual resistance and, 240
  website design and, 311, 312–313,
    314, 315, 320*p. See also*
    Website design
Aesthetics, 6, 13, 17
  photo-elicited interviews
    and, 208
  video and, 302
  websites and, 308, 316–317,
    325, 28
Agee, J., 30
Alianza, 128, 138nn 19
Alvelos, H., 240
American Behavioral Science, 307
Andall, J., 283, 284
Angle of view, 69
Anthropology, 3, 5, 44

empirical inquiry and, 52
filmmaking and, 143
new knowledge and, 50
observational studies and, 56
video diaries and, 256
Apertures, 68–69
Arbus, D., 73
Archives, 19
  churches and, 84–89, 90–91
  digital photography and, 147
  Internet and, 83–89
  LBJ Library and, 122, 123,
    128, 129, 136–137
  missionaries and, 83–89.
    See also Missionaries
  political images and, 229–230
  text-based materials and,
    83, 89, 112, 115, 118,
    122, 127, 128, 129, 136
  video diaries and, 277
  website design and, 342
  See also Digital archives
Audio, 19
  archives and, 128
  audiovisual texts and, 317–319
  editing and, 143
  hypertext and, 326–327.
    See also Hypertext
  interviews and, 262
  video diaries and, 258, 262,
    269, 276
  website design and, 308, 310,
    315, 316, 317–319

345

About the Contributors

Marisol Clark-Ibáñez, PhD, is an Assistant Professor in the Department of Sociology at California State University, San Marcos. She has published an article on photo elicitation interviews and ethnography in the journal *American Behavioral Scientist*. Her current book project is a photo elicitation study of urban childhoods. Recently, she has presented her research on photo elicitation interviews at *Childhoods 2005*, in Oslo, Norway, at the International Visual Sociology Association Conference, and at the American Sociological Association Conference. In addition, she has published in the areas of urban schooling, classroom microinteractions, qualitative methodology, and social relationships.

Emmanuel A. David is a doctoral student in sociology at the University of Colorado at Boulder, where he is an adjunct graduate part-time instructor in the Department of Women and Gender Studies. He holds a BA from Loyola University of New Orleans, where he studied sociology and photojournalism. He is currently completing dissertation fieldwork in post-Katrina New Orleans on the intersection between emergent behavior in mitigation, preparedness, and recovery phases of disaster and the pervasiveness of women's participation in these efforts.

Erina Duganne is an Assistant Professor in the Department of Art and Design at Texas State University, San Marcos. Her essays have appeared in the *New Thoughts on the Black Arts Movement* and in the exhibition catalogue *Beautiful Suffering: Photography and the Traffic in Pain* for which she also served as a co-curator. Currently she is completing a book project entitled *Looking In/Looking Out: Photography and the Black Subject* which explores the complex and often contradictory ways in black subjects were used to represent the self in photography during the 1950s through 1970s.

Steven J. Gold is professor and associate chair in the Department of Sociology at Michigan State University. He is co-editor of *Immigration Research for a New Century: Multidisciplinary Perspectives* (with Rubén G. Rumbaut and Nancy Foner), the author of *Refugee Communities: A Comparative Field Study, From the Worker's State to the Golden State, Ethnic Economies* (with Ivan Light), and *The Israeli Diaspora,* which won the Thomas and Znaniecki Award in 2003. He is currently involved in studies of Black self-employment in Detroit and refugee resettlement in the Midwest.

Robert Goldman teaches sociology and cultural studies at Lewis & Clark College in Portland, Oregon. He is the author of *Reading Ads Socially* and the co-author with Stephen Papson of *Sign Wars* and *Nike Culture: the Sign of the Swoosh.*

Barry M. Goldstein, MD, PhD, is Associate Professor of Biochemistry and Biophysics and Associate Professor of Medical Humanities at the University of Rochester Medical Center, Rochester, New York; Visiting Professor of Art at Williams College, Williamstown, Massachusetts; and Adjunct Professor of Humanism in Medicine at New York University Medical Center, New York City. He teaches photography at Rochester, and the New York University Medical School. He is the author of *Being There* (2005), a collection of photographic portraits of and interviews with NYU medical student morgue volunteers following 9/11. He is currently working on a companion project photographing Iraq war veterans. His photographic work can be seen at www.bgoldstein.net.

Yolanda Hernandez-Albujar is originally from Barcelona, Spain, where she received a bachelor's degree in special education. In 2000, she moved to Gainesville, Florida, where she obtained a master's degree in Latin American Studies from the University of Florida. She is currently a doctoral student in sociology at the University of Pittsburgh. She is interested in feminist and postmodern approaches to sociological research as applied to migrant and minority populations.

Ruth Holliday is Director of the Centre for Interdisciplinary Gender Studies at the University of Leeds in the United Kingdom. She has published in the areas of organizational culture, representations of work, queer identities, the body and sexuality, and video methods. She is currently completing a book on kitsch and the cultural politics of taste.

Noah Kersey presently works as the Administrative Coordinator and Trip Leader for the Outdoor Program at Lewis & Clark College. With interests in Web and graphic design, he explores the ways that emerging technologies can intersect the academic realm and be used to develop new teaching tools.

Jon Miller is Research Professor at the University of Southern California. Most of his scholarly work is conducted at the University of Southern California's Center for Religion and Civic Culture, where he serves as Director of Research. Miller has focused on the history of the international evangelical missionary movement, using that movement as a lens for understanding the global relationships among religion, politics, and economics. Recently, he has been working with an international team to create the Internet Mission Photography Archive, hosted by USC's Archival Research Center. Miller also collaborates with Donald E. Miller and Grace Dyrness in an ongoing investigation of the importance of religion in the lives of recent immigrants to California. Miller's books include *Missionary Zeal and Institutional Control* (2003), *The Social Control of Religious Zeal* (1994), *Pathways in the Workplace* (1986), and *Immigrant Religion in the City of Angels* (in progress).

Stephen Papson teaches sociology and film studies at St. Lawrence University in Canton, New York. With Robert Goldman, he has co-authored *Sign Wars* and *Nike Culture: The Sign of the Swoosh*. He is currently exploring the use of hypertext in pedagogy.

Jeffrey Samuels is Assistant Professor in the Department of Philosophy and Religion at Western Kentucky University. He earned his PhD degree in the history of religions from the University of Virginia in 2002. In addition to having published numerous peer-reviewed articles on Buddhist monastic culture and training in contemporary Sri Lanka, he has coedited (with Anne M. Blackburn) *Approaching the Dhamma: Buddhist Texts and Practices in South and Southeast Asia*. His current project—examining monastic recruitment, monastic training, and the interactions between monks and lay people—seeks to locate a place for the emotions and the heart in encounters with Buddhism in contemporary Sri Lanka.

Gregory C. Stanczak is a sociologist working in Southern California. He is a Research Fellow at the Center for Religion and Civic Culture at the University of Southern California. His primary research areas are culture and religion. Stanczak is the author of *Engaged Spirituality* (2005), an in-depth sociological analysis of the personal motivations for sustained commitment to social change. He recently extended this research along with Grace Dyrness and Donald Miller by employing digital video elicitation as a tool for studying sustainability among workers in faith-based nongovern-mental organizations in Tanzania. He is currently exploring the historical use of charitable photographs of children by missionary and faith-based organizations. Stanczak received his PhD from the University of Southern California and has taught sociology at Pitzer College and Williams College.

Jon Wagner is Professor in the School of Education at the University of California, Davis, where he teaches courses on qualitative and visual research methods, material culture and children's lives, school change, and the social and philosophical foundations of education. His current research focuses on teacher-initiated school change and on children's learning and material culture. He is a past president of the International Visual Sociology Association and the founding image editor for *Contexts* magazine.